TRAVEL GUIDE

Formerly Mobil Travel Guide

GREAT PLAINS

2011

ACKNOWLEDGMENTS

We gratefully acknowledge the help of our representatives for their efficient and perceptive inspections of the lodgings listed. Forbes Travel Guide is also grateful to the talented writers who contributed to this book.

Some of the information contained herein is derived from a variety of third-party sources. Although every effort has been made to verify the information obtained from such sources, the publisher assumes no responsibility for inconsistencies or inaccuracies in the data or liability for any damages of any type arising from errors or omissions.

Neither the editors nor the publisher assume responsibility for the services provided by any business listed in this guide or for any loss, damage or disruption in your travel for any reason.

Front Cover image: ©Veer.com
All maps: Mapping Specialists

ISBN: 9781936010851
Manufactured in the USA
10 9 8 7 6 5 4 3 2 1

CONTENTS

GREAT PLAINS
Acknowledgments 2
Star Attractions 4
Star Ratings 5-7
Top Hotels, Restaurants and Spas 9
Your Questions Answered 10

IOWA
Welcome to Iowa 12
Iowa's Best Attractions 13

EASTERN IOWA 13
Bettendorf
Cedar Falls
Cedar Rapids
Clear Lake
Davenport
Decorah
Dubuque
Iowa City

CENTRAL IOWA 24
Ames
Des Moines
Grinnell
Madrid
Newton

WESTERN IOWA 31
Arnolds Park/Lake Okoboji Area
Council Bluffs
Sioux City

KANSAS
Welcome to Kansas 34
Kansas' Best Attractions 35

NORTHEASTERN WOODED HILLS 35
Lawrence
Topeka

NORTH FLINT HILLS/ CENTRAL PRAIRIE 41
Abilene
Council Grove
Emporia
Manhattan
Salina

WICHITA 46
What to See
Where to Stay
Where to Eat

MISSOURI
Welcome to Missouri 52
Missouri's Best Attractions 53

NORTHERN MISSOURI 53
Excelsior Springs
Hannibal
Mark Twain's Hannibal
Independence

ST. LOUIS 59
What to See
Where to Stay
Where to Eat

CENTRAL MISSOURI 72
Columbia
Jefferson City
Lake Ozark
Rolla

SOUTHWEST MISSOURI 75
Branson
Springfield

KANSAS CITY 83
What to See
Where to Stay
Where to Eat
Where to Shop

MONTANA
Welcome to Montana   95
Montana's Best Attractions   96

GLACIER COUNTRY   96
Bigfork
Missoula
West Glacier
West Yellowstone
Whitefish

BILLINGS   98

GOLD WEST COUNTRY/ RUSSELL COUNTRY   103
Anaconda
Great Falls
Helena

NEBRASKA
Welcome to Nebraska   109
Nebraska's Best Attractions   110

METROPOLITAN AREA   110
Lincoln
Omaha

NORTH DAKOTA
Welcome to North Dakota   119
North Dakota's Best Attractions   120

WESTERN NORTH DAKOTA   120
Bismarck
Mandan
Williston
The Little Missouri Badlands
Theodore Roosevelt National Park

OKLAHOMA
Welcome to Oklahoma   128

NORTHEAST/GREEN COUNTRY   129
Bartlesville
Claremore
Grove
Musckogee
Tulsa

OKLAHOMA CITY   137
What to See
Where to Stay
Where to Eat

SOUTH DAKOTA
Welcome to South Dakota   144
South Dakota's Best Attractions   145

WESTERN SOUTH DAKOTA   145
Deadwood
Keystone
Rapid City

WYOMING
Welcome to Wyoming   150
Wyoming's Best Attractions   151

GRAND TETON NATIONAL PARK AREA   152
Jackson
Jackson Hole
Moose
Moran
Teton Village

YELLOWSTONE NATIONAL PARK AREA   160
Cody
Yellowstone National Park

INDEX   167

MAPS   187

STAR ATTRACTIONS

If you've been a reader of Mobil Travel Guide, you will have heard that this historic brand partnered in 2009 with another storied media name, Forbes, to create a new entity, Forbes Travel Guide. For more than 50 years, Mobil Travel Guide assisted travelers in making smart decisions about where to stay and dine when traveling. With this new partnership, our mission has not changed: We're committed to the same rigorous inspections of hotels, restaurants and spas—the most comprehensive in the industry with more than 500 standards tested at each property we visit—to help you cut through the clutter and make easy and informed decisions on where to spend your time and travel budget. Our team of anonymous inspectors are constantly on the road, sleeping in hotels, eating in restaurants and making spa appointments, evaluating those exacting standards to determine a property's rating.

What kinds of standards are we looking for when we visit a property? We're looking for more than just high-thread count sheets, pristine spa treatment rooms and white linen-topped tables. We look for service that's attentive, individualized and unforgettable. We note how long it takes to be greeted when you sit down at your table, or to be served when you order room service, or whether the hotel staff can confidently help you when you've forgotten that one essential item that will make or break your trip. Unlike any other travel ratings entity, we visit each place we rate, testing hundreds of attributes to compile our ratings, and our ratings cannot be bought or influenced. The Forbes Five Star rating is the most prestigious achievement in hospitality—while we rate more than 5,000 properties in the U.S., Canada, Hong Kong, Macau and Beijing, for 2011, we have awarded Five Star designations to only 54 hotels, 23 restaurants and 20 spas. When you travel with Forbes, you can travel with confidence, knowing that you'll get the very best experience, no matter who you are.

We understand the importance of making the most of your time. That's why the most trusted name in travel is now Forbes Travel Guide.

STAR RATED HOTELS

Whether you're looking for the ultimate in luxury or the best value for your travel budget, we have a hotel recommendation for you. To help you pinpoint properties that meet your needs, Forbes Travel Guide classifies each lodging by type according to the following characteristics:

★★★★★These exceptional properties provide a memorable experience through virtually flawless service and the finest of amenities. Staff are intuitive, engaging and passionate, and eagerly deliver service above and beyond the guests' expectations. The hotel was designed with the guest's comfort in mind, with particular attention paid to craftsmanship and quality of product. A Five-Star property is a destination unto itself.

★★★★These properties provide a distinctive setting, and a guest will find many interesting and inviting elements to enjoy throughout the property. Attention to detail is prominent throughout the property, from design concept to quality of products provided. Staff are accommodating and take pride in catering to the guest's specific needs throughout their stay.

★★★These well-appointed establishments have enhanced amenities that provide travelers with a strong sense of location, whether for style or function. They may have a distinguishing style and ambience in both the public spaces and guest rooms; or they may be more focused on functionality, providing guests with easy access to local events, meetings or tourism highlights.

Recommended: These hotels are considered clean, comfortable and reliable establishments that have expanded amenities, such as full-service restaurants.

For every property, we also provide pricing information. All prices quoted are accurate at the time of publication; however, prices cannot be guaranteed. Because rates can fluctuate, we list a pricing range rather than specific prices.

STAR RATED RESTAURANTS

Every restaurant in this book has been visited by Forbes Travel Guide's team of experts and comes highly recommended as an outstanding dining experience.

★★★★★Forbes Five-Star restaurants deliver a truly unique and distinctive dining experience. A Five-Star restaurant consistently provides exceptional food, superlative service and elegant décor. An emphasis is placed on originality and personalized, attentive and discreet service. Every detail that surrounds the experience is attended to by a warm and gracious dining room team.

★★★★These are exciting restaurants with often well-known chefs that feature creative and complex foods and emphasize various culinary techniques and a focus on seasonality. A highly-trained dining room staff provides refined personal service and attention.

★★★Three Star restaurants offer skillfully prepared food with a focus on a specific style or cuisine. The dining room staff provides warm and professional service in a comfortable atmosphere. The décor is well-coordinated with quality fixtures and decorative items, and promotes a comfortable ambience.

Recommended: These restaurants serve fresh food in a clean setting with efficient service. Value is considered in this category, as is family friendliness.

Because menu prices can fluctuate, we list a pricing range rather than specific prices. The pricing ranges are per diner, and assume that you order an appetizer or dessert, an entrée and one drink.

STAR RATED SPAS

Forbes Travel Guide's spa ratings are based on objective evaluations of more than 450 attributes. About half of these criteria assess basic expectations, such as staff courtesy, the technical proficiency and skill of the employees and whether the facility is clean and maintained properly. Several standards address issues that impact a guest's physical comfort and convenience, as well as the staff's ability to impart a sense of personalized service. Additional criteria measure the spa's ability to create a completely calming ambience.

★★★★★Stepping foot in a Five Star Spa will result in an exceptional experience with no detail overlooked. These properties wow their guests with extraordinary design and facilities, and uncompromising service. Expert staff cater to your every whim and pamper you with the most advanced treatments and skin care lines available. These spas often offer exclusive treatments and may emphasize local elements.

★★★★Four Star spas provide a wonderful experience in an inviting and serene environment. A sense of personalized service is evident from the moment you check in and receive your robe and slippers. The guest's comfort is always of utmost concern to the well-trained staff.

★★★These spas offer well-appointed facilities with a full complement of staff to ensure that guests' needs are met. The spa facil ties include clean and appealing treatment rooms, changing areas and a welcoming reception desk.

TOP HOTELS, RESTAURANTS AND SPAS

HOTELS

★★★★★FIVE STAR
Four Seasons Resort Jackson Hole
(Jackson Hole, Wyoming)

★★★★FOUR STAR
Four Seasons Hotel St. Louis
(St. Louis, Missouri)
The Ritz-Carlton, St. Louis
(Clayton, Missouri)
Amangani
(Jackson Hole, Wyoming)

RESTAURANTS

★★★★FOUR STAR
The American Restaurant
(Kansas City, Missouri)
Tony's
(St. Louis, Missouri)

SPAS

★★★★FOUR STAR
The Spa at Four Seasons Resort Jackson Hole
(Jackson Hole, Wyoming)

YOUR QUESTIONS ANSWERED

WHICH NATIONAL PARKS ARE FOUND IN THE GREAT PLAINS?

BADLANDS NATIONAL PARK

Located in Interior, South Dakota, the park is a moonscape of steep canyons, spires, pinnacles and flat-topped tables sits amid a sea of the largest protected prairie in the United States. The Badlands National Park occupies 244,000 acres in South Dakota's southwest corner, and its stark and simple beauty is the result of the geologic processes of deposition and erosion. Located 88 miles east of Rapid City and other attractions, including the Black Hills and Mt. Rushmore, the Badlands can be seen as a stand-alone trip or as a day trip among other South Dakota highlights.

GLACIER NATIONAL PARK

Located in West Glacier, Montana this national park is vast, rugged, primitive and majestic. It is nature's unspoiled domain. This is the place for a midsummer snowball fight, honing photography skills with a lens trained on glacier-wrapped peaks, enjoying the pure solitude on a wilderness trail bordered by alpine wildflowers and then settling in for all the tranquility that a remote campsite on a fir-fringed lake affords. This is the place to come simply to gawk at nature and gain an appreciation for everything that created it. The park is a living textbook in geology from 800 million-year-old rocks that show millions of years of sea patterns and marine environments to stromatolites, ancient fossils of blue-green algae that give evidence of the earth's earliest physical and chemical compositions. There are even the findings from recent archaeological surveys that show evidence of humans in the Glacier area dating back more than 10,000 years.

THEODORE ROOSEVELT NATIONAL PARK

Located in Medora and Watford City, North Dakota, the park was established in 1947 as a monument to the 26th U.S. president, Theodore Roosevelt, who first came to the badlands of North Dakota in September 1883 to hunt buffalo and other large game. Wind and water have carved curiously sculptured formations, tablelands, buttes, canyons and rugged hills from a thick series of flat-lying multihued sedimentary rocks, which were first deposited here by waters flowing from the freshly risen Rocky Mountains between 55 and 60 million years ago. The park is unique in that its sections are not connected; substantial distance lies between the two main units. The North Unit is located 70 miles above the South Unit. Between the two sections lies the small Elkhorn Ranch Unit, which connects to the South Unit via gravel roads.

YELLOWSTONE NATIONAL PARK

Located in Cody, Wyoming, Yellowstone is the world's first national park. Covering 3,000 square miles of rambling wilderness, Yellowstone National Park has been open to exploration since 1872, welcoming visitors from all over the globe through its five entrances in three states (Wyoming, Montana and Idaho) onto 370 miles of scenic public roads. You'll travel past impressive granite peaks and through lodgepole pine forests that open onto meadows dotted with wildflowers and elk. Beyond the beautiful panorama, Yellowstone boasts a marvelous list of sights and attractions: a big freshwater lake that ranks as the largest in North America at high elevation (7,733 feet); a waterfall almost twice as high as Niagara; a dramatic, 1,200-foot-deep river canyon; and the world's most famous geyser, Old Faithful.

WELCOME TO IOWA

PROBABLY MORE THAN ANY OTHER HEARTLAND STATE,

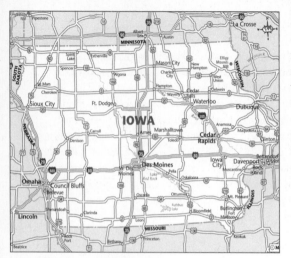

Iowa conjures up images of table top-flat cornfields dotted with silos and farmhouses. And while in some parts of the state you will find yourself driving through a sea of corn that stretches to the horizon (Iowa grows more of it than any state except Illinois), with a bit of exploring, you'll find ski slopes, towering bluffs above the Mississippi River and six wildlife refuges.

The Sioux called Iowa the "Beautiful Land" and it's a fitting name. Every region of the state has a loop of Scenic Byways, well-marked routes that reveal the beauty of the countryside. Iowa has miles of bike trails, many built on the gentle grades of old railroad lines. Hikers can retreat into the tranquility of nature preserve trails that retrace historical journeys such as those of Louis and Clark or the Mormons as they moved west.

History abounds in Iowa. This is the birthplace of Buffalo Bill Cody, John Wayne and Herbert Hoover. In Des Moines, visitors to the State Historical Museum are greeted by a 16,000-year-old Hebior mammoth, while airplanes "buzz" overhead in the atrium. To the northeast in Dubuque, freshwater creatures and habitats get their due in the National River Museum and Aquarium.

You won't need a guidebook to discover Iowa's essential charm, the friendly character of people who are by heritage tied to the land and the value of work. To find this, sit down in a local café in a small town at lunchtime. Or, in the summer, make your way to one of the fairs held in each of the 99 counties. Buy yourself a corn dog and head to the agricultural barn where kids display their meticulously groomed cows, pigs and sheep. From the dedication and pride you'll see in these young people's faces, you'll learn what Iowa is about.

BEST ATTRACTIONS

IOWA'S BEST ATTRACTIONS

EASTERN IOWA
This region offers a slew of one-of-a-kind tourist spots, including Buffalo Bill's childhood home, the excellent Cedar Rapids Museum of Art and the original ball field from *Field of Dreams*.

DES MOINES
Des Moines is Iowa's industrial, retail, financial and political hub. It's also a great place to visit for its many museums, restaurants and other attractions.

EASTERN IOWA

Located on and surrounding the Mississippi River, Eastern Iowa covers the Quad Cities metropolitan area, which includes Davenport and Bettendorf, each of which offer restaurants and attractions looking out onto the river.

West of the Quad Cities is Iowa City, which is referred to as "the river city," and is the home of the University of Iowa and the state's first capital. It has a small-town feel accented by the kind of cultural amenities and fun restaurants that a university presence delivers. In the fall, the town is mesmerized by football when the Hawkeyes are playing at home on Saturdays.

To the north lies Cedar Rapids. This vibrant smaller city has all the amenities you need for a cosmopolitan lifestyle that rivals other Midwestern cities twice its size. From dining and shopping to the arts and nightlife, this city has it all in a comfortable and very livable atmosphere. To the northwest lies Clear Lake, an ancient Native American fishing and hunting ground and a popular resort town. In the northeast is Decorah, located in one of the state's most picturesque areas with towering spires of limestone along the Upper Iowa River nearby.

WHAT TO SEE

BETTENDORF
BUFFALO BILL CODY HOMESTEAD
28050 230th Ave., Princeton, 563-225-2981; www.scottcountyiowa.com
Visit the restored and furnished boyhood home of Buffalo Bill Cody, built by his father in 1847. Buffalo and longhorn cattle graze on the grounds surrounding the property.
Admission: adults $2, children 16 and under free. April-October, daily 9 a.m.-5 p.m.

FAMILY MUSEUM OF ARTS & SCIENCE

2900 Learning Campus Drive, Bettendorf, 563-344-4106; www.familymuseum.org

This interactive museum features hands-on exhibits as well as a traveling exhibit gallery for children and adults alike.

Admission: adults $6, children under 2 free. Monday-Thursday 9 a.m.-8 p.m., Friday-Saturday 9 a.m.-5 p.m., Sunday noon-5 p.m.

ISLE OF CAPRI CASINO

777 Isle Parkway, Bettendorf, 563-359-7280, 800-724-5825; www.isleofcapricasino.com

A big draw for locals and students from the surrounding colleges, this casino features more than 35,000 square feet of gaming options as well as various entertainment choices such as the Osmond Brothers, WAR and the Commodores. Dining options abound with three onsite restaurants.

CEDAR FALLS

CEDAR FALLS HISTORICAL SOCIETY VICTORIAN HOME MUSEUM

308 W. Third St., Cedar Falls, 319-266-5149;

This Victorian house is furnished in period style. The Carriage House Museum contains a library, archives, fashions, Lenoir train exhibit and memorabilia of the first permanent settlement in Black Hawk County.

Admission: donation. Wednesday-Saturday 10 a.m.-4 p.m., Sunday 1-4 p.m.

GEORGE WYTH HOUSE

303 Franklin St., Cedar Falls, 319-266-5149; www.cedarfallshistorical.org

The residence of George Wyth, founder of the Viking Pump Company, was built in 1907. It's now furnished in the Art Deco style of the 1920s and includes pieces by Gilbert Rhode. The Viking Pump Company museum is housed on the third floor.

Admission: donation. Tours: May-September, Sunday; also by appointment.

LITTLE RED SCHOOL

First and Clay streets, Cedar Falls, 319-266-5149; www.cedarfallshistorical.org

To see what life was once like, this country school has been authentically furnished to reflect turn-of-the century education.

Admission: donation. May-October, Wednesday, Saturday-Sunday.

CEDAR RAPIDS

CEDAR RAPIDS MUSEUM OF ART

410 Third Ave. S.E., Cedar Rapids, 319-366-7503; www.crma.org

The Cedar Rapids Museum of Art houses an extensive collection of works by Grant Wood, Marvin Cone and Mauricio Lasansky. The largest collection of Grant Wood's work is here and his original studio is a few blocks away for anyone interested in seeing how the artist worked. They also feature rotating exhibits such as one that includes Monet and Picasso from a local collection.

Admission: adults $5, seniors and students $4, children 18 and under free. Free Thursday 4 p.m.-8 p.m. Tuesday-Saturday 10 a.m.-4 p.m., Thursday 10 a.m.-8 p.m., Sunday noon-4 p.m.

CZECH VILLAGE

48 16th Ave. S.W., Cedar Rapids, 319-362-2846; www.czechvillageiowa.com

Near downtown, this is an intriguing area with shops, restaurants and businesses

HIGHLIGHT

WHAT ARE THE TOP THINGS TO DO IN EASTERN IOWA?

VISIT THE BUFFALO BILL CODY HOMESTEAD

Old West buffs will want to make a trip out to this homestead, the place where sharpshooter Buffalo Bill grew up.

CHECK OUT THE WORK AT THE CEDAR RAPIDS MUSEUM OF ART

The museum houses the largest collection of works from artist Grant Wood, most known for his iconic painting *American Gothic*.

PLAY CATCH AT THE FIELD OF DREAMS MOVIE SITE

If you build it, tourists will come. Fans of the baseball flick *Field of Dreams* will want to throw the ball around at this field, which was featured in the movie.

PERUSE THE NATIONAL MISSISSIPPI RIVER MUSEUM AND AQUARIUM

This is one of the region's best attractions. It includes six historical museums that center around the city's river history.

SEE AMISH CULTURE AT KALONA HISTORICAL VILLAGE

This village preserves Amish traditions and lifestyles with museums, a log house, a country store, a Victorian house and more.

celebrating the cultural history of the area. A bakery, a meat market, gift shops, restaurants and historic structures preserving Czech heritage are featured here.

INDIAN CREEK NATURE CENTER
6665 Otis Road S.E., Cedar Rapids, 319-362-0664; www.indiancreeknaturecenter.org
On this 210-acre nature preserve is an observatory and museum offering changing exhibits in a remodeled dairy barn as well as hiking trails.
Admission: donation. Monday-Friday.

PALISADES-KEPLER STATE PARK

700 Kepler Drive, Mount Vernon, 319-895-6039; www.iowadnr.gov

This 970-acre park includes limestone palisades that rise 75 feet above the Cedar River as well as timbered valleys and wildflowers. You can come here for fishing, boating, nature and hiking trails, snowmobiling, picnicking and camping.

PARAMOUNT THEATRE

123 Third Ave. S.E., Cedar Rapids, 319-398-5211; www.uscellularcenter.com

A restored theater built in the 1920s, the Paramount hosts stage productions, films and Broadway series, and is the home of the Cedar Rapids Symphony.

SCIENCE STATION

427 First St. S.E., Cedar Rapids, 319-363-4629; www.sciencestation.org

The science and technology museum features unusual hands-on exhibits, including a working hot air balloon and giant kaleidoscope.

Mid-April-May, Tuesday-Sunday; June-August 30, daily; August 31-mid-April, Tuesday-Saturday.

US CELLULAR CENTER

370 First Ave. N.E., Cedar Rapids, 319-398-5211; www.uscellularcenter.com

This 10,000-seat entertainment center features sports events, concerts, exhibits, rodeos, ice shows and more.

CLEAR LAKE

CLEAR LAKE STATE PARK

2730 S. Lakeview Drive, Clear Lake, 641-357-4212; www.iowadnr.gov

Swimming, fishing, boating, snowmobiling, picnicking and camping are all available at this park.

SURF BALLROOM

460 North Shore Drive, Clear Lake, 641-357-6151; www.surfballroom.com

This was the site of Buddy Holly's last concert before Holly, Ritchie Valens and J. P. Richardson (the Big Bopper) died in a plane crash nearby on February 2, 1959. The ballroom features entertainment on weekends and a museum of musical history.

Tours are available.

DAVENPORT

FIGGE ART MUSEUM

1737 W. 12th St., Davenport, 563-326-7804; www.figgeartmuseum.org

Rotating displays from a permanent collection of 19th- and 20th-century paintings, Mexican Colonial, Asian and native Haitian art are displayed here, as well as works by regional artists Grant Wood and Thomas Hart Benton.

Admission: adults $7, seniors $6, children ages 3-12 $4. Tuesday-Sunday.

PUTNAM MUSEUM OF HISTORY & NATURAL SCIENCE

1717 W. 12th St., Davenport, 563-324-1933; www.putnam.org

The museum houses permanent and changing exhibits of regional history, natural science and world cultures.

Admission: adults $6, seniors $5, children ages 3-12 $4. Exhibit Hall hours: Monday-Saturday 10 a.m.-5 p.m., Sunday noon-5 p.m.

DECORAH

FORT ATKINSON STATE PRESERVE
10225 Ivy Road, Decorah, 563-425-4161; www.iowadnr.com

The fort was built in 1840 as federal protection for the Winnebago from the Sac, Fox and Sioux. Restored buildings include barracks and a blockhouse. Museum exhibits highlight Native American and pioneer relics.

Admission: free. Mid-May-mid-October, daily.

SEED SAVERS HERITAGE FARM
3094 N. Winn Road, Decorah, 563-382-5990; www.seedsavers.org

This 173-acre farm features displays of endangered vegetables, apples, grapes and ancient White Park cattle. Preservation Gardens house 15,000 rare vegetable varieties; the Cultural History Garden exhibits old-time flowers and vegetables. Historic Orchard has 650 19th-century apples and 160 hardy grapes.

Admission: Donation. April-December, daily.

VESTERHEIM NORWEGIAN-AMERICAN MUSEUM
523 W. Water St., Decorah, 563-382-9681; www.vesterheim.org

Extensive exhibits relate the history of Norwegians in America and Norway. Pioneer objects, handicrafts, a ship gallery, and arts are displayed in a complex of 13 historic buildings with a restored mill.

Admission: adults $7, seniors and children ages 7-18 $5. Free Thursday. Daily.

DUBUQUE

BELLEVUE STATE PARK
24668 Highway 52, Dubuque, 563-872-4019; www.iowadnr.com

This state part covers approximately 540 acres on a high bluff above the Mississippi. Enjoy a day here exploring Native American mounds, hiking through the rugged woodlands on trails, snowmobiling, picnicking and camping. The South Bluff nature center also is open seasonally with displays and programs in the summer.

CATHEDRAL SQUARE
Second and Bluff streets, Dubuque, 563-582-7646

Surrounding the square are stylized figures of a lead miner, farmer, farmer's wife, priest and river hand. Opposite the square is the architecturally and historically significant St. Raphael's Cathedral.

CRYSTAL LAKE CAVE
7699 Crystal Lake Cave Drive, Dubuque, 563-556-6451; www.crystallakecave.com

A network of passageways carved by underground streams surrounds a lake with glittering stalactites and stalagmites, with water that is crystal clear. Guided tours are available; be sure to bring a jacket as it gets very cool in the cave.

Admission: adults $12, children 4-11 $6, children 3 and under free. Memorial Day-late October, daily; May, Saturday-Sunday.

DUBUQUE ARBORETUM AND BOTANICAL GARDENS
3800 Arboretum Drive, Dubuque, 563-556-2100;
www.dubuquearboretum.com

Annual and perennial gardens are featured here, as well as ornamental trees and a prairie wildflower walk. It's a very popular place for weddings. In the summer,

HIGHLIGHT

A WALK THROUGH DAVENPORT

Davenport is one of the Quad Cities, a four-city metropolitan area that straddles the Mississippi River and includes Moline and Rock Island in Illinois, plus Bettendorf, just up the river from Davenport. Begin this walk on Credit Island Park, the site of a turn of-the-century amusement park. Scenic trails loop around the island, and a number of public art pieces are found here, part of the Quad Cities Art in the Park project. Cross over to the Iowa mainland from the east end of Credit Island Park and walk along the Mississippi through two more riverside parks. Centennial Park features riverside walkways past sports fields and stadiums. Atop the bluff on Division Street is Museum Hill, home of the Putnam Museum of Science and Natural History (*1717 W. 12th St.*) and the Davenport Museum of Art (*1737 W. 12th St.*). The Putnam houses two permanent exhibits about the Mississippi River. The art museum's permanent collection includes works by Midwestern painters, including Thomas Hart Benton and Grant Wood, an Iowa native famous for his painting *American Gothic*. Just to the east is LeClaire Park, home to summer outdoor events and concerts.

The Davenport Downtown Levee area includes a riverboat casino, restaurants, nightclubs and the renovated Union Station railroad depot, which houses the Quad Cities Convention and Visitors Center. A local Farmers' Market (*www.freighthousefarmersmarket.com*) is also held here on Tuesday and Saturday throughout the year (in winter, it's in the Freight House Building).

Just downstream from the historic Government Bridge, Dam 15 provides a pool for commercial shipping on the Mississippi. Lock 15 allows boats to transfer between the river pools. Cross Government Bridge to Arsenal Island, which was acquired by the U.S. Government in 1804 under a treaty with the Sauk and Fox Indians. Fort Armstrong was established in 1816 on the tip of the island, where a replica now stands. The island contains a number of historic homes and structures, including the Rock Island Arsenal Museum; the restored Colonel George Davenport Mansion, filled with furnishings from the mid-1800s; and the Mississippi River Visitors Center, with exhibits about the history of navigation on the river. A Confederate Soldiers Cemetery and National Military Cemetery date back to the 1800s. Hikers and bikers can enjoy a five-mile trail around the island.

it features a free outdoor music series on Sunday.
Admission: free. May-October, daily 7 a.m.-dusk; November-May, Monday-Friday 10 a.m.-3 p.m.

DUBUQUE COUNTY COURTHOUSE
720 Central Ave., Dubuque, 563-589-4445; www.dubuquecounty.org
This gold-domed courthouse is on the National Register of Historic Places and was built in 1891 (it replaced the original, built in 1839).
Monday-Friday.

DUBUQUE MUSEUM OF ART/OLD COUNTY JAIL

701 Locust St., Dubuque, 563-557-1851

This museum is housed in a brand-new facility. The gallery is an example of Egyptian Revival architecture and features a sound and light show and plenty of artifacts, including a Union flag from the Civil War.

Tuesday-Sunday.

EAGLE POINT PARK

2200 Bunker Hill Road, Dubuque, 563-589-4263; www.dbq.com

On a high bluff above the Mississippi, this 164-acre park overlooks three states. A Works Progress Administration project, the park's Prairie School pavilions and naturalistic landscaping were designed by Alfred Caldwell, who studied under Frank Lloyd Wright.

Mid-May-mid-October, daily.

FENELON PLACE ELEVATOR

512 Fenelon Place, Dubuque, 563-582-6496; www.dbq.com

In operation since 1882, one of the world's shortest, steepest incline railways connects Fenelon Place with Fourth Street, providing a three-state view. Bikes are allowed.

Admission: adults $2 (roundtrip), children 5-12 $1, children 4 and under free. April-November, daily 8 a.m.-10 p.m.

FIELD OF DREAMS MOVIE SITE

28995 Lansing Road, Dyersville, 563-875-8404; www.fieldofdreamsmoviesite.com

If you're a fan of the movie *Field of Dreams* or just a baseball fan, you'll want to make a stop here in Dyersville to check out the field featured in the movie. Hang out on the bleachers or play a little ball.

April-November, daily 9 a.m.-6 p.m.

FIVE FLAGS THEATER

405 Main St., Dubuque, 563-589-4254; www.fiveflagscenter.com

Designed by Rapp and Rapp, premier theater architects of their day, the Five Flags Theater was modeled after Parisian music halls.

Tours by appointment.

GRAND OPERA HOUSE

135 Eighth St., Dubuque, 563-588-1305; www.thegrandoperahouse.com

This century-old opera house was recently restored and offers a variety of entertainment throughout the year, such as the musical *Chicago*.

Box office: Monday-Friday noon-4 p.m. and two hours before each show.

HERITAGE TRAIL

13606 Swiss Valley Road, Dubuque, 563-556-6745; www.dubuquecounty.com

This trail provides 26 miles of scenic hiking, biking and cross-country skiing on an old railroad along rugged Little Maquoketa River valley. Level, surfaced trails cross from wooded, hilly, "driftless" areas to rolling prairie near Dyersville. A self-guided tour identifies railroad landmarks and includes water-powered mill sites.

Daily.

JULIEN DUBUQUE MONUMENT

Grandview Avenue and Julien Dubuque Drive, Dubuque, 563-556-0620

The tower was built in 1897 at the site of Julien Dubuque's mine and the spot where Native Americans buried him in 1810. The monument provides an excellent view of the Mississippi River.

MATHIAS HAM HOUSE HISTORIC SITE

2241 Lincoln Ave., Dubuque, 563-583-2812

An 1857 Italianate/Victorian mansion with a cupola, this house has spectacular views of the Mississippi River. Grounds include Iowa's oldest log cabin and a one-room schoolhouse.

Admission: adults $5, children $3.50, children 6 and under free. June-October, daily; May, Saturday-Sunday.

NATIONAL MISSISSIPPI RIVER MUSEUM AND AQUARIUM

350 E. Third St., Dubuque, 563-557-9545; www.mississippirivermuseum.com

One of the region's outstanding attractions, this complex offers six Dubuque County Historical Society museums that all emphasize the city's river history. Included here is the Woodward Discovery Center, which features six aquariums where you can see catfish, sturgeon, ducks, frogs, turtles and more from the river. Other exhibits dramatize 300 years of Mississippi River history, from Native American culture to explorers to lead miners. A RiverWorks display offers hands-on water-based activities for children to learn about how a river works.

Admission: adults $15, seniors $13, youth 3-17 $10, children 2 and under free.
Memorial Day-Labor Day, daily 9 a.m.-6 p.m., Labor Day-October, daily 9 a.m.-5 p.m., November-Memorial Day, daily 10 a.m.-5 p.m.

SUNDOWN MOUNTAIN SKI AREA

16991 Asbury Road, Dubuque, 563-556-6676, 888-786-3696; www.sundownmtn.com

Skiing in Iowa? You bet. And at this spot, the lodge is at the top of the run. There are five chairlifts, towrope, patrol, school, rentals and snowmaking. The resort includes 21 runs, with the longest run being a half mile with a vertical drop of 475 feet.

Late November-mid-March, daily.

IOWA CITY

CORALVILLE LAKE

2850 Prairie du Chien Road, Iowa City, 319-338-3543; www.mvr.usace.army.mil

This 5,400-acre lake offers swimming, boating and fishing. Flooding that occurred during the summer of 1993 eroded a 15-foot-deep channel exposing the underlying bedrock. Now called Devonian Fossil Gorge, it offers a rare opportunity to view Iowa's geological past. The site is an Army Corps of Engineers project.

Visitor Center: October 16-April 14, Monday-Friday 8 a.m.-4 p.m.; April 15-October 15, Saturday-Sunday 10 a.m.-5 p.m.

HERBERT HOOVER NATIONAL HISTORIC SITE

110 Parkside Drive, West Branch, 319-643-2541; www.nps.gov

The 187-acre park includes the restored house in which President Hoover was born, the Quaker meeting house where he worshipped as a boy, a school, a blacksmith shop and the graves of the President and his wife, Lou Henry Hoover.

Daily 9 a.m.-5 p.m.

HERBERT HOOVER PRESIDENTIAL LIBRARY-MUSEUM

210 Parkside Drive, West Branch, 319-643-5301; www.hoover.nara.gov

Administered by the National Archives and Records Administration, this place features a museum with re-created historic settings in China, Belgium, Washington and other places prominent in Hoover's 50 years of public service. The research library is open by appointment only.

Admission: adults $6, seniors $3, children 16 and under free. Daily 9 a.m.-5 p.m.

IOWA CHILDREN'S MUSEUM

1451 Coral Ridge Ave., Coralville, 319-625-5500; www.theicm.org

This museum has interactive exhibits for kids such as the CityWorks exhibit which features a kid-sized village set up for children to play and learn in a grocery store, pizza shop, television station and other real-life situations. There's also a Puppet Kingdom exhibit where kids put on plays.

Admission: adults and children $7, seniors $6, children under 1 free. Tuesday-Thursday 10 a.m.-6 p.m., Friday-Saturday 10 a.m.-8 p.m., Sunday 11 a.m.-6 p.m.

KALONA HISTORICAL VILLAGE

411 Ninth St., Kalona, 319-656-3232; www.kalonaiowa.org

Amish traditions and lifestyle are preserved in this village containing the Wahl Museum, the Mennonite Museum and Archives, a restored 110-year-old depot, a log house, a one-room school, a country store, Victorian house, working windmill, post office and church. See antique farm machinery, historic quilts and much more.

Admission: adults $6, children 7-12 $2.50 and children 6 and under free. April-October, Monday-Saturday 9:30 a.m.-4 p.m.; November-March 11 a.m.-3 p.m.

PLUM GROVE HISTORIC FARM

1030 Carroll St., Iowa City, 319-337-6846; www.uiowa.edu

The 1844 residence of the territory's first governor, Robert Lucas, has been restored and furnished with period furniture and is a memorial to him.

Memorial Day-October, Wednesday-Sunday 1-5 p.m.

WHERE TO STAY

CEDAR RAPIDS

★★★CROWNE PLAZA

350 First Ave. N.E., Cedar Rapids, 319-363-8161, 800-227-6963; www.crowneplaza.com

Located in downtown Cedar Rapids, this hotel is near shopping, restaurants, and entertainment. In inclement weather, the convenient 12-block skywalk system leads to many great local restaurants. Rooms feature neutral tones, comfortable bedding and lavender sprays and eye masks to aid in restful sleep.

275 rooms. Restaurant, bar. Business center. Fitness center. Pool. $61-150

WHICH IOWA
CITY HOTEL HAS
THE BEST ROOM
AMENITIES?

HotelVetro:
This chic property crams
its suites with amenities,
including complimen-
tary Internet access and
flat-screen TVs. The full
kitchens have an oven, a
microwave and a fridge.
Bathrooms come with
Gilchrist & Soames
products, a tub for
two and a glass-walled
shower. The box of
truffles on the bed is a
sweet touch.

DECORAH

★★★HOTEL WINNESHIEK
104 E. Water St., Decorah, 563-382-4164; www.hotelwinn.com

The Hotel Winneshiek is a gem: an elegantly restored 1905 hotel in the heart of downtown. Guests are greeted at a concierge desk in an entryway decorated with fresh flowers and displays of antique glassware and porcelain figurines. The lobby has an octagonal three-story atrium, set under a large stained-glass skylight. Rooms are simple but decorated with antique reproductions.

31 rooms. Restaurant, bar. Complimentary breakfast. $61-150

IOWA CITY

★★★SHERATON IOWA CITY HOTEL
210 S. Dubuque St., Iowa City, 319-337-4058, 800-848-1335; www.starwoodhotels.com

Located one block from the University of Iowa, rooms at this hotel have been updated with the Sheraton Sweet Sleeper beds, HD flat-screen TVs and soaking tubs. Enjoy wine and small plates at the new dining lounge, Share. The cozy and modern business center makes it easy for business travelers to keep up with work and the fitness center offers state-of-the-art equipment so you don't have to miss a workout. The many area bars and restaurants offer a variety of options for a night out.

234 rooms. Restaurant, bar. Business center. Fitness center. Pool. Pets accepted. $61-150

ALSO RECOMMENDED

IOWA CITY

HOTELVETRO
201 S. Linn St., Iowa City, 800-592-0355; www.hotelvetro.com

For chic digs, book one of the studio suites in hotel-Vetro. The rooms come stocked with an oven, a microwave, a fridge, a plasma TV, Gilchrist & Soames toiletries, a tub for two plus a glass-walled shower and a pillow-topped bed. But what steals your attention is the contemporary décor, with earth tones, light wood, modern art works on the walls and retro chaise lounges.

54 rooms. Restaurant, bar. Business center. Fitness center. Pets accepted. $151-250

WHERE TO EAT

BETTENDORF
★★★THE FAITHFUL PILOT CAFÉ
117 N. Cody Road, Le Claire, 563-289-4156;
www.faithfulpilotcafe.com

This restaurant features progressive American cuisine served in an elegant and modern dining room. Menu highlights include buttermilk-brined chicken breast with creamy red bell pepper polenta, beer-battered pickled okra and grilled scallions; and citrus seared scallops with sweet potato and chorizo hash, sliced avocado and cilantro salad. The restaurant also features special events like wine tastings.

American. Lunch (Wednesday-Saturday), dinner, Saturday-Sunday brunch. $16-35

★★★THE LODGE RESTAURANT
900 Spruce Hills Drive, Bettendorf, 563-359-1607;
www.lodgehotel.com

This restaurant features an extensive collection of American and German fare. Specialties include Regensburg goulash, chicken von jumer and rack of lamb. The bourbon pork chop is not to be missed. The Sunday brunch is also very popular.

American, German. Breakfast, lunch, dinner, Sunday brunch. Children's menu. Bar. $16-35

RECOMMENDED

IOWA CITY
LINN ST. CAFÉ
121 N. Linn St., Iowa City, 319-337-7370; www.linnstreetcafe.com

Locals celebrate their special occasions at this cozy eatery with tables topped with white linens and candles. They gather over appetizers such as smoked trout pâté with lemon dressing and entrées such as pecan-crusted chicken with Dijon-cream reduction, and seared duck breast with bacon and sweet potato hash. Delicious cuisine like this is worthy of celebration on its own.

American. Lunch (Monday-Friday), dinner. $16-35

MOTLEY COW CAFÉ
160 N. Linn St, Iowa City, 319-688-9177; www.motleycowcafe.com

Diners flock to this local favorite to nosh on inventive contemporary American cuisine with ingredients from local farms. Try dishes like the roasted ruby trout and barley salad with yams parsley and pistachios, or

---

WHICH RESTAURANT HAS THE BEST CONTEMPORARY AMERICAN FOOD IN EASTERN IOWA?

Dine on updated classic American dishes at **The Faithful Pilot Café.** Buttermilk-brined chicken gets an upgrade with creamy red bell pepper polenta and scallops take a yummy twist with sweet potato and chorizo hash.

a pork chop that gets a Mexican makeover with seared polenta, roasted tomatillo salsa and queso fresco. Finish with a carnival-inspired dessert: cardamom funnel cake with orange cranberry ice cream.

American. Breakfast, lunch (Monday-Friday), dinner, Sunday brunch. Outdoor seating. $16-35

CENTRAL IOWA

The most well-known city in Central Iowa is Des Moines, the capital and largest city in the state. This city is the industrial, retail, financial and political hub of Iowa. A military garrison established Fort Des Moines at a point on the Raccoon and Des Moines rivers in 1843. The word "fort" was abandoned when the community became a city in 1857; the next year it became the state capital. Today more than 60 insurance companies have their home offices here, as does media giant Meredith Corporation, publishers of *Better Homes & Gardens* and *Ladies' Home Journal*. To the north is Grinnell, a thriving small college town. When Horace Greeley said "Go west, young man, go west and grow up with the country!" he was talking to Josiah Bushnell Grinnell, who took the advice, went west to a bit of prairie between the Iowa and Skunk rivers, and established the town of Grinnell. The city of Newton was once known as the home of the Maytag Corporation and now is the headquarters for Whirlpool. People with a need for speed come out to the city to see cars battle it out at the Iowa Speedway.

WHAT TO SEE

AMES
GRANT WOOD MURALS
Parks Library, Morrill Road, Ames

Considered among the best works of this Iowa artist, the nine murals began as a Works Projects Administration project during the Great Depression. They depict various academic divisions of the school as well as the breaking of sod by pioneer farmers.

MAMIE DOUD EISENHOWER BIRTHPLACE
709 Carroll St., Boone, 515-432-1907; www.mamiesbirthplace.homestead.com

This one-story frame house includes period furnishings such as the bed in which Mamie Eisenhower was born.

Admission: adults $4, children 6-17 $1. June-October, Monday-Saturday, 10 a.m.-5 p.m.

DES MOINES
ADVENTURELAND PARK
305 34th Ave. N.W., Altoona, 515-266-2121, 800-532-1286; www.adventurelandpark.com

This amusement park has more than 100 rides, shows and attractions. Older children and adults can enjoy the Tornado rollercoaster and other thrill rides while younger children can enjoy bumper cars, a carousel and many other fun rides. There are also kiddie rides that cater to infants. Also offered are gaming areas, an arcade and a bingo parlor. Of course, there's plenty of fun food to enjoy as well from funnel cakes and cotton candy to nachos and hot dogs.

Admission: adults $35, seniors and children ages 4-9 $30, children 3 and under free. June-late August, daily; May and September, Saturday-Sunday.

HIGHLIGHT

WHAT ARE THE TOP THINGS TO DO IN CENTRAL IOWA?

TAKE IN THE GRANT WOOD MURALS
Artist Grant Wood, who created the masterpiece *American Gothic*, painted these murals, which are considered among his best works.

GO ON CRAZY RIDES AT ADVENTURELAND AMUSEMENT PARK
Thrill-seekers have their choice of more than 100 attractions, including water rides and coasters. The Dragon is the state's only upside-down, double-looping coaster.

SEE THE ANIMALS AT THE BLANK PARK ZOO
Iowa's only accredited zoo lets you get up close to the animals. Be sure to visit the rare red pandas, which look more like raccoons than black-and-white pandas.

VISIT THE DES MOINES ART CENTER
The striking modern white building houses a great collection of works from Henri Matisse, Edward Hopper and Georgia O'Keeffe. Best of all, admission is free.

RACE OVER TO THE IOWA SPEEDWAY
NASCAR fans will want to head to this state-of-the-art racetrack. It's open year round so that you can get your racing fix.

BLANK PARK ZOO
7401 S.W. Ninth St., Des Moines, 515-285-4722, 515-323-8383; www.blankparkzoo.com

The animal and bird habitats at this zoo are designed for close viewing. It includes Australian and African walk-through displays, a farm animal contact area, camel rides and an Old West train ride. There are 1,484 animals here from red pandas and African lions to river otters and alligators.

Admission: adults $10.95, seniors $8.95, children 3-12 $5.95, children 2 and under free. May-September, daily 10 a.m.-5 p.m.; Friday until 8 p.m. June-August.

DES MOINES ART CENTER
4700 Grand Ave., Des Moines, 515-277-4405; www.desmoinesartcenter.org

Exhibits of 19th- and 20th-century paintings and sculptures are displayed in a contemporary building designed by Eliel Saarinen, with additions by Richard Meier and I.M. Pei. Gaze upon collections from Henri Matisse, Edward Hopper and Georgia O'Keeffe, among others. Enjoy lunch at the outdoor courtyard that surrounds a reflecting pool and sculptures.

Admission: free. Tuesday, Wednesday, Friday 11 a.m.-4 p.m., Thursday 11 a.m.-9 p.m., Saturday 10 a.m.-4 p.m., Sunday noon-4 p.m.

DES MOINES BOTANICAL CENTER

909 Robert D. Ray Drive, Des Moines, 515-323-6290; www.botanicalcenter.com

Displays of nearly 1,500 species from around the world are located here along with seasonal floral displays. There are also galleries, which display various artists' work, and special events are offered, including storytime in the gardens for children and gardening classes on Saturdays.

Admission: adults $5, seniors $4, and children 4-17 $3, children 3 and under free. Daily 10 a.m.-5 p.m.

HOYT SHERMAN PLACE

1501 Woodland Ave., Des Moines, 515-244-0507; www.hoytsherman.org

This 1877 house was once the home of Gen. William Tecumseh Sherman's brother. It now features the city's oldest art gallery, including artifacts, antique furniture and an art collection. It also hosts entertainment including theatrical productions, musical acts such as Tegan and Sara and comedians such as the Second City comedy troupe of Chicago.

Tours by appointment. Monday-Friday 9 a.m.-4 p.m.

IOWA HISTORICAL MUSEUM

Capitol Complex, 600 E. Locust, Des Moines, 515-281-5111; www.iowahistory.org

This modern cultural center houses a state historical museum with displays portraying Iowa's history and heritage. The library contains county, state and family history materials; rare books and manuscripts about Iowa; census records and newspapers.

Tuesday-Saturday 9 a.m.-4:30 p.m., Sunday noon-4:30 p.m.

LIVING HISTORY FARMS

11121 Hickman Road, Urbandale, 515-278-5286; www.lhf.org

This complex has three farms and a town set on 600 acres. A Native American settlement includes gardens, shelters and crafts of the Ioway tribe. The pioneer farm of 1850 features a log cabin and outbuildings. The horse-powered farm of 1900 depicts farm and household chores typical of the period. The 1875 town of Walnut Hill includes a Victorian mansion, schoolhouse, pottery, blacksmith and carpentry shops, church, bank, newspaper, doctor's offices and a general store.

Admission: adults $11.50, seniors $10.50, children 3-12 $7. Monday-Saturday 9 a.m.-5 p.m.

PRAIRIE MEADOWS RACETRACK AND CASINO

1 Prairie Meadows Drive, Altoona, 800-325-9015; www.prairiemeadows.com

Live thoroughbred, quarter horse and harness racing occur late April to October. Also featured are simulcasts of thoroughbred and greyhound racing, and a 24-hour casino with more than 1,500 slots, a poker room and video poker machines.

SCIENCE CENTER OF IOWA
Science Center of Iowa, 401 W. Martin Luther King, Jr. Parkway, Des Moines, 515-274-6868, 515-274-4138; www.sciowa.org

Natural and physical science exhibits are the draw at this center, as are live demonstrations, Digistar planetarium shows and laser shows.

Admission: adults $9, seniors $8, children 2-12 $7. Daily.

STATE CAPITOL
1005 Grand Ave., Des Moines, 515-281-5591; www.legis.state.ia.us

The towering central dome of this 1871 building is covered with 23-karat gold leaf and the four smaller domes have golden seam marks. The building holds State offices, the Supreme Court, House and Senate chamber, a law library as well as beautiful paintings, mosaics and a collection of war flags.

Daily.

TERRACE HILL
2300 Grand Ave., Des Moines, 515-281-3604; www.terracehill.org

This extravagant Italianate/Second Empire mansion, now the residence of Iowa governors, is situated on a commanding knoll above downtown. The restored house is an outstanding example of Victorian residential architecture. Tours include first and second floors, carriage house and gardens.

March-December, Tuesday-Saturday 10 a.m.-1:30 p.m.

GRINNELL

GRINNELL HISTORICAL MUSEUM
1125 Broad St., Grinnell, 641-236-3732; grinnellmuseum.org

Historical furnishings, relics and documents of J. B. Grinnell and aviator Billy Robinson are housed in this late Victorian house.

Admission: donation. June-August, Tuesday-Sunday; rest of year, Saturday-Sunday or by appointment.

WELLS FARGO BANK OF IOWA—POWESHIEK COUNTY
Downtown, Grinnell

The second in the series of "jewel box" banks that architect Louis Henri Sullivan designed late in his career, this building was constructed in 1914. This unique structure, one of the more important designs in the series, has been restored within the confines of a working bank environment.

MADRID

IOWA ARBORETUM
1875 Peach Ave., Madrid, 515-795-3216; www.iowaarboretum.org

This arboretum includes 378 acres of trees, shrubs and gardens. Meander along trails and enjoy horticultural plantings, scenic overlooks, ravines and streams.

Admission: Donation. Daily dawn-dusk.

NEWTON

FRED MAYTAG PARK
301 S. 11th Ave. West, Newton, 641-792-1470; www.newtongov.org

Donated by the founder of the Maytag Company, this park covers 40 acres. It features tennis courts, picnicking areas, a playground, an amphitheater, an outdoor pool, a basketball court and a disc golf course. A log cabin originally built in 1848 also sits on the property. The outdoor pool features two water-slides, lap lanes, fountains and diving boards.

Park: Daily. Pool: June-August, Monday and Wednesday noon-9:30 p.m.; Tuesday, Thursday-Saturday noon-7 p.m.; Sunday noon-5 p.m.

IOWA SPEEDWAY

3333 Rusty Wallace Drive, Newton, 641-791-8000; www.iowaspeedway.com

Former NASCAR champion Rusty Wallace designed this state-of-the-art racetrack, which is operated by the U.S. Motorsport Corporation. Cars hit the track year round and fans fill the 25,000 grandstand seats to see all of the action. You can watch NASCAR races here.

JASPER COUNTY HISTORICAL MUSEUM

I-80 Exit 164, Newton, 641-792-9118; www.jaspercountymuseum.net

This museum holds local historical displays, which include a bas-relief sculpture of the natural history of the county, a Victorian home, a schoolroom, chapel and tool/farm equipment collections. There's also a Maytag historical display of washing machines with models from as far back as 1907.

Admission: adults $2, children $.50. May-September, daily 1-5 p.m.

WHERE TO STAY

DES MOINES
★★★DES MOINES MARRIOTT DOWNTOWN

700 Grand Ave., Des Moines, 515-245-5500, 800-228-9290; www.marriott.com

Connected to the Iowa Events Center by skywalk, this downtown hotel is close to the city's top shopping and restaurants. Rooms have been updated with luxury bedding, including down duvets and pillow-top mattresses as well as flat-screen TVs. Enjoy breakfast, lunch or dinner in the Rock River Grill & Tavern, featuring American cuisine in a casual setting.

417 rooms. Restaurant, bar. Pool. Pets accepted. $61-150

NEWTON
★★★LA CORSETTE MAISON INN

629 First Ave. E., Newton, 641-792-6833; www.lacorsette.com

This family-run historic mission-style mansion from 1909 is decorated with stained glass and oak. Guest suites are unique in styles and have French furnish-ings; some have wood-burning fireplaces. The onsite restaurant is a destination in its own right.

5 rooms. Restaurant. Complimentary breakfast. $151-250

RECOMMENDED

DES MOINES
RENAISSANCE DES MOINES SAVERY HOTEL

401 Locust St., Des Moines, 515-244-2151, 800-514-4706; www.marriott.com

This downtown hotel is an architectural landmark and is on the National Register of Historic Places. Rooms have a whimsical air, with walls sporting a cream and tan checkerboard pattern and striped rugs. You'll also get complimentary wireless Internet access and an in-room fitness package customized to your workout preferences. Business travelers will like the easy access to the Polk County Convention Center, since a climate-controlled skywalk connects the hotel to the building. It also links to the Iowa Events Center & Wells Fargo Arena.

218 rooms. Restaurant, bar. Fitness center. Pool. $61-150

THE SUITES OF 800 LOCUST

800 Locust St., Des Moines, 515-288-5800; www.800locust.com

For classy digs, try this European-inspired hotel. The classic rooms have crown molding, dark wood and are filled with reds, browns and cream. Request one of the 31 fireplace suites or 11 whirlpool suites for even cozier rooms. If you want to indulge yourself a little, get a treatment at the full-service spa and stop by the onsite bar for one of its signature martinis.

51 rooms. Bar. Complimentary breakfast. Business center. Fitness center. Spa. $151-250

WHERE TO EAT

DES MOINES

★★★CHRISTOPHER'S

2816 Beaver Ave., Des Moines, 515-274-3694;
www.christophers-restaurant.com

Located in a charming and historic neighborhood, family-owned Christopher's serves Italian-American cuisine, including pastas, steaks and seafood. Dishes are made from scratch, some from old family recipes. Try the Sophia pasta, penne with fresh garlic, basil, tomatoes, mushrooms and a light cream sauce or the chicken velouté served with king crab meat, mashed potatoes and grilled asparagus. It has been a local favorite for many years and now features three dining rooms, a large bar and lounge area as well as a private dining room.

American, Italian. Dinner. Closed Sunday. Children's menu. Bar. $16-35

★★★TROSTEL'S GREENBRIAR RESTAURANT AND BAR

5810 Merle Hay Road, Johnston, 515-253-0124;
www.greenbriartrostels.com

The menu from chef Troy Trostel offers a broad selection of seafood, chicken, pasta and specialty prime rib as well as specialty dishes that are seasonal

WHICH DES MOINES HOTEL IS BEST FOR BUSINESS TRAVELERS?

The Renaissance Des Moines Savery Hotel is in a convenient downtown spot for those on business. Even better, a skywalk connects it to the convention center. The hotel itself has a business center and complimentary wireless Internet, great perks for business travelers.

WHAT ARE THE BEST ITALIAN RESTAURANTS IN DES MOINES?

Centro:
Centro's George Formaro was a semifinalist for a James Beard Award in the Best Chef category for his inspired Italian cuisine. Taste it for yourself.

Christopher's:
What's the secret to this family-run restaurant's delish Italian dishes? It uses recipes handed down from generation to generation. It's food that grandma would make.

and locally grown or raised in Iowa. Dishes include halibut stuffed with havarti and crab meat, Iowa pork chops and broiled New Zealand orange roughy. Choose a glass from the extensive wine list to accompany your meal.

American. Lunch (Wednesday-Friday), dinner. Closed Sunday. Outdoor seating. Children's menu. $16-35

NEWTON
★★★LA CORSETTE MAISON INN
629 First Ave. E., Newton, 641-792-6833; www.lacorsette.com

Located inside La Corsette Maison Inn, guests are served by tuxedoed waiters and entertained with music from the baby grand piano. Four- or six-course prix fixe menus are offered, including entrée creations such as roasted pork loin with prune chutney, pheasant braised in apple cider and onions or orange roughy with walnut cream sauce. Many of the ingredients come from the surrounding Iowa farms and all breads, pastries and desserts are housemade.

American, French. Lunch, dinner. Reservations recommended. $36-85

RECOMMENDED

DES MOINES
CENTRO
1007 Locust St., Des Moines, 515-248-1780; www.centrodesmoines.com

Diners pack this popular restaurant to gorge on mouth-watering Italian eats. Centro specializes in New York-style thin-crust pizza that comes out piping hot from the coal-fired brick oven. Try the Pizza Bianco, topped with roasted garlic, mozzarella, ricotta and Parmesan. But it also serves more unconventional fare, like Portobello fries with truffle aioli, fettuccine studded with shrimp and prosciutto, and Parmesan-crusted pork chop Milanese. Whichever route you choose, cap off your meal with polenta crêpes with pistachio ice cream, honey and toasted pistachios.

Italian. Lunch, dinner. Children's menu. Bar. $16-35

LA MIE
841 42nd St. Des Moines, 515-255-1625; www.lamiebakery.com

A local favorite for breakfast and brunch, La Mie serves up dishes like fromage blanc quiche and a flank steak sandwich with arugula and horseradish mayo. But the desserts are the standouts at this small eatery. The restaurant/bakery makes all of its own artisan bread and pastries in house. No one would blame you if you ordered the chocolate brioche, some macarons or the blueberry danish with a hot mug of coffee and made that your morning meal.

French. Breakfast, lunch, Saturday-Sunday brunch. Closed Sunday. $15 and under

PROOF

1301 Locust St., Des Moines, 515-244-0655; www.proofrestaurant.com

Proof may be primarily a lunchtime spot, but you won't find pedestrian sandwiches on the menu. That's because James Beard Rising Star Chef semifinalist Carly Groben is at the helm. Grab a seat in the stark white dining room for Moroccan chicken, vegetable falafel or merguez sausage flatbread sandwiches. Or go for the salmon and risotto cake or the scallops with tabbouleh. The Friday three-course dinner menu changes weekly but features ingredients from local farms. Expect dishes like butternut squash and cheddar bisque and duck-basil gnocchi.

Mediterranean. Lunch (Monday-Friday), dinner (Friday). $15 and under

WESTERN IOWA

Located on the western border of Iowa where it meets Nebraska is Council Bluffs. The Lewis and Clark expedition stopped here in 1804 to hold the first "council bluff" with local Native American tribes. To the north is Sioux City, which lies at the heart of a tri-state region bordered by the Sioux and Missouri rivers. It has historically been a center for shipping, transportation and agriculture. The Lewis and Clark expedition followed the Missouri River; the only fatality of that historic trek is commemorated here with the Sergeant Floyd Monument, the first registered U.S. historic landmark. Today, the Missouri River is important to the city from a recreational standpoint, with a developed riverfront with parks, a dance pavilion and a riverboat casino. Further north is Lake Okoboji, one of the Iowa great lakes and a vacationer's paradise. Lake Okoboji is among the most popular resort areas in Iowa. Visitors will find everything from golf to fishing to shopping and every expected water sport available.

WHAT TO SEE

ARNOLDS PARK/LAKE OKOBOJI AREA
ARNOLDS PARK AMUSEMENT PARK

37 Lake St., Arnolds Park, 712-332-2183; www.arnoldspark.com

This century-old amusement park features classic old rides like the wooden Legend roller coaster, which was built in 1927, a Ferris wheel and newer favorites. Kids of all ages will enjoy the bumper cars, tilt-a-whirl and other fun rides as well as amusement games like skee ball and tons of great food. There is also entertainment, like a free concert series featuring national and local artists.

Admission: adults $25, children $17. Mid-June-mid-August, daily; May-mid-June and late August, Saturday-Sunday; hours vary.

OKOBOJI QUEEN II
37 Lake St., Arnolds Park, 712-332-5159

Take one of several steamship cruises on West Okoboji Lake, which are offered in the summer. Tours last a little more than an hour and you'll learn about the surrounding historical landmarks and enjoy the lake breeze.

Admission: adults $15, seniors $13, children under 36 inches tall free. May-September; hours vary.

COUNCIL BLUFFS
GOLDEN SPIKE MONUMENT
S. 21st Street and Ninth Avenue, Council Bluffs; www.cbparksandrec.org

Erected in 1939, this 56-foot golden concrete spike commemorates the junction of the Union Pacific and Central Pacific railroads in Council Bluffs.

HISTORIC POTTAWATTAMIE COUNTY SQUIRREL CAGE JAIL
226 Pearl St., Council Bluffs, 712-323-2509; www.thehistoricalsociety.org

This unique three-story rotary jail is sometimes referred to as the "human squirrel cage" or "lazy Susan jail." It acted as the jail from 1885 until 1969 with 18 revolving cells covering three stories. It is only one of three revolving jails still existing in the United States today.

Admission: adults $7, seniors $6, children 6-12 $5, children 5 and under free. April-October, Wednesday-Saturday, 10 a.m.-4 p.m., Sunday 1-4 p.m.; November-March, Saturday noon-4 p.m.

LEWIS AND CLARK MONUMENT
19962 Monument Road, Council Bluffs, 712-328-4650

This monument of native stone located on the bluffs depicts Lewis and Clark holding council with the Otoe and Missouri tribes and was dedicated to honor their expedition in 1804.

LINCOLN MONUMENT
323 Lafayette Ave., Council Bluffs; www.parksandrec.councilbluffs-ia.gov

Erected in 1911, this granite pylon marks the spot from which Lincoln designated the town as the eastern terminus of the Union Pacific Railroad.

RAILSWEST RAILROAD MUSEUM
16th Avenue and S. Main Street, Council Bluffs, 712-323-5182; www.thehistoricalsociety.org

For anyone interested in trains, this would be an interesting place to stop. The historic Rock Island depot was built in 1899 and today displays railroad memorabilia and HO gauge model trains. The last time the depot was used was in 1970, and the last time the Rock Island Railroad ran was in 1980.

Admission: adults $6, seniors $5, children 6-16 $4, children 5 and under free. April-October, Tuesday-Saturday 10 a.m.-4 p.m., Sunday 1-4 p.m.; November-March, Friday-Saturday 10 a.m.-4 p.m., Sunday 1-4 p.m.

SIOUX CITY
SERGEANT FLOYD MONUMENT
Glenn Avenue and Highway 75, Sioux City

This was the first registered national historic landmark in the United States. The 100-foot obelisk marks the burial place of Sgt. Charles Floyd, the only casualty of the Lewis and Clark expedition.

SIOUX CITY PUBLIC MUSEUM
2901 Jackson, Sioux City, 712-279-6174; www.siouxcitymuseum.org

Exhibits show Sioux City history and life in pioneer days as well as geological, archaeological and Native American materials. It's located in a Romanesque 23-room mansion.

Tuesday-Saturday 9 a.m.-5 p.m., Sunday 1-5 p.m.

WOODBURY COUNTY COURTHOUSE
620 Douglas St., Sioux City, 712-279-6601

This courthouse was the largest structure ever completed in the architectural style of Chicago's Prairie School. Designed by Purcell and Elmslie, long-time associates of Louis Sullivan, the city-block-long building was constructed in 1918 of Roman brick and ornamented with massive pieces of terracotta, stained glass and relief sculpture by Alfonso Ianelli, who also worked with Frank Lloyd Wright. Both the exterior and highly detailed interior are in near-pristine condition. Courtrooms still contain original architect-designed furniture and lighting fixtures.

WELCOME TO KANSAS

IN THE MOVIE THE WIZARD OF OZ, KANSAS IS A DUSTY,

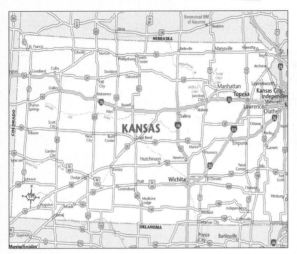

empty landscape in black and white. In real life, no one will deny Kansas has plenty of open space (the state uses the slogan "As Big As You Think" to promote itself), but the curious visitor will find that Kansas is full of interesting places and natural attractions. And yes, it's in color: the gold and black of sunflowers growing by the thousands in a field, the green of vast swaths of native prairie grass (dappled with splashes of brightly colored wildflowers) and of course, the amber waves of grain—wheat—that is grown on so much of Kansas' ground.

For more life in Technicolor, check out the annual Wah-Shun-Gah Days powwow in a Santa Fe Trail town, where tribal dancers don beautiful, brilliantly colored native costumes and dip and sway to drums. Or if you like your colors loud and your timing is right, you can catch the spectacle of car racing at the Kansas Speedway in Kansas City.

Native Americans inhabited Kansas thousands of years before Spanish conquistador Francisco Vasquez de Coronado explored the territory in 1541. Other early explorers of Kansas were Meriwether Lewis and William Clark.

By the 1840s, traders and immigrants had established the Santa Fe and Chisholm Trails across the region. Kansas' pre-Civil War activities included the exploits of John Brown, who operated part of the Underground Railroad for slaves escaping through the state. Many clashes occurred between antislavery and proslavery forces as Kansas was being admitted to the Union. The Abolitionists were determined that Kansas be a "free" state. As railroads expanded westward, the era of cattle drives made such towns as Abilene, Hays, Wichita and Dodge City centers of the legendary Old West, as did such men as Bat Masterson, Wyatt Earp, "Wild Bill" Hickok and the Dalton Gang.

BEST ATTRACTIONS

KANSAS' BEST ATTRACTIONS

TOPEKA
As Kansas' capital, Topeka is a hub for culture, politics and sightseeing. Gage Park is a good place to start, since it houses a zoo, an aquatic center, a rose garden and more.

WICHITA
Wichita is the largest city in the state. You'll find a plethora of things to see and do, especially in Old Town, the city's thriving downtown entertainment district.

Eastern Kansas is green, fertile and hilly, with woods, streams and lakes. Western Kansas is a part of the Great Plains, once the grass-covered haunt of the buffalo. In 1874, Mennonite immigrants from Russia introduced their Turkey Red wheat seed to Kansas soil, helping to establish Kansas as the breadbasket of the nation.

When you want to rub elbows with civilization, Topeka, the state's largest city with a 600,000 metro area population, has galleries and museums. Its historic Delano District, once known for its brothels and saloons, is a place to find martini lounges and jazz. If you're looking for the laid-back vibe of a college town, head to Lawrence, home of the University of Kansas.

NORTHEASTERN WOODED HILLS

In the Northeastern Wooded Hills area, you'll find the city of Lawrence, which had a stormy history in the territorial years. It was founded by the New England Emigrant Aid Company, which aimed to populate the area with antislavery proponents transplanted from New England and other "free states" as a means of warding off slavery. The center of Free State activities, the town was close to a state of war from 1855 until the Free Staters triumphed in 1859. The Confederate guerrilla leader, William Quantrill, made one of his most spectacular raids on Lawrence in 1863, burning the town and killing 150 citizens. After the Civil War, the town experienced a gradual and peaceful growth. Today, it is the site of the University of Kansas. North of Lawrence is Topeka, the capital city of Kansas, located on the Kansas River (locally called the Kaw). World-famous psychiatric clinic and research center, the Menninger Foundation, is located here. Herbert Hoover's vice president, Charles Curtis, who was part Kaw and a descendant of one of Topeka's earliest settlers, was born here.

WHAT TO SEE

LAWRENCE
LAWRENCE ARTS CENTER
940 New Hampshire St., Lawrence, 785-843-2787; www.lawrenceartscenter.com

This art center hosts two galleries featuring the work of local artists and craftspeople, and a performance hall for theater, dance and music performances. The center offers art classes and workshops for all ages.

Monday-Saturday 9 a.m.-5 p.m.

OLD WEST LAWRENCE HISTORIC DISTRICT
402 N. Second St., Lawrence, 785-865-4499

Take a self-guided tour through this area (from Sixth and Eight streets and Tennessee and Indiana streets) of about 50 notable 19th-century homes. The district itself is on the National Register of Historic Places.

TOPEKA
BROWN V. BOARD OF EDUCATION NATIONAL HISTORIC SITE
1515 S.E. Monroe St., Topeka, 785-354-4273; www.nps.gov

This site commemorates the U.S. Supreme Court's groundbreaking 1954 decision declaring segregation in public schools unconstitutional. Here you'll find Monroe Elementary School, one of Topeka's four formerly segregated elementary schools for African-American children, along with interpretive exhibits and educational programs.

Daily 9 a.m.-5 p.m.

CEDAR CREST GOVERNOR'S MANSION
1 S.W. Cedar Crest Road, Topeka, 785-296-3636; www.governor.ks.gov

This massive house features period architecture with Loire Valley overtones spread out on 244 acres. Built in 1928 and bequeathed to the state in 1955, it became the governor's residence in 1962.

Guided tours: Monday afternoons, 1-3:30 p.m.

COMBAT AIR MUSEUM
Forbes Field, Hangars 602 and 604, J St., Topeka, 785-862-3303; www.combatairmuseum.org

Jets, cargo transports, fighters and trainers from 1917-1980 are displayed here, as well as military artifacts. There are also exhibits featuring uniforms from specific wars along with other items like artillery and photographs.

Admission: adults $6, active military and children 5-17 $4, children under 5 free. June-September, Monday-Saturday 9 a.m.-4:30 p.m.; October-May, Monday-Saturday noon-4:30 p.m.

GAGE PARK
9635 S.W. Gage Blvd., Topeka, 785-368-9180; www.topeka.org

Head to Gage Park, which covers 160 acres, for a fun day outside where you

HIGHLIGHT

WHAT ARE THE TOP THINGS TO DO IN NORTHEASTERN WOODED HILLS?

TAKE A WALK THROUGH THE OLD WEST LAWRENCE HISTORIC DISTRICT

Amble along the sidewalks to see charming 19th-century homes in this historic district, which is listed on the National Register of Historic Places.

SEE THE BROWN V. BOARD OF EDUCATION NATIONAL HISTORIC SITE

This historic site, which includes schools, exhibits and programs, pays homage to the landmark 1954 Supreme Court decision that ended segregation in schools.

SPEND THE DAY IN GAGE PARK

The 160-acre park is home to the Blaisdell Family Aquatic Center, the Topeka Zoo, the Reinisch Rose Garden and the Helen Hocker Center for the Performing Arts.

can play tennis, softball and volleyball; go swimming; and take your kids to the playground, which features equipment for different ages and abilities. Take your whole family on the newly restored carousel, which was built in 1908 (rides are $1). The Blaisdell Family Aquatic Center is also here; it features an outdoor pool with a diving board, four water slides, a baby pool and picnicking areas. Kids can also enjoy taking a ride on a mini-train and a visit to the Topeka Zoo, which resides here along with a dog park, the Reinisch Rose Garden and Helen Hocker Center for the Performing Arts.

Carousel: April-late May, Thursday-Saturday 10 a.m.-4:45 p.m., Sunday 11 a.m.-4:45 p.m.; late-May-mid-August, Monday-Saturday 10 a.m.-5:45 p.m., Sunday 11 a.m.-5:45 p.m.; mid-August-October, Thursday-Saturday 10 a.m.-4:45 p.m., Sunday 11 a.m.-4:45 p.m. Pool: Mid-May-early August, daily 1-8 p.m.; mid-August, Saturday-Sunday 1-8 p.m.

KANSAS STATE HISTORICAL SOCIETY
6425 S.W. Sixth Ave., Topeka, 785-272-8681; www.kshs.org
The Kansas Museum of History includes the Library of Kansas and information on Native American and Western history and genealogy. Exhibits at the museum include "Cars: the Need for Speed," which showcases various cars and uniforms worn by race car drivers.

Admission: adults $6, students $4, children 5 and under free. Tuesday-Saturday 9 a.m.-5 p.m., Sunday 1-5 p.m.

STATE CAPITOL

300 W. 10th St., Topeka, 785-296-3966; www.kshs.org

The design of the beautiful Kansas State Capitol was based on the U.S. Capitol. On the grounds are the statues Abraham Lincoln The Man of Sorrows and The Pioneer Mother and Child, both by Topeka-born sculptor Merrell Gage. Murals on the second floor are by John Steuart Curry and include his famous Tragic Prelude; those on the first floor are by David H. Overmyer. Note that due to renovations, tours have been canceled until June 2012 and some murals may be covered.

Monday-Friday 8 a.m.-4:30 p.m.

TOPEKA ZOO

Gage Park, 635 S.W. Gage Blvd., Topeka, 785-368-9180; www.topeka.org

Located within Gage Park, the Topeka Zoo was built in 1833 as part of the 80 acres donated by the Gage family and today features more than 380 animals. Features include an orangutan and gorilla exhibit, a black bear exhibit, jungle cats such as the African black leopard and the Sumatran tiger, a lion exhibit, and a tropical rain forest. The children's zoo allows children to get closer to the animals and interact with farm animals such as goats, cows, sheep and pigs.

Admission: adults $5.75, seniors $4.75, children 3-12 $4.25, children 2 and under free. Daily 9 a.m.-5 p.m.

WHERE TO STAY

LAWRENCE

★★★THE ELDRIDGE HOTEL

701 Massachusetts St., Lawrence, 785-749-5011, 800-527-0909; www.eldridgehotel.com

This hotel, with a history dating to the Civil War, is located in the heart of quaint downtown Lawrence, near the University of Kansas. The setting is charming, but the décor is crisp and contemporary, including guest suites that featuring neutral tones with a splash of color. The original ceilings and woodwork have been nicely maintained. Spacious suites feature separate sitting rooms and the Premier King Suite has French doors. The sleek restaurant, Ten, serves breakfast, lunch and dinner and the bar, the Jayhawker, features a long list of tasty martinis (Thursday night is half-off martinis), if you're up for a cocktail. While the hotel is more modern, it still carries on an interesting past; a ghost supposedly lives here and it is said to possibly be the ghost of Col. Eldridge, after whom the hotel is named.

48 rooms. Restaurant, bar. $151-250

RECOMMENDED

TOPEKA

HYATT PLACE TOPEKA

6021 S.W. Sixth Ave., Topeka, 785-273-0066; www.hyatt.com

These stylish, spacious rooms come in earthy browns, cream and bright blue. They all have a comfortable sitting area with an L-shaped sleeper sofa. Rooms also come with a 42-inch flat-screen HDTV and free wireless Internet access. Business travelers will make good use of a media center that allows you to plug a laptop, MP3 player or DVD player directly into the television.

126 rooms. Complimentary breakfast. Fitness center. Pool. $61-150

THE SENATE LUXURY SUITES
900 S.W. Tyler St., Topeka, 785-233-5050, 800-488-3188; www.senatesuites.com

Everyone from Aerosmith to Dustin Diamond, a.k.a. Screech from *Saved by the Bell*, has checked into this hotel with its beautiful brick Victorian façade. Architecture is a strong suit for 1920s hotel, which has its original stucco-walled hallways with unusual woodwork, arched doorways and courtyards sprinkled with bronze statues. All of the classic rooms are individually decorated, but each has a balcony where you can see the Capitol Building, which is a block away. Rooms also come with complimentary wireless Internet access.

51 rooms. Bar. Complimentary breakfast. Fitness center. $61-150

WHERE TO EAT

ALSO RECOMMENDED
LAWRENCE
FREE STATE BREWING COMPANY
636 Massachusetts St., Lawrence, 785-843-4555; www.freestatebrewing.com

When Free State opened in 1989, it had the unique distinction of being the first legally operating brewery in Kansas in more than a hundred years. So of course, you have to drink to that. Pay homage to Kansas by ordering the Wheat State Golden, a light, refreshing wheat beer, but don't forget about the food. Go for the local favorite, the gumbo, which is brimming with andouille sausage, Cajun crawfish tails and chicken. For dessert, have another beer.

American. Lunch, dinner. Outdoor seating. Bar. $16 and under

WHEATFIELD'S BAKERY CAFÉ
904 Vermont St., Lawrence, 785-841-5553; www.wheatfieldsbakery.com

You won't be able to stop munching on the addictive bread here. The good-for-you, from-scratch artisan breads, baked daily in the wood-fired brick oven, are the café's specialty. That explains why the menu centers on the numerous loaf varieties; the dinner menu is composed of sandwich selections. You can get Genoa salami, provolone, red peppers and red

---

WHICH HOTEL IS BEST FOR BUSINESS TRAVELERS?

The Hyatt Place Topeka seems made for business travelers. Rooms have nice-sized workstations, a media center where you can plug your laptop into the TV and hotel-wide complimentary wireless Internet access, giving you the option to work in bed or in the modern lobby.

onions on kalamata olive bread or turkey and cranberry relish on walnut sage bread. The gravlax plate will give you an assortment of the delicious breads along with house-cured salmon, cornichons, red onions and mustard dill sauce.

American. Breakfast (Monday-Friday), lunch, dinner (Monday-Saturday).

TOPEKA
LONGHORN STEAKHOUSE
1915 S. Wanamaker Road, Topeka, 785-228-9900; www.longhornsteakhouse.com

This chain is all about hearty, sizzling steaks. The tender filet is a guest favorite, but if you want some surf with your turf, go for the filet stuffed with lump crab and slathered with an herb-cheese sauce. If you have enough room for dessert, try the Chocolate Stampede, a rich cake layered with six different types of chocolate and a scoop of vanilla bean ice cream on the side.

American, steak. Lunch, dinner. Bar. $16-35

NEW CITY CAFÉ
4005 S.W. Gage Center Drive, Topeka, 785-271-8646; www.newcityonline.biz

This hip restaurant adds Latin flair to Topeka's dining scene. An eclectic starter is the Caribbean quesadilla stuffed with jerk chicken, Monterey Jack cheese, peppers red onions and mango. For the main course, try lamb chops with guava-tequila chutney over Parmesan risotto or pan-seared tilapia with mango-chipotle salsa with black beans, rice and fried green plantains. Check out the hefty wine list as well.

Caribbean, Latin. Lunch (Monday-Friday), dinner. $36-85

ROWHOUSE RESTAURANT
515 S.W. Van Buren St., Topeka, 785-235-1700; www.rowhouserestaurant.net

Tucked inside a real row house, this cozy, elegant restaurant has three levels and a number of dining rooms. The seasonal menu changes weekly, but typical entrées include mac and cheese with goat, Swiss and Parmesan cheeses as well as seared marinated chicken breast with butternut squash, Brussels sprouts and beurre blanc. Save room for in-season desserts like pumpkin crème brûlée and blueberry cobbler topped with whipped sour cream. On Thursdays, try to reserve a spot in the restaurant's wine tasting; for $15, you get three pours and a tasting portion of one of the week's entrées.

Contemporary American. Dinner. Closed Monday-Tuesday. Bar. $36-85

NORTH FLINT HILLS/CENTRAL PRAIRIE

As the last outfitting place on the Santa Fe Trail between the Missouri River and Santa Fe, Council Grove, now a National Historic Landmark, holds historic significance in the development of the West. The town grew up around a Native American campground in a grove of oaks near the Neosho River and has many turn-of-the-century buildings, several parks and two lakes. South of Council Grove is Emporia, which was once the home of one of America's most famous newspaper editors, William Allen White. His *Emporia Gazette* editorials, written from the 1890s to the 1940s, attracted nationwide attention and earned White a Pulitzer Prize.

To the north, Manhattan is a thriving center for trade, education, government, healthcare and entertainment. Several early settlements were combined to form Manhattan. Kansas State University is in Manhattan, making it a popular college town. Abilene, once famous as a Kansas "cow town" in 1867, is the terminal point of the Kansas Pacific (later Union Pacific) Railroad and the nearest railhead for the shipment of cattle brought north over the Chisholm Trail in 1867. The number of cattle shipped east from here between 1867 and 1871 has been estimated at more than a million, and often 500 cowboys were paid off at a time. City marshals Tom Smith and "Wild Bill" Hickok brought in law and order in the 1870s. Today, Abilene is a wheat center, perhaps best known as the boyhood home of Dwight D. Eisenhower.

Salina got its start as a trading post for gold hunters stopping through on their way to Pikes Peak. The arrival of the Union Pacific Railroad in 1867 brought new growth, and the wheat crops in the 1870s established a permanent economy. The city was rebuilt in 1903 after the Smoky Hill flood destroyed most of the community. Aviator Steve Fossett made history in 2005 when he launched the first solo, nonstop, round-the-world, non-refueled flight in the Virgin Atlantic GlobalFlyer from the Salina airport.

WHAT TO SEE

ABILENE

ABILENE & SMOKY VALLEY RAIL ROAD

200 S. Fifth St., Abilene, 785-263-1077, 888-426-6687; www.asvrr.org

This 100-year-old wooden diner coach makes trips through the historic countryside and offers dinner trips featuring cuisine from the area's restaurants while you enjoy the scenery (check website for schedule and prices).

Memorial Day-Labor Day, Wednesday-Saturday 10 a.m. and 2 p.m., Sunday 2 p.m.; May-October, Saturday 10 a.m. and 2 p.m., Sunday 2 p.m.

DICKINSON COUNTY HISTORICAL MUSEUM

412 S. Campbell St., Abilene, 785-263-2681; www.heritagecenterdk.com

Exhibits at this museum depict life in early pioneer days and include antique toys and household items used at the turn of the century. Also onsite is a heritage center, carousel and log cabin.

Daily.

HIGHLIGHT

WHAT ARE THE TOP THINGS TO DO IN NORTH FLINT HILLS/CENTRAL PRAIRIE?

VISIT THE EISENHOWER CENTER

If you like Ike, or just want to learn more about the 34th U.S. president, come to this center. It houses his birthplace, presidential library and final resting place.

GET OUTSIDE AT THE FLINT HILLS NATIONAL WILDLIFE REFUGE

The scenic grounds of this 18,500-acre refuge are great for hiking and camping. If you make the trek in the fall or winter, you can catch a glimpse of bald eagles.

SEE THE ANIMALS AT THE SUNSET ZOO

The zoo's most famous resident is Brownie, who's believed to be the oldest grizzly bear in the world. Visit him and Nia, the adorable baby chimpanzee.

EISENHOWER CENTER

200 S.E. Fourth St., Abilene, 785-263-4751; www.dwightdeisenhower.com

President Dwight D. Eisenhower's birthplace is also the location of his presidential library. Visitors can tour the 1887 house where Eisenhower was raised; the interior and most furnishings are original. The museum houses changing exhibits of mementos, souvenirs and gifts received during Eisenhower's career. The library contains presidential papers, photographs, manuscripts and more from the President's time in the White House and after. President and Mrs. Eisenhower are buried in the Meditation Chapel.

Admission: adults $8, seniors $6, children 8-15 $1. Mid-August-Memorial Day, 9 a.m.-4:45 p.m.; Memorial Day-mid-August, 8 a.m.-5:45 p.m.

SEELYE MANSION AND MUSEUM

1105 N. Buckeye Ave., Abilene, 785-263-1084; www.seelyemansion.org

This 25-room Georgian mansion is listed on the National Register of Historic Places. It was built in 1905 by A. B. Seelye, a patent medicine entrepreneur. The home features original furniture, a Steinway Grand piano, 25 bedrooms, 11 bathrooms, a bowling alley and a Tiffany-designed fireplace. The museum depicts a turn-of-the-century medicine business with artifacts from 1890.

Admission: adults $10, children 6-12 $5. Monday-Saturday 10 a.m.-6 p.m., Sunday 1-6 p.m.

COUNCIL GROVE
COUNCIL OAK SHRINE
313 E. Main St., Council Grove

The treaty of 1825 was signed here between U.S. government commissioners and the Osage.

CUSTER'S ELM SHRINE
South Neosho Street, Council Grove

This elm trunk stands as a shrine to a tree that was 100 feet tall, 16 feet in circumference and reputedly sheltered the camp of Gen. George Custer in 1867 when he was leading an expedition to western Kansas.

MADONNA OF THE TRAIL MONUMENT
Union and Main streets, Council Grove

This is one of 12 statues erected in each of the states through which the National Old Trails Roads passed. The Madonna pays tribute to pioneer mothers and commemorates the trails that opened the West.

POST OFFICE OAK
East Main Street, Council Grove

This mammoth oak tree with a cache at its base served as an unofficial post office for pack trains and caravans on the Santa Fe Trail from 1825 to 1847.

EMPORIA
DAVID TRAYLOR ZOO OF EMPORIA
75 Soden Road, Emporia, 620-341-4365; www.emporiazoo.org

Located in Soden's Grove Park, the David Traylor Zoo is small but still offers a lot to see. You'll encounter cougars, elk, badgers, buffalo, deer and much more in more natural settings than at larger zoos. Take a ride on the miniature train (during summer evenings) and enjoy the rest of what Soden's Grove Park has to offer.

Memorial Day-October, daily 10 a.m.-4:30 p.m.; until 8 p.m. Sunday and Wednesday.

EMPORIA GAZETTE BUILDING
517 Merchant St., Emporia, 620-342-4800

This building houses William Allen White's widely quoted newspaper and has been its headquarters for more than a century. Located here is a small one-room museum that displays newspaper machinery used during White's time.

Monday-Friday 7:30 a.m-5:30 p.m.

FLINT HILLS NATIONAL WILDLIFE REFUGE
530 W. Maple Ave., Hartford, 620-392-5553; www.fws.gov

Consisting of 18,500 acres on the upstream portion of John Redmond River, this park offers hiking and camping. You'll see plenty of waterfowl here, and bald eagles can be spotted in fall and winter. Fishing and hunting are permitted only during legal seasons.

Monday-Friday 8 a.m.-4:30 p.m.

MANHATTAN
SUNSET ZOO
2333 Oak St., Manhattan, 785-587-2737; www.ci.manhattan.ks.us

Sunset Zoo is home to more than 300 animals, including Brownie, thought to be the oldest living grizzly bear in the world. He's kept company by snow leopards, cheetahs, red pandas, bobcats, reptiles, birds and more. Be sure to visit the baby chimpanzee, Nia, who is only a year old. There are also baby snow leopard cubs, sloth bear cubs and other darling baby animals to see.

Admission: adults $4, children 3-12 $2, children under 2 free. April-October, daily 9:30 a.m.-5 p.m.; November-March, daily noon-5 p.m.

TUTTLE CREEK STATE PARK
5800 A River Pond Road, Manhattan, 785-539-7941; www.stateparks.com

This 1,200-acre park is on a 13,350-acre lake and there's a 12,000-acre wildlife area nearby. There is a special observation area with distant views of the Blue River Valley and Randolph Bridge, the largest in Kansas. Enjoy swimming on the beach (which has a bathhouse), fishing, boating and camping.

SALINA
SALINA ART CENTER
242 S. Santa Fe, Salina, 785-827-1431; www.salinaartcenter.org

The Salina Art Center features art exhibits as well as a hands-on art laboratory for children and a movie theater featuring a range of art-house films. The gallery has exhibits such as "Photographic," which displays photographs from Anne Collier and Melanie Schiff and sound installations from composer and sound artist Stephen Vitiello. The art lab is a free place for children to make art often related to the current exhibition, and the center also offers other educational classes for kids.

Wednesday-Saturday noon-5 p.m., Sunday 1-5 p.m.

SMOKY HILL MUSEUM
211 W. Iron Ave., Salina, 785-309-5776; www.smokyhillmuseum.org

The history of Salina is told through photos and artifacts at this museum. Changing exhibits feature the Prairie Education Lab with a pioneer sod dugout home from 1858 that parents and children can sit in to imagine what life was like on the frontier, a general store period room and much more.

Admission: free. Tuesday-Friday noon-5 p.m., Saturday 10 a.m.-5 p.m., Sunday 1-5 p.m.

WHERE TO STAY

RECOMMENDED
MANHATTAN
FAIRFIELD INN MANHATTAN
300 Colorado St., Manhattan, 785-539-2400; www.marriott.com

The rooms at this Marriott brand hotel are simple and bright, with white walls and a red and green color motif in the rest of the space. Take advantage of the free continental breakfast and the complimentary wireless Internet access. If you like to stay fit on the road, hit the onsite gym or do some laps in the indoor pool.

98 rooms. Complimentary breakfast. Fitness center. Pool. $61-150

PARKWOOD INN & SUITES
505 S. 17th St., Manhattan, 785-320-5440;
www.parkwoodinnmanhattan.com

The exterior of this hotel is unremarkable, but inside you'll find a cozy spot. Rooms are bathed in chocolate brown, beige and dark wood, but they get a spark with touches like a gold comforter and a fire-engine-red armchair. They also have flat-screen HDTVs, DVD players, complimentary wireless Internet access, mini-fridges and microwaves. If you want to laze around, hunker down in front of the lobby's double-sided fireplace, sit in the patio overlooking Longs Park or borrow one of the 250-plus DVDs and watch it in your welcoming room.

78 rooms. Complimentary breakfast. Business center. Fitness center. Pets accepted. $61-150

SALINA
COURTYARD SALINA
320 Riffel Drive, Salina, 785-309-1300, 800-919-4795;
www.marriott.com

The basic rooms have light wood and décor in orange and blue. Rooms come outfitted with a mini-refrigerator, a microwave and complimentary wireless Internet access. For something a bit more indulgent, reserve the whirlpool suite.

80 rooms. Restaurant, bar. Business center. Fitness center. Pool. $61-150

WHERE TO EAT

ABILENE
★★★KIRBY HOUSE
205 N.E. Third St., Abilene, 785-263-7336;
www.kirby-house.com

Built as a home in 1885, this Victorian-style restaurant has a friendly atmosphere popular with large groups and anyone celebrating a special occasion. The menu features American classics and house specialties such as country fried steak and prime rib.

American. Lunch, dinner. Closed Sunday. Children's menu. Bar. $16-35

MANHATTAN
★★★HARRY'S
418 Poyntz Ave., Manhattan, 785-537-1300;
www.harrysmanhattan.com

The historic Wareham hotel is the setting for this restaurant, named in honor of the hotel's first owner, Harry Wareham. Though the restaurant has been

---

WHERE'S THE BEST PLACE TO GET A GLASS OF WINE?

4 Olives Wine Bar will surely satisfy every wine drinker, since it boasts a list with 700 selections. The eatery has consistently won accolades from *Wine Spectator* for its great selection. If you need a nosh with your vino, order from the cheese menu.

restored to look much as it did when it first opened in the 1920s, the menu is decidedly up-to-date, with dishes such as a prosciutto and fig salad with candied walnuts and bleu cheese, risotto and grilled portobellos, or trout breaded in pecan focaccia with a spicy almond, crawfish and green bean cream sauce.

American. Lunch, dinner. Closed Sunday. Reservations recommended. Children's menu. Bar. $36-85

RECOMMENDED

MANHATTAN
4 OLIVES WINE BAR
3033 Anderson Ave., Manhattan, 785-539-1295; www.4olives.biz

The restaurant's olive-colored walls frame a glass wine cave in the middle of the room, which holds 700 wines. The dishes are all crafted to be wine-friendly, and a wine recommendation is listed for each menu item—even desserts like gourmet s'mores get a pairing. If you favor small plates, go for seared foie gras with black cherries and local pork tacos in blue corn tortillas. But if you want an entrée-sized dish, try the grilled filet mignon with Portobello ragout or shiraz-braised lamb shank.

Italian. Dinner. Children's menu. Bar. $16-35

DELLA VOCE
405 E. Poyntz Ave., Manhattan, 785-532-9000; www.dellavoce.com

This restaurant goes for an East Coast bar vibe, and you can belly up to the bar and order one of the specialty martinis, but the mood turns Italian when it comes to the food. The menu features osso buco and housemade ravioli stuffed with spinach and ricotta with a wine-spinach cream sauce. For something a bit different, try the pizza with figs, prosciutto, goat cheese, balsamic reduction and béchamel. Classic Italian desserts are on offer as well, including tiramisu and cannoli.

Italian. Lunch (Monday-Friday), dinner, Sunday brunch. Bar. $16-35

WICHITA

The largest city in Kansas has a metropolitan flavor, with its tall buildings and wide streets. Still a major marketing point for agricultural products, the city is now best known as an aircraft production center. McConnell Air Force Base is here. The town's first settlers were the Wichita, who built a village of grass lodges on the site. The following year James R. Mead set up a trading post and in 1865 sent his assistant, Jesse Chisholm, on a trading expedition to the Southwest. His route became famous as the Chisholm Trail, over which longhorn cattle were driven through Wichita to the Union Pacific at Abilene. As the railroad advanced to the southwest, Wichita had its turn as a "cow capital" in the early 1870s. By 1880, farmers drawn by the land boom had run fences across the trail and the cattle drives were shifted west to Dodge City. Wheat production and the discovery of oil after World War I revived the city.

WHAT TO SEE

ALLEN-LAMBE HOUSE MUSEUM AND STUDY CENTER
255 N. Roosevelt St., Wichita, 316-687-1027; www.allenlambe.org

Frank Lloyd Wright designed this house in 1915 as a private residence.

HIGHLIGHT

WHAT ARE THE TOP THINGS TO DO IN WICHITA?

SNIFF THE FLOWERS AT BOTANICA, THE WICHITA GARDENS

Meander through these gardens, which have flowers and plants native to Kansas. On the grounds, you'll also see sculptures, streams and waterfalls.

HANG WITH THE ANIMALS AT SEDGWICK COUNTY ZOO

Animal exhibits will give you a peek into foreign lands. Check out wallabies from Australia and the Amur and Malayan tigers from Asia.

SEE NOTED ART AT THE WICHITA ART MUSEUM

Gaze at paintings and sculptures from Charles M. Russell, who captured the spirit of the Old West; pre-Columbian pieces; and works from Kansas artists at this museum.

Considered the last of Wright's prairie houses, it features furniture designed by Wright in collaboration with interior designer George M. Niedecken. The center hosts special events, which have included lectures with Eric Lloyd Wright, the grandson of Frank Lloyd Wright.

Admission: $10. No children under 16 allowed.

BOTANICA, THE WICHITA GARDENS

701 Amidon, Wichita, 316-264-0448; www.botanica.org

Spend the day taking in the beauty of these botanical gardens with displays of exotic flowers and plants native to Kansas. The gardens cover nine acres with 3,600 different species. Among the gardens are sculptures, streams, fountains and waterfalls. Springtime brings in 43,000 tulip bulbs and 62,000 daffodils, making it a great time to visit. Visit gardens such as the Wildflower Meadow to see flowers native to the Great Plains or the Butterfly/Pansy House to take in hundreds of beautiful butterflies in an enclosed space, which also has thousands of pansies.

Admission: adults $7, seniors and military personnel $6, children 3-12 $3, Gardens: Monday-Saturday daily 9 a.m.-5 p.m.; extended hours April-October, Tuesday and Thursday until 8 p.m., Sunday 1-5 p.m.

CORBIN EDUCATION CENTER

Wichita State University, 1845 Fairmount, Wichita; www.wichita.edu

This Prairie-style structure, located on the campus of Wichita State University, was designed by Frank Lloyd Wright and built in 1963, making it one of his last. The center was named for the President of the University at that time, Harry Corbin.

LAKE AFTON PUBLIC OBSERVATORY

Wichita State University, 25000 W. 39th St. South, Wichita, 316-978-7827; www.webs.wichita.edu

Public programs offer the opportunity to view a variety of celestial objects through a 16-inch reflecting telescope. The observatory is only open to the public on Friday and Saturday evenings but also offers special programs and events.

Admission: adults $4, children 6-12 $3, children 5 and under free. Friday-Saturday; see website for schedule.

MID-AMERICA ALL-INDIAN CENTER MUSEUM

650 N. Seneca, Wichita, 316-262-5221; www.theindiancenter.org

This museum features changing exhibits of past and present Native American art. The Gallery of Nations features the flags of tribes in the United States, and exhibits have included everything from Navajo rugs and pottery to ancient artifacts, weapons and tools from Plains tribes.

Admission: adults $7, seniors $5, children 6-12 $3, children 5 and under free. Tuesday-Saturday 10 a.m.-4 p.m.

OLD COWTOWN MUSEUM

1865 Museum Blvd., Wichita, 316-660-1871; www.oldcowtown.org

This 40-building historic village museum depicts Wichita life in the 1870s with everything from a blacksmith and drugstore to a train depot and a fur trader's cabin complete with animal skins. Don't miss the Diamond W Chuckwagon Supper, which features all-you-can-eat barbecue and a performance by the Prairie Wranglers, a country-western band (see website for details).

April 15-December Wednesday-Saturday 9:30 a.m.-4:30 p.m., Sunday, noon-4:30 p.m.; December-April 15, Wednesday-Saturday 10 a.m.-4 p.m.

SEDGWICK COUNTY ZOO

5555 Zoo Blvd., Wichita, 316-660-9453; www.scz.org

See more than 2,500 animals in their natural habitats at this Wichita zoo. Head to the Australian portion of the zoo to see a cassowary bird, cockatoos, wallabies and more. Or head to the new Asian tiger exhibit, Slawson Family Tiger Trek, which features Amur and Malayan tigers in a natural habitat. The Children's Farm is the perfect way to introduce children to farm animals and get up close to pet them.

Admission: adults $11.50, seniors $7, children 3-11 $7, children 2 and under free. March-November, daily 8:30 a.m.-5 p.m.; November-April, daily 10 a.m.-5 p.m.

WICHITA ART MUSEUM

1400 W. Museum Blvd., Wichita, 316-268-4921; www.wichitaartmuseum.org

This museum features traveling exhibits, a collection of American art, paintings and sculpture by Charles M. Russell, pre-Columbian art and works by contemporary and historic Kansas artists. Past exhibits have included sculptures by Michael Aurbach, a Wichita native and professor at Vanderbilt University and illustrations of the Book of Job by William Blake.

Admission: adults $7, seniors $5, children 6-17 $3, children 5 and under free. Tuesday-Saturday 10 a.m.-5 p.m.,
Sunday noon-5 p.m.

WICHITA CENTER FOR THE ARTS
9112 E. Central Ave., Wichita, 316-634-2787; www.wcfta.com

With changing and permanent exhibits, this center features a gallery, theater and art school. The Irene Vickers Baker Theatre has featured performances such as *Art* by Yasmin Reza and *Lost in Yonkers* by Neil Simon (see website for tickets).

Admission: free. Tuesday-Sunday 1-5 p.m.

WICHITA-SEDGWICK COUNTY HISTORICAL MUSEUM
204 S. Main St., Wichita, 316-265-9314; www.wichitahistory.org

Learn about local Wichita history through Native American artifacts, period rooms, a costume collection and more on display here. Past exhibits have included "The French Connection: Fashions from Paris to Wichita," displaying French clothing worn during the 1880s to the 1980s from designers such as Chanel and Christian Dior.

Admission: adults $4, children 6-12 $2, children 5 and under free. Tuesday-Friday 11 a.m.-4 p.m., Saturday-Sunday 1-5 p.m.

WHERE TO STAY

★★★HYATT REGENCY WICHITA
400 W. Waterman, Wichita, 316-293-1234, 800-633-7313; www.wichita.hyatt.com

Perched on the Arkansas River, this contemporary hotel has updated rooms with duvet-topped beds, flat-screen TVs, iHome stereos or iPod docks, Portico bath amenities and most have either river or city views. Get in a workout at the fitness center or have a swim in the indoor pool. Enjoy contemporary American cuisine at Harvest Kitchen and Bar, which uses local and regional ingredients in dishes such as herb-roasted chicken, natural-fed Kansas City strip or flatbread pizzas.

303 rooms. Restaurant, bar. Business center. Fitness center. Pool. $61-150

★★★MARRIOTT WICHITA
9100 E. Corporate Hills Drive, Wichita, 316-651-0333, 800-610-0673; www.marriott.com

After a complete renovation in 2007, this hotel has updated guest rooms that feature luxury beds, flat-screen TVs and wireless Internet access. Hotel amenities include a fitness center and both outdoor and indoor pools. The Black Angus Grille serves steakhouse classics, while Corrigan's Sports Bar is a prime place for catching up on the latest scores and noshing on pub fare.

294 rooms. Restaurant, bar. Business center. Fitness center. Pool. $61-150

RECOMMENDED

THE CASTLE INN AT RIVERSIDE
1155 N. River Blvd., Wichita, 316-263-9300; www.castleinnriverside.com

This inn is tucked inside the stunning historic Campbell Castle, which even has a tower. The stone structure, a replica of an 1888 Scottish castle, is listed on the National Register of Historic Places. Inside, the public spaces preserve the castle's grandeur; there's hand-carved oak ornamentation adorning the turret entry and the main hallway, a 275-year-old staircase imported from London and a 700-year-old Grecian fireplace. The rooms are just as lovely, and each has its own theme. The popular Royal Court is done up in a Greco-Roman motif, with pillars framing the marble Jacuzzi and an antique white couch. But don't worry, although the rooms have a period feel, they come with modern-day amenities like complimentary wireless Internet access and TVs.

14 rooms. Complimentary breakfast. $151-250

COURTYARD WICHITA AT OLD TOWN

820 E. Second St. N., Wichita, 316-264-5300; www.marriott.com

This hotel has a convenient spot near Old Town's hopping entertainment district. Rooms are decked out in orange and royal blue and have pillow-top beds, mini-fridges and marble bathrooms. The airy atrium lobby near the clock tower provides a nice spot to kick back, as does the indoor whirlpool.

128 rooms. Business center. Fitness center. $61-150

FAIRFIELD INN WICHITA EAST

333 S. Webb Road, Wichita, 316-685-3777; www.marriott.com

The white-walled rooms at this hotel have accents of kelly green and come with complimentary wireless Internet access. Start your day off with a dip in the outdoor pool, and then head to the dining area for the complimentary continental breakfast.

104 rooms. Complimentary breakfast. Pool. $61-150

WHERE TO EAT

WICHITA

★★★OLIVE TREE

2949 N. Rock Road, Wichita, 316-636-1100;
www.olivetree-bistro.com

This family-owned, European-style bistro has an extensive wine list and a menu with both small and large plates of Mediterranean-inspired dishes. Entrées are eclectic and include everything from Thai green curry made with eggplant to fennel pollen roasted chicken.

Mediterranean. Dinner, Sunday brunch. $36-85

RECOMMENDED

CHESTER'S CHOPHOUSE & WINE BAR

1550 N. Webb Road, Wichita, 316-201-1300;
www.chesterschophouse.com

Sitting along Beech Lake, the warm dining room is full of mahogany and has stone fireplaces. Order comforting dishes like maple mustard salmon with spinach and white bean sauté, bacon and lemon caper butter or the 12-ounce chopped steak smothered with onions and steak sauce. Top off your homey meal with a fun dessert, like limoncello cheesecake with strawberries, lemon cream and mint syrup or apple beignets with vanilla ice cream, butterscotch-caramel sauce and whipped cream. Be sure to peruse the wine list. It may be hard to decide though, since the restaurant carries a whopping 1,000 bottles in the cellar.

American, steak. Dinner. Outdoor seating. Bar. $36-85

LARKSPUR

904 E. Douglas Ave., Wichita, 316-262-5275; www.larkspuronline.com

Usually filled with a mix of businessmen and women as well as tourists, this popular restaurant has a prime spot in Wichita's Old Town entertainment district. You can watch the action from the patio while you nosh on lamb chops with a rosemary-balsamic reduction or a sesame-crusted, pan-seared ahi tuna.

Continental. Lunch (Monday-Saturday), dinner. Outdoor seating. $36-85

SCOTCH & SIRLOIN

5325 E. Kellogg Ave., Wichita, 316-685-8701-5300; www.scotchandsirloin.net

This steak house is a local favorite, thanks to its juicy cuts of meat. The succulent slow-roasted prime rib is a must-try dish, but you can opt for the Kansas City strip or marbled rib-eye. There's also a selection of seafood, like the deep-fried catfish or the deep-fried jumbo frog legs.

Steak. Lunch (Monday-Saturday), dinner. Reservations recommended. $36-85

WHICH RESTAURANT IN WICHITA SERVES THE BEST STEAK?

Scotch & Sirloin
has been serving quality cuts of meat for more than 40 years. Don't miss the prime rib, the house's best carnivore delight, which is slow roasted and offered in three different cuts to satisfy every appetite.

WELCOME TO MISSOURI

WHEN THE UNITED STATES PURCHASED ALL OF THE VAST French territory of Louisiana in 1803, Missouri, with its strategic waterways and the

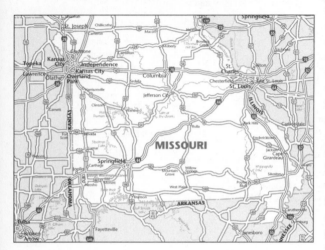

already-thriving town of St. Louis, became a gateway to the West and remained one throughout the entire westward expansion. Its two largest cities, St. Louis and Kansas City, sit on its eastern and western edges like bookends. St. Louis was the Midwest's first great city, the center of commerce and transportation thanks to its location on two major rivers.

Kansas City was once the quintessential cow town and, the Gateway Arch notwith-standing, was the true way station to the West—to cattle trails and to the frontier.

Today, Missouri offers a diverse array of sights. St. Louis and Kansas City have fine dining (and great barbecue), nightlife and music (especially blues and jazz). St. Louis has a world-famous zoo and one of the largest city parks in the nation. It has a significant art museum as well as the International Bowling Hall of Fame. Home to the Cardinals and a legion of knowledgeable fans, the city is often hailed as the nation's best baseball town. Kansas City has the world's first planned shopping center (Country Club Plaza), a 60-acre water park, and did we mention barbecue?

For outdoor recreation, Missouri could vie for the title of Land of Awesome Lakes. Its largest one, Lake of the Ozarks, is 92 miles end to end and has 1,150 miles of shoreline. There's also the 55,000-acre Truman Lake, part of the Harry S. Truman State Park, southeast of Kansas City, and Pomme de Terre Lake, 78 acres of water near Springfield.

Then there are the rivers, and we don't just mean the Mississippi and Missouri. Four state parks dot the Meramec River, which runs for nearly 100 miles. Nearly 90 percent of the river is shallow, which makes it a perfect waterway for float trips. Another of Missouri's river gems is the Black, running through Poplar Bluff and north into the Arcadia Valley. It too promises great floating.

Wherever you are in the state, there's something to explore. Around Hannibal by the

BEST ATTRACTIONS

MISSOURI'S BEST ATTRACTIONS

BRANSON
This resort town is the entertainment capital of Missouri. It's the place to go if you enjoy country music, old-fashioned acts, and variety and comedy shows, all of which happen nightly.

KANSAS CITY
From the great shopping at City Market and Country Club Plaza to the galleries in the Crossroads District and the top-notch restaurants sprinkled in between, this city has it all.

ST. LOUIS
You'll be saying, "Meet me in St. Louis," so that you can see the iconic Gateway Arch, visit the St. Louis Zoo and check out the other attractions this fun city has to offer.

Mississippi, you can recapture Mark Twain's riverboat days. Southwest is Springfield, a gateway to both the Ozarks and to Branson, that one-of-a-kind capital of cornpone, country and crooning. In the middle is Jefferson City, a prototypical sleepy capital town with a beautiful capitol standing astride the Missouri River.

NORTHERN MISSOURI

This region is steeped in history and culture. Maybe the most well-known town in the area is Hannibal, the hometown of the great novelist Samuel Clemens (Mark Twain) as well as the setting of *The Adventures of Tom Sawyer*, which records many actual events of Clemens' boyhood. He served his printer's apprenticeship here and gained a fascination with steamboats in the days when the river was the source of the town's prosperity. Excelsior Springs was established in 1880 when two settlers, Anthony W. Wyman and J. V. D. Flack, discovered various natural springs on Wyman's property. Today the city is a health resort offering visitors bottled water from the springs and medicinal baths in the city-operated bathhouse. Independence was an outfitting point for westbound wagon trains from 1830-1850. The scene of much of the Mormon Wars in the early 1830s, it was ravaged by raiders and occupied by Union and Confederate troops during the Civil War. Today, it's best known as the hometown of President Harry S. Truman.

WHAT TO SEE

EXCELSIOR SPRINGS
JESSE JAMES'S FARM
21216 James Farm Road, Kearney, 816-736-8500; www.jessejamesmuseum.org

On this farm, you can see the house where outlaw Jesse James was born and raised with his brother Frank. There's also a video about the history of the James brothers and Jesse's original burial site.

Admission: adults $7.50, seniors $6.50, children 8-15 $4, children 7 and under free. May-September, daily 9 a.m.-4 p.m.; October-April, Monday-Saturday 9 a.m.-4 p.m., Sunday noon-4 p.m.

WATKINS WOOLEN MILL STATE PARK AND STATE HISTORIC SITE
26600 Park Road N. Lawson, 816-580-3387; www.mostateparks.com

This woolen factory and gristmill, built and equipped in 1854, still contains original machinery along with the original owner's house, summer kitchen, ice house, smokehouse and school.

Admission: adults $3, children 6-12 $1.50, children 5 and under free. April-October, daily 10 a.m.-3 p.m.; November and March, daily 10 a.m.-2 p.m., December-February, Friday-Sunday 10 a.m.-2 a.m.

HANNIBAL
BECKY THATCHER HOUSE
209-211 Hill St., Hannibal

This is the house where Laura Hawkins (Becky Thatcher) lived during Samuel Clemens' boyhood. The upstairs rooms have authentic furnishings.

Daily.

JOHN M. CLEMENS JUSTICE OF THE PEACE OFFICE
205 Hill St., Hannibal

The restored courtroom is where Twain's father presided as justice of the peace.

MARK TWAIN CAVE
7097 Country Road 453, Hannibal, 573-221-1656; www.marktwaincave.com

This is the cave in *The Adventures of Tom Sawyer* in which Tom and Becky Thatcher were lost and where Injun Joe died.

Tours: daily.

MARK TWAIN MUSEUM AND BOYHOOD HOME
208 Hill St., Hannibal, 573-221-9010

The museum houses Mark Twain memorabilia, including books, letters, photographs and family items.

Daily.

MARK TWAIN RIVERBOAT EXCURSIONS
Center St., Hannibal, 573-221-3222, 800-621-2322; www.marktwainriverboat.com

Go on a one-hour cruise on the Mississippi River or a two-hour dinner cruise.

Early May-October, daily.

HIGHLIGHT

WHAT ARE THE TOP THINGS TO DO IN NORTHERN MISSOURI?

VISIT THE BOYHOOD HOME OF THE OUTLAW JESSE JAMES
See where Jesse James grew up and learn about how he became a famous outlaw.

TOUR MARK TWAIN'S HANNIBAL
Walk through the town that inspired Mark Twain to write *The Adventures of Tom Sawyer*. Spots like the Mark Twain Cave and the Becky Thatcher house are mentioned in the tome.

EXPLORE THE HARRY S. TRUMAN PRESIDENTIAL MUSEUM AND LIBRARY
Learn about the life and presidency of Harry S. Truman with exhibits that include a reproduction of Truman's White House oval office. You can also pay your respects at his and Mrs. Truman's graves.

WANDER THROUGH THE TRUMAN FARM HOME
Look through the white frame house that President Truman lived in during what he considered to be "the best years," when he farmed the surrounding 600 acres, worked as a mason and postmaster, served as a soldier and courted Bess Wallace.

MOLLY BROWN BIRTHPLACE AND MUSEUM
600 Butler St., Hannibal, 573-221-2100; www.visitmollybrown.com
The antique-filled home has memorabilia of the "unsinkable" Molly Brown, who survived the Titanic disaster.
Monday 10 a.m.-3 p.m., Thursday-Saturday 10 a.m.-4 p.m., Sunday 11 a.m.-4 p.m.

PILASTER HOUSE AND GRANT'S DRUGSTORE
Hill and Main streets, Hannibal
The Clemens family lived in this Greek Revival house, which contains a restored old-time drugstore, a pioneer kitchen, a doctor's office and more.

ROCKCLIFFE MANSION
Hill Street, Hannibal, 573-221-4140; www.rockcliffemansion.com
This restored Beaux Arts mansion overlooks the river. Its 30 rooms contain

many of the original furnishings. Samuel Clemens addressed a gathering here in 1902. Guided tours: daily.

INDEPENDENCE

1859 MARSHAL'S HOME AND JAIL MUSEUM
217 N. Main St., Independence, 816-252-1892; www.jchs.org

This restored building contains dungeon-like cells, a marshal's living quarters, a regional history museum and a one-room schoolhouse. The Jackson County jailhouse held famous outlaw Frank James for almost six months.

Admission: adults $5, seniors $4.50, children 5-15 $2, children 4 and under free. November-March, Monday-Saturday 10 a.m.-4 p.m.; April-October, Monday-Saturday 10 a.m.-4 p.m., Sunday 1-4 p.m.

BINGHAM-WAGGONER ESTATE
313 W. Pacific, Independence, 816-461-3491; www.bwestate.org

Famous Missouri artist George Caleb Bingham lived here from 1864-1870. It's also the homestead of the Waggoner family, millers of "Queen of the Pantry" flour.

Admission: adults $5, seniors $4.50, children $2. April-October and late November-December, Monday-Saturday 10 a.m.-4 p.m., Sunday 1-4 p.m.

HARRY S. TRUMAN COURTROOM AND OFFICE MUSEUM
Jackson County Courthouse, 112 W. Lexington, Independence, 816-795-8200

This is the restored office and courtroom where Truman began his political career as presiding county judge. Watch the short film, *The Man from Independence*, about Harry Truman's life and hometown.

Admission: adults $2, children 6-15 $1, children 5 and under free. Sunday-Thursday, by appointment.

HARRY S. TRUMAN PRESIDENTIAL MUSEUM AND LIBRARY
500 W. Highway 24, Independence, 816-268-8200; www.trumanlibrary.org

This museum explores the life and presidency of Harry S. Truman with exhibits displaying presidential papers, mementos of public life and a reproduction of President Truman's White House oval office. The graves of President and Mrs. Truman are here.

Admission: adults $8, seniors $7, children 6-15 $3, children 5 and under free. Monday-Saturday 9 a.m.-5 p.m., Sunday noon-5 p.m.

NATIONAL FRONTIER TRAILS CENTER
318 W. Pacific, Independence, 816-325-7575; www.ci.independence.mo.us

This partially restored flour mill at the site of the Santa Fe, California and Oregon trails serves as a museum, interpretive center, library and archive of westward pioneer expansion.

Admission: adults $5, seniors $3, children 6-17 $3, children 5 and under free. Monday-Saturday 9 a.m.-4:30 p.m., Sunday 12:30 p.m.-4:30 p.m.

TRUMAN FARM HOME
12301 Blue Ridge Blvd., Grandview, 816-254-2720; www.nps.gov

Harry Truman lived in this two-story, white frame house in the decade preceding World War I. During these years—"the best years," according to Truman—he farmed the surrounding 600 acres, worked as a mason and postmaster, served as a soldier and courted Bess Wallace. The interior features period furnishings, including original family pieces. For information, visit the Truman Visitor Center at 223 N. Main St. in Independence.

Tours: Memorial Day-Labor Day, Friday-Sunday 9:30 a.m.-4 p.m.

WHERE TO STAY

EXCELSIOR SPRINGS
★★★THE INN ON CRESCENT LAKE
1261 St. Louis Ave., Excelsior Springs, 816-630-6745, 866-630-5253; www.crescentinn.com

This inn was built in 1915 on 22 acres of landscaped yard, surrounded by two crescent-shaped ponds (known as Crescent Lake). The rooms are individually decorated and have private baths. For a bit more privacy, rent the more modern cottage which offers two floors with a kitchen, dining area, a living room, two-person whirlpool tub and walk-in shower. Guests can enjoy swimming in the outdoor pool or take a paddleboat out on Crescent Lake.

10 rooms. Restaurant. Complimentary breakfast. Fitness center. Pool. No children under 12. $61-150

HANNIBAL
★★★GARTH WOODSIDE MANSION BED AND BREAKFAST
11069 New London Road, Hannibal, 573-221-2789, 888-427-8409; www.garthmansion.com

With eight guest rooms, each with its own private bath, this Second Empire/Victorian mansion where Mark Twain was often a guest is located on 33 acres of grass, woodland, gardens and ponds. For a more private getaway, rent the three-story Dawager House, a quiet cottage that features a king-sized bed with 1,200 thread count linens, a luxurious rainshower, fireplaces in the bedroom and bathroom and a whirlpool bath. Guests receive a full breakfast each morning and are welcome to snacks in the house refrigerator (and warm chocolate chip cookies out of the oven). Explore the beautiful property and take in the scenery.

8 rooms. Complimentary breakfast. $61-150

RECOMMENDED

INDEPENDENCE
HILTON GARDEN INN INDEPENDENCE
19677 E. Jackson Drive, Independence, 816-350-3000; www.hilton.com

These simple rooms are clean and spacious, and

WHICH NORTHERN MISSOURI HOTEL IS THE MOST ICONIC?

Samuel Clemens was a frequent guest at the **Garth Woodside Mansion Bed and Breakfast**. To channel the writer, reserve the cozy Samuel Clemens Room, bathed in maroon and cream with floral wallpaper, a canopy bed and a fireplace.

WHICH NORTHERN MISSOURI RESTAURANT IS BEST FOR FAMILIES?

V's Italiano
is a perfect spot for family dining, since the classic Italian fare is served family-style. You and your brood can share delicious dishes including veal parmigiana, eggplant parmigiana and osso buco.

come with refrigerators, microwaves, complimentary wireless Internet access and nice-sized work desks. Take a swim in the pool, or soak your jetlagged body in the Jacuzzi, and don't forget to visit the grill for the free breakfast. Instead of the usual spread of cold prepared foods, you can get eggs, waffles, hash browns and more made to order.

201 rooms. Restaurant, bar. Complimentary breakfast. Business center. Fitness center. Pool. $61-150

WHERE TO EAT

INDEPENDENCE
★★★V'S ITALIANO
10819 Highway 40 E., Independence, 816-353-1241;
www.vsrestaurant.com
This family-style Italian restaurant serves up heaping portions of classic dishes like veal parmigiana and osso buco as well as steak and seafood options. You'll get plenty of food as entrées come with a house salad, Italian and pumpernickel bread, a baked potato or a side of spaghetti, steak fries or vegetables and a fresh slice of homemade Italian rum cake.

American, Italian. Lunch, dinner, Sunday brunch. Children's menu. Bar. $16-35

RECOMMENDED

INDEPENDENCE
OPHELIA'S RESTAURANT & INN
201 N. Main St., Independence, 816-461-4525;
www.opheliasind.com
Overlooking Independence Square, Ophelia's has a convenient spot for dinner. The restaurant offers fun takes on homey Midwestern cuisine. For the starters, tempura shrimp gets a rice krispies batter and Idaho and sweet potatoes become housemade chips with toasted onion, curry aioli and apple pico de gallo dips. While airplane food is far from appetizing, the restaurant's airline chicken, with caramelized shallots, fingerling potatoes and truffle-corn sauce, is a craveworthy entrée. On the weekends, you can hear some live jazz with your meal.

American. Lunch (Monday-Saturday), dinner (Monday-Saturday), Sunday brunch. Bar. $16-35

LONGHORN STEAKHOUSE
17800 39th St., Independence, 816-373-0716;
www.longhornsteakhouse.com
This steak house chain delivers reliably succulent steaks.

HIGHLIGHT

MARK TWAIN'S HANNIBAL

Start a tour of Hannibal, an old Mississippi riverboat stop and hometown to Samuel Longhorn Clemens—better known as Mark Twain—at the Hannibal Convention and Visitors Bureau (505 N. Third St.). Towering above the visitor center is the Mark Twain Lighthouse, located at the crest of Cardiff Hill. This is the largest inland lighthouse in the United States, offering great views of Hannibal and the Mississippi from the top.

A block south of the Visitors Bureau is the Mark Twain Boyhood Home and Museum (208 Hill St.), which features the original 1843 Clemens home, restored to look as it did when Twain lived here in the 1840s. Next door (211 Hill St.) is the period home of Laura Hawkins, Mark Twain's childhood sweetheart and the inspiration for the character Becky Thatcher in Twain's novels. On the corner of Hill and Main streets is the Clemens Law office, where Twain's father, J. M. Clemens, presided as Hannibal's justice of the peace. Attached to the building is a historic courtroom, which served as the model for scenes from *The Adventures of Tom Sawyer*. At the base of Cardiff Hill at Main Street is the Tom and Huck Statue, which commemorates Twains most famous characters, Huck Finn and Tom Sawyer. Frederick Hibbard sculpted this bronze statue in 1926.

Stretching along Main Street are a number of historic buildings and shops. Follow Main Street south, passing boutiques in historic storefronts. A worthy stop is Mrs. Clemens' Antique Mall (305 N. Main), which features two floors of antiques and an ice cream parlor. At Bird and Main streets stands the handsome Pilaster House/Grant's Drug Store, dating from the 1830s. The Clemens family lived here briefly in the 1940s, and Judge Clemens died here in 1847. Today, the building is preserved as an 1890s apothecary.

At Main and Center streets is the Mark Twain Museum, a restored structure that contains a collection of original Norman Rockwell paintings used for illustrated editions of *Adventures of Huckleberry Finn*. The museum also serves as a memento of Hannibal's riverboat past.

The restaurant's signature is the Outlaw, the 18-ounce bone-in rib-eye. You also have a plethora of other meaty choices, including porterhouse, filet, sirloin, prime rib and Kansas City strip. Pair your favorite cut with sides like jalapeño coleslaw, brandied cinnamon apples or that steak staple, mashed potatoes. *American, steak. Lunch, dinner. Bar. $16-35*

ST. LOUIS

One of the oldest settlements in the Mississippi Valley, St. Louis was founded by Pierre Laclede as a fur trading post and was named for Louis IX of France. Early French settlers, a large German immigration in the mid-1800s and a happy mix of other nationalities contribute to the city's cosmopolitan flavor. In 1804, it was the scene of the transfer of Louisiana to the United States, which opened the way to westward expansion. During the Civil War, though divided in sympathy, the city was a base of Union operations. In 1904, the Louisiana Purchase Exposition, known as the St. Louis World's Fair, brought international fame to the city.

For more than 200 years, St. Louis has been the dominant city in the state. It's the home of St. Louis University, the University of Missouri-St. Louis and Washington University. After the steamboat era, St. Louis grew westward away from the riverfront, which deteriorated into slums. This original center of the city has now been redeveloped as the Jefferson National Expansion Memorial. Recent redevelopment of downtown and the riverfront is revitalizing the city. Busch Stadium brings St. Louis Cardinals fans into the downtown area and the rehabilitated Union Station offers visitors a vast shopping experience within a restored turn-of-the-century railroad station that was one of the nation's most magnificent.

WHAT TO SEE

ANHEUSER-BUSCH BREWERY
12th and Lynch streets, St. Louis, 314-577-2626; www.budweisertours.com
Trace the making of Budweiser beer from farm fields to finished product in a free tour of the nation's largest brewery. Inside the 159-year-old plant, you'll also experience a historic brewhouse, beechwood aging cellars, a packing facility and Clydesdale stables. Adults can sample Budweiser products. Guests can also take the Beermaster Tour (make a reservation online) to get a better look at what goes on behind the scenes, including visiting the packaging center and tasting beer directly from the finishing tank.
Admission: free. Beermaster Tour: adults $25, children 13-20 $10. September-April, Monday-Saturday 10 a.m.-4 p.m., Sunday 11:30 a.m.-4 p.m.; May, Monday-Saturday 9 a.m.-4 p.m., Sunday 11:30 a.m.-4 p.m.; June-August, Monday-Saturday 9 a.m.-5 p.m., Sunday 11:30 a.m.-5 p.m. Beermaster Tours: Monday-Saturday 10 a.m., 12:30 p.m., 1:45 p.m., 3 p.m., Sunday 12:30 p.m., 1:45 p.m., 3 p.m.

BUTTERFLY HOUSE
Faust Park, 15193 Olive Blvd., Chesterfield, 636-530-0076; www.butterflyhouse.org
This three-story crystal palace acts as a conservatory with more than 2,000 butterflies of more than 60 different species in free flight. Butterflies live among almost 100 species of tropical plants and flowers. Also offered are educational programs; films focusing on the butterfly life cycle and metamorphosis; and a miracle of metamorphosis display where visitors can watch as butterflies emerge from chrysalides. A gift shop offers butterfly-themed souvenirs to take home with you.
Admission: adults $6, seniors $4.50, children 3-12 $4, children 2 and under free. Memorial Day-Labor Day, daily 9 a.m.-5 p.m.; Wednesday until 7 p.m.; Labor Day-Memorial Day, Tuesday-Sunday 9 a.m.-4 p.m. Half-price admission 5-7 p.m. Memorial Day-Labor Day.

CATHEDRAL BASILICA OF ST. LOUIS
4431 Lindell Blvd., St. Louis, 314-373-8242; www.cathedralstl.org
The city's cathedral, built in 1907, is a fine example of Romanesque architecture with Byzantine details. The beautiful interior mosaic work is among the most extensive in the world. Pope John Paul II designated it the Cathedral

Basilica in 1997 and then visited later in 1999.

Mass: Monday-Friday 7 a.m., 8 a.m., 12:05 p.m., Saturday 8 a.m., 5 p.m., Sunday 8 a.m., 10 a.m., noon, 5 p.m.

CHRIST CHURCH CATHEDRAL

1210 Locust St., St. Louis, 314-231-3454

Founded in 1819, this was the first Episcopal parish west of the Mississippi River. An English Gothic sandstone building, its altar was carved in England from stone taken from a quarry in Caen, France and there are Tiffany windows on the north wall.

Worship schedule: Labor Day-Memorial Day, Sunday 8 a.m., 9 a.m., 11:15 a.m.; Memorial Day-Labor Day, Sunday 8 a.m., 10 a.m. Tours: by appointment.

EADS BRIDGE

St. Louis Riverfront area

Designed in 1874 by engineer James B. Eads, the Eads was the first bridge to span the wide southern section of the Mississippi and the first bridge in which steel and the cantilever were used extensively. The approach ramps are carried on enormous Romanesque stone arches.

THE EUGENE FIELD HOUSE AND ST. LOUIS TOY MUSEUM

634 S. Broadway, St. Louis, 314-421-4689; www.eugenefieldhouse.org

A National Historic Landmark, this was the birthplace of the famous children's poet, Eugene Field. The museum includes mementos, manuscripts, antique toys and many original furnishings from when Field lived here.

Admission: adults $5, children 4-11 $1, children 3 and under free. Wednesday-Saturday 10 a.m.-4 p.m., Sunday noon-4 p.m.; Monday-Tuesday and January-February by appointment only.

GATEWAY ARCH

The Gateway Arch Riverfront, St. Louis, 877-982-1410; www.gatewayarch.com

Eero Saarinen's Gateway Arch is a 630-foot stainless steel arch that symbolizes the starting point of the westward expansion of the United States. Purchase tickets in the visitor center to take a tram to the observation deck at the top of the arch, where you can get a great view of the city and the Mississippi River. There are also exhibits within the visitor center.

Admission: adults $10, children 3-15 $5. Memorial Day-Labor Day, daily 8 a.m.-10 p.m.; Labor Day-Memorial Day, daily 9 a.m.-6 p.m. Tours: Labor Day-Memorial Day, daily 9:20 a.m.-5:10 p.m., every 10 minutes; Memorial Day-Labor Day, daily 8:20 a.m.-9:10 p.m., every 10 minutes.

GRANT'S FARM

10501 Gravois Road, St. Louis, 314-843-1700; www.grantsfarm.com

This 281-acre wooded area contains a log cabin and land once owned by Ulysses S. Grant. On the property, there is a barn, carriage house and trophy room. Children will love watching the deer, antelope, buffalo, longhorn steer and other animals roam freely in their natural habitat in Deer Park. There are also animal shows in the Tier Garden and you can see the Budweiser Clydesdale Stables. Enjoy Anheuser-Busch beer and German fare, like bratwurst and

HIGHLIGHT

WHAT ARE THE TOP THINGS TO DO IN ST. LOUIS?

TAKE A TOUR OF ANHEUSER-BUSCH BREWERY
Kick back with some suds on a tour of the nation's largest brewery. But before you do some taste testing, learn how your Budweiser goes from farm fields to bottles.

STAND UNDERNEATH THE GATEWAY ARCH AND THEN RIDE TO THE TOP
The brilliant 630-foot stainless steel arch is synonymous with St. Louis. Admire it from below and then take a tram to the observation deck for breathtaking city vistas.

VISIT THE ANIMALS AT THE ST. LOUIS ZOO
Considered one of the best in the country, the St. Louis Zoo is home to 24,000 animals, many of which are endangered. Don't miss the cute critters at the Penguin & Puffin Coast.

pretzels, at the Brat Haus and sit and relax at the patio by the Bauernhof. *Admission: free. Mid-April-early-May, Saturday 9 a.m.-3:30 p.m., Sunday 9:30 a.m.-3:30 p.m.; Early-May-mid-August, Tuesday-Friday 9 a.m.-3:30 p.m., Saturday 9 a.m.-4 p.m., Sunday 9:30 a.m.-4 p.m., Sunday 9:30 a.m.-4 p.m.; mid-April-August-October, Friday 9:30 a.m.-2:30 p.m., Saturday-Sunday 9:30 a.m.-3:30 p.m.*

JEFFERSON NATIONAL EXPANSION MEMORIAL
11 N. Fourth St., St. Louis, 314-655-1700; www.nps.gov
The Jefferson National Expansion Memorial park, located along the Mississippi River, pays tribute to Thomas Jefferson and his influence on freedom and democracy. Located here are the Gateway Arch, the Museum of Westward Expansion and the Old Courthouse.

OLD COURTHOUSE
11 N. Fourth St., St. Louis, 314-655-1600; www.nps.gov
Construction on this historical courthouse began in 1837 and was completed in 1862. The first two trials of the Dred Scott case were held in this building. It houses five museum galleries on St. Louis history, including various displays, dioramas and films. The courtrooms have also been restored to give a glimpse

into what they were like during the 19th century.
Admission: free. Daily 8 a.m.-4:30 p.m.

LACLEDE'S LANDING
720 N. Second St., St. Louis, 314-241-1155; www.lacledeslanding.com

This early St. Louis commercial district (mid-1800s) includes a nine-block area of renovated pre-Civil War and Victorian buildings that house specialty shops, restaurants and nightclubs. Cobblestone streets and its location on the riverfront add to the charm. The area also hosts events throughout the year from an Independence Day celebration with fireworks, live music and a festival to the Big Muddy Blues Festival over Labor Day weekend featuring a blues festival.

MISSOURI BOTANICAL GARDEN
4344 Shaw Blvd., St. Louis, 314-577-9400, 800-642-8842; www.mobot.org

The oldest botanical garden in the United States, this 79-acre park includes rose, woodland and herb gardens; a greenhouse conservatory containing camellias; tram tours; a butterfly house and more. Visit the largest traditional Japanese garden in North America, with a lake landscaped with many varieties of water irises, waterfalls, bridges and a teahouse. Sections of the botanical garden are more than a century old. Children will love the Climatron, a 70-foot high, prize-winning geodesic dome—the first of its kind to be used as a conservatory—that houses a two-level, half-acre tropical rain forest with canopies, rocky outcrops, waterfalls and mature tree collection. Exhibits explain the many facets of a rain forest. The entrance to Climatron is through a series of sacred lotus and lily pools. When you're done exploring, head to Sassafras, the garden's certified green restaurant featuring delicious sustainable cuisine including burgers, sandwiches, salads, soups and more.
Admission: adults $8, residents $4, senior residents $3, children 12 and under free. Tram Tours: $4. Daily 9 a.m.-5 p.m. Tram Tours: April-October, daily.

MISSOURI HISTORY MUSEUM-MISSOURI HISTORICAL SOCIETY
5700 Lindel Blvd., St. Louis, 314-746-4599; www.mohistory.org

This history museum contains exhibits on St. Louis and the American West, including artwork, costumes and decorative arts; toys, firearms; 19th-century firefighting equipment; a St. Louis history slide show; a ragtime-rock 'n' roll music exhibit; and 1904 World's Fair and Charles A. Lindbergh collections. A theater offers one-person plays about a significant people who once lived in St. Louis such as abolitionist and newspaper editor Elijah Lovejoy or a Civil War spy.
Admission: free. Mid-September-mid-May, daily 10 a.m.-5 p.m., Tuesday until 8 p.m.; Mid-May-mid-September, daily 10 a.m.-6 p.m., Tuesday until 8 p.m.

MUSEUM OF TRANSPORTATION
3015 Barrett Station Road, Kirkwood, 314-965-7998; www.transportmuseumassociation.org

The Museum of Transportation houses an extensive collection of passenger and freight train equipment (ranging from elevated cars from Chicago to the last steam locomotive to operate in Missouri), as well as the riverboats and airplanes.
Admission: adults $6, children 5-12 and military personnel $4, children 4 and under free. May-Labor Day, Monday-Saturday 9 a.m.-5 p.m., Sunday 11 a.m.-5 p.m.; Labor Day-April, Tuesday-Saturday 9 a.m.-4 p.m., Sunday 11 a.m.-4 p.m.

NASCAR SPEEDPARK

5555 St. Louis Mills Blvd., Hazelwood, 314-227-5600; www.nascarspeedpark.com

This mini amusement park is northwest of downtown and is one of five now open across North America. The park features everything from an arcade to a rock-climbing wall to a NASCAR merchandise store. But its main draw is its multitude of racetracks. You can climb into a mock stock car and experience centrifugal forces, turns and crash impacts as you "drive" a full-motion NASCAR Silicon Motor Speedway simulator.

Admission: unlimited daily rides $30; pay per rides. Daily, hours vary.

OLD CATHEDRAL

209 Walnut St., St. Louis, 314-231-3250; www.catholic-forum.com

The 1831 basilica of St. Louis, King of France, is on the site of the first church built in St. Louis in 1770. The museum on the west side contains the original church bell and other religious artifacts.

Mass: Monday-Friday 7 a.m., 12:10 p.m., Saturday 7 a.m., Sunday 8 a.m., 10:30 a.m., noon, 5 p.m.

SAINT LOUIS SYMPHONY ORCHESTRA

Powell Symphony Hall, 718 N. Grand Blvd., St. Louis, 314-534-1700; www.slso.org

Decorated in ivory, red and 24-karat gold leaf, Powell Symphony Hall was built in 1925 as a movie and vaudeville house, And after a $2 million renovation, it's now home of the St. Louis Symphony Orchestra. Concerts range from classical to family-focused and holiday-themed. Past productions have included Beethoven, Mozart, an Abba tribute band with the orchestra and an evening with Renee Fleming.

Check website for concert schedule and pricing.

SIX FLAGS ST. LOUIS

I-44 and Six Flags Road, Eureka, 636-938-4800; www.sixflags.com

This edition of the theme park franchise has rides and attractions for kids and grownups, plus live shows throughout summer. Among the two dozen or so rides here are several roller coasters, such as the Ninja, Batman the Ride and the Boss, a wooden roller coaster; Tony Hawk's Big Spin, which spins you on 360s like when Tony's skateboarding; Tidal Wave, a coaster that drops you over a waterfall; antique cars for younger kids to ride around on; and much more. There's plenty of other fun to take part in here, including games and entertainment, as well as a water park featuring a wave pool, a raft ride, slides and a children's play area.

Admission: adults $42.99, children under 48" $32.99, children 2 and under free; after 4 p.m. admission $24.99. Hours vary; see website for calendar.

ST. LOUIS ART MUSEUM

1 Fine Arts Drive, St. Louis, 314-721-0072; www.stlouis.art.museum

Built for the 1904 World's Fair as the Palace of Fine Arts, this museum has collections of American and European paintings, prints, drawings and decorative arts. Modern artists include Manet, van Gogh, Gauguin, Monet, Picasso, Chagall and more. Exhibitions vary and have included things such as textiles, film, needleworking and more. The museum is undergoing an expansion but remains open.

Admission: free. Tuesday-Sunday 10 a.m.-5 p.m., Friday until 9 p.m. Tours: Tuesday-Friday 10:30 a.m., Saturday-Sunday 1:30 p.m.

ST. LOUIS CARDINALS (MLB)

Busch Stadium, 250 Stadium Plaza, St. Louis, 314-421-3060; www.cardinals.mlb.com

The Cardinals, St. Louis' professional baseball team, play at Busch Stadium (which opened in 2006), located downtown near Laclede's Landing, the Gateway Arch and the riverfront.

ST. LOUIS SCIENCE CENTER

5050 Oakland Ave., St. Louis, 314-289-4444, 800-456-7572; www.slsc.org

This science center features three buildings with more than 700 exhibits, including an OMNIMAX theater, a planetarium and a children's discovery room. A Life Science Lab lets visitors explore hands-on experiments and studies; the Flight! Gallery is a tunnel that leads to the planetarium where you can see yourself in different forms just like if you were in space; and Cyberville focuses on understanding technology. The planetarium has telescopes for viewing, space shows and exhibits, and the OMNIMAX theater features films like *Under the Sea*, which looks into the Indo-Pacific region and *Hubble*, about the space telescope.

Admission: free. Monday-Saturday 9:30 a.m.-5:30 p.m.

ST. LOUIS UNION STATION

1820 Market St., St. Louis, 314-421-6655; www.stlouisunionstation.com

This block-long stone chateauesque railroad station was the world's busiest passenger terminal from 1905 to the late 1940s. After the last train pulled out on October 31, 1978, the station and train shed were restored and redeveloped as a marketplace with more than 100 specialty shops and restaurants, night-clubs and a hotel. The architecture of the building is beautiful as it was modeled after the medieval city in France, Carcassone. It features an Allegorical Window in the Grand Hall, which is a Tiffany stained glass window with beautiful archways and mosaics. The Marriott St. Louis Union Station is located here and restaurants include the Hard Rock Café, Station Grille and Key West Café among others.

ST. LOUIS ZOO

1 Government Drive, St. Louis, 314-781-0900, 800-966-8877; www.stlzoo.org

The St. Louis Zoo is considered one of the best in the country. Lions, cheetahs and giraffes roam in natural African settings while other areas showcase exotic species from the poles to the tropics. Head to the River's Edge, a 10-acre exhibit, to see animals from Africa, Asia and North America hanging out in a natural habitat. Here you can see cheetahs and hyenas running among tall grasses, hippos swimming and elephants playing in water. The Wild features bears, penguins, gorillas, orangutans and the Conservation Carousel, where children and adults can enjoy riding on wooden animals ($3 per person). There is so much to explore at this zoo. Hop aboard the mini-train and take a narrated tour around the exhibits. Check for special exhibits and performances, such as the sea lion show, and 3-D movies.

Admission: free. Memorial Day-Labor Day, Monday-Thursday 8 a.m.-5 p.m., Friday-Sunday 8 a.m.-7 p.m.; Labor Day-Memorial Day, daily 9 a.m.-5 p.m.

ULYSSES S. GRANT NATIONAL HISTORIC SITE

7400 Grant Road, St. Louis, 314-842-3298; www.nps.gov

The White Haven property was a focal point in Ulysses' and his wife Julia's lives for four decades. Grounds feature more than 50 species of trees and are a haven for a variety of wildlife. The visitor's center includes exhibits and information on the Grants and White Haven.

Guided tours: daily 9:30 a.m.-4 p.m., every half-hour.

WHERE TO STAY

★★★THE CHASE PARK PLAZA

212-232 N. Kingshighway Blvd., St. Louis, 314-633-3000; 877-587-2427; www.chaseparkplaza.com

Recently renovated, this historic hotel in St. Louis's Central West End exudes more of a resort-like feel with its five-screen movie theater, spa and salon, courtyard with outdoor pool and 24-hour concierge. Guest rooms are sleek and sophisticated with neutral color schemes with splashes of blue. You'll find pillow-top mattresses, cotton linens, Internet access and luxurious bathroom amenities. Relax in the outdoor heated pool surrounded by a piazza with fountains, a fireplace and carved stone walkways and columns. The theater offers a variety of movies to watch while relaxing in a cozy seat—there are even concessions available. The salon and spa offers an array of treatments and you can enjoy a workout at the Santé fitness center. For dinner, head to Eau Bistro for delicious international cuisine.

250 rooms. Restaurant, bar. Business center. Fitness center. Pool. Spa. $151-250

★★★★FOUR SEASONS HOTEL ST. LOUIS

999 N. Second St., St. Louis, 314-881-5800; www.fourseasons.com

St. Louis has not been this exciting since the Cardinals won the World Series in 2006. The arrival of the Four Seasons brings new levels of both energy and luxury to the city. The airy guest rooms have contemporary furnishings and a light wood color palette, plus amenities such as an LCD television and an iPod docking station. Just be sure to request a room facing south to get a view of the Gateway Arch. If you venture out, head for the Vegas-style casino Lumière Place just at your doorstep. Or if you feel like staying in, retreat to the outdoor pool with hot tub overlooking downtown St. Louis, or make for the spa and indulge in the signature Caviar Serum Facial. Grab a drink or dinner at Italian restaurant Cielo at sunset to capture the striking urban vista from the terrace.

186 rooms. Restaurant, bar. Business center. Fitness center. Pool. Spa. $251-350

★★★HILTON ST. LOUIS AT THE BALLPARK

1 S. Broadway, St. Louis, 314-421-1776, 800-228-9290; www.hilton.com

As its name suggests, this hotel is across the street from the home of the Cardinals, Busch Stadium. The entire space has been recently renovated in a contemporary style, with rooms outfitted with granite bathrooms and duvet-topped beds. Some rooms have amazing views of the skyline and Gateway Arch. Enjoy a slice at Imo's Pizza place or American cuisine at Market Street Bistro and Bar.

675 rooms. Restaurant, bar. Business center. Fitness center. Pool. Pets accepted. $151-250

★★★HILTON ST. LOUIS DOWNTOWN

400 Olive St., St. Louis, 314-436-0002, 800-445-8667; www.hilton.com

A historic landmark, the Hilton St. Louis occupies the original Merchant Laclede building. All of dowtown St. Louis' attractions are within walking distance of this hotel, including the Gateway Arch, Busch Stadium and America's Center. Guest rooms feature Serenity Beds, flat-screen TVs and complimentary Internet. Dine at 400 Olive, which features fresh American cuisine in a relaxed atmosphere.

195 rooms. Restaurant, bar. Business center. Fitness center. Pets accepted. $61-150

★★★HILTON ST. LOUIS FRONTENAC

1335 S. Lindbergh Blvd., St. Louis, 314-993-1100, 800-325-7800; www.hilton.com

Located between downtown St. Louis and Lambert International Airport, this hotel is near the St. Louis Zoo, the Science Center, Six Flags Amusement Park and adjacent to the upscale Plaza Frontenac shopping mall. The grand lobby features a large crystal chandelier and two staircases. While the rooms feature outdated floral bedding and curtains, they have modern amenities such as flat-screen TVs, Internet access and MP3 alarm clocks. The hotel offers two dining options, the pub-like Provinces Grille and the more casual bistro, Provinces Restaurant.

263 rooms. Restaurant, bar. Fitness center. Pool. Pets accepted. $151-250

★★★ST. LOUIS UNION STATION MARRIOTT

1 St. Louis Union Station, St. Louis, 314-621-5262, 800-410-9914; www.marriott.com

Located in the renovated Union Station railroad terminal, the main lobby and lounge of this hotel occupy the Grand Hall. The mall in the station has many stores and restaurants. Décor here is traditional, but contemporary details include an updated fitness center and guest rooms featuring luxury linens and flat-screen TVs.

539 rooms. Restaurant, bar. Business center. Fitness center. Pool. $151-250

★★★ST. LOUIS AIRPORT MARRIOTT

10700 Pear Tree Lane, St. Louis, 314-423-9700, 877-264-8771; www.marriott.com

This airport hotel provides complimentary shuttle service and updated business and fitness centers. Guest rooms feature classic décor and luxurious

---

WHAT ARE THE MOST LUXURIOUS HOTELS IN ST. LOUIS?

The Chase Park Plaza: This is a historic hotel, but it has the crème de la crème of modern-day amenities. The most noteworthy among them is a five-screen movie theater with plush seats.

Four Seasons Hotel St. Louis: The new Four Seasons has upped the ante among St. Louis hotels. The swanky rooms have LCD televisions, DVD players and marble bathrooms. Plus, the Lumière Place entertainment complex is right downstairs.

The Ritz-Carlton, St. Louis The Ritz piles on the luxe perks: hydrotherapy pools, a steam room and sauna, private balconies overlooking the city, feather beds—and the list goes on.

Revive bedding. The Rock River Grill and newly renovated Rock River Tavern serve a variety of classic American fare in a casual environment.

601 rooms. Restaurant, bar. Business center. Fitness center. Pool. $151-250

★★★OMNI MAJESTIC HOTEL

1019 Pine St., St. Louis, 314-436-2355, 800-843-6664; www.omnihotels.com

This European-style hotel is in downtown St. Louis and is listed on the National Register of Historic Places. Guest rooms feature poster beds with luxurious linens, dark wood, Italian marble in the bathroom, flat-screen TVs and sitting areas. Dine in the Mahogany Grille, a warm and cozy spot serving up your typical pub fare. The Omni Sensational Kids program welcomes children with a backpack filled with goodies upon arrival and gives parents a kit with a nightlight and outlet covers. If you're a workout buff, stay in one of the Get Fit rooms, which offer an in-room workout set-up.

91 rooms. Restaurant, bar. Business center. Fitness center. Pets accepted. $151-250

★★★RENAISSANCE ST. LOUIS GRAND HOTEL

800 Washington Ave., St. Louis, 314-621-9600, 800-397-1282; www.renaissancehotels.com

This historic and elegant downtown hotel is close to St. Louis' top attractions, making it a great choice for those who will be sightseeing. Guest rooms feature amazing views of the city, along with Aveda amenities in the spacious bathrooms. There are four onsite restaurants, including An American Place, an upscale local favorite serving American cuisine in an elegant atmosphere. A full fitness center and an indoor pool provide guests with a way to keep up their workouts and unwind.

1,083 rooms. Restaurant, bar. Business center. Fitness center. Pool. Pets accepted. $61-150

★★★RENAISSANCE ST. LOUIS HOTEL AIRPORT

9801 Natural Bridge Road, St. Louis, 314-429-1100, 800-340-2594; www.renaissancehotels.com

This hotel is adjacent to the Lambert International Airport and has been recently updated with pillow-top mattresses, down comforters and flat-screen TVs. The spacious rooms are more classic and sleek with neutral tones of honey and cream. An onsite Espresso Café serves up Starbucks and lighter food and T-Bone Trattoria cooks up Italian cuisine and steaks.

393 rooms. Restaurant, bar. Business center. Fitness center. Pool. $151-250

★★★★THE RITZ-CARLTON, ST. LOUIS

100 Carondelet Plaza, Clayton, 314-863-6300, 800-241-3333; www.ritzcarlton.com

This sophisticated hotel features spacious and plush guest rooms, all with private balconies with views of the city skyline. The elegant guest rooms also feature Comfort Essentials feather beds, luxurious linens, marble baths, iPod docking stations and 42-inch flat-screen TVs. A comprehensive fitness center includes lap and hydrotherapy pools, a Jacuzzi, a steam room, a sauna, a private sun deck and massage services. Enjoy one of the delicious dining options, from the Grill, serving steaks and seafood, to the Lobby Lounge, offering light fare, sushi and afternoon tea. For Sunday brunch, head to the Restaurant, a bright and casual spot. Enjoy a cocktail at the cozy Cigar Club or for a more private experience, go to the Wine Room, a unique spot for sampling one of the hotel's more than 7,000 bottles of wine.

300 rooms. Restaurant, bar. Business center. Fitness center. Pool. Pets accepted. $351 and up

★★★SHERATON ST. LOUIS CITY CENTER HOTEL AND SUITES
400 S. 14th St., St. Louis, 314-231-5007, 800-325-3535; www.sheraton.com

Located in a 1929 landmark building, this downtown hotel has oversized guest rooms with queen-size sleeper sofas for extra guests. Other amenities include a fitness center, an indoor Olympic-sized pool and a rooftop sun deck for guests who want to sunbathe. Grab a drink in the sleek onsite lounge, Column's, before heading to dinner at Bistro 14, where you can sample American cuisine.

288 rooms. Restaurant, bar. Business center. Fitness center. Pool. Pets accepted. $151-250

★★★THE WESTIN ST. LOUIS
811 Spruce St., St. Louis, 314-621-2000, 800-228-3000; www.westin.com

Adjacent to Busch Stadium and convenient to shopping and restaurants, this contemporary hotel has a spa, a health club and an acclaimed restaurant and bar. Guest rooms feature Heavenly beds, high ceilings and soaking tubs in the bathrooms. Dogs will be able to relax in their own Heavenly pet bed. Solera Spa and Health Club offers a wide range of treatments in a soothing environment. For a bite to eat, head to Clark Street Bar & Grill, which serves international cuisine in a modern warehouse-like space.

255 rooms. Restaurant, bar. Business center. Fitness center. Spa. Pets accepted. $151-250

RECOMMENDED

HYATT REGENCY ST. LOUIS AT THE ARCH
315 Chestnut St., St. Louis, 314-655-1234.

Having just undergone a $63 million renovation, this Hyatt is not only in a perfect spot, but it also features updated and luxe amenities. The guest rooms now feature modern décor, with cream, red, brown and blue hues; Hyatt Grand Beds with pillow-top mattresses; flat-screen TVs; iHome alarm clock radios; and Portico bathroom toiletries. The sleek lobby features a Starbucks and plenty of lounging space. Red Kitchen and Bar serves seasonal American cuisine, but if you crave a good steak, head to the new Ruth's Chris Steak House. If you're just looking to enjoy a beer, visit the Brewhouse Historical Sports Bar, where you can sip a brew and watch the game. The new state-of-the-art fitness center has everything you need to get in a good workout or try YogaAway, the Hyatt's in-room yoga set-up.

910 rooms. Restaurant, bar. Business center. Fitness center. Pets accepted. $251-350

WHERE TO EAT

★★★CARDWELL'S AT THE PLAZA
94 Plaza Frontenac, St. Louis, 314-997-8885; www.cardwellsattheplaza.com

St. Louis natives love this friendly bistro whose focus is on seasonal, local cuisine. You'll find everything from hearth-baked pizzas, fresh seafood and more on the menu. It also offers a variety of vegetarian and vegan dishes. Try the smoked baby-back ribs with housemade barbecue sauce, baked macaroni and vegetable coleslaw or the seafood stew with fresh fish, mussels, Gulf shrimp, calamari and scallops in a truffled fish broth with potatoes and veggies. For dessert, try one of Cardwell's seasonal pies with housemade ice cream. Artwork lines the walls in the relaxing dining room and a lovely patio is the perfect spot to enjoy a summer evening with your family.

International. Lunch, dinner. Reservations recommended. Outdoor seating. Children's menu. Bar. $36-85

★★★DOMINIC'S RESTAURANT

5101 Wilson Ave., St. Louis, 314-771-1632; www.dominicsrestaurant.com

Friendly service and a menu of well-crafted, traditional Italian cuisine have earned this restaurant a loyal following since it opened in 1971. Entrées include breast of chicken alla Romano, lobster picante and veal T-bone chop with truffle sauce. Pasta dishes range from pappardelle with mushrooms to risotto with lobster. The wine list is Italian-focused with many exceptional vintages.

Italian. Dinner. Closed Sunday. Reservations recommended. Children's menu. Bar. $36-86

★★★THE GARDENS AT MALMAISON

3519 St. Albans Road, St. Albans, 636-458-0131; www.gardensmalmaison.com

This restaurant, a rustic replica of a French inn tucked away in the countryside outside of St. Louis, offers a small, fresh seasonal menu. Enjoy dishes such as Southern fried chicken, grilled lamb chops, pan-seared chicken with garlic-herb Boursin cheese, and baby-back ribs. After your meal, take a stroll through the gardens on the grounds.

French. Lunch (Sunday), dinner. Closed Monday-Thursday. Outdoor seating. Jacket required. Bar. $36-85

★★★GIOVANNI'S ON THE HILL

5201 Shaw Ave., St. Louis, 314-772-5958; www.giovannisonthehill.com

This restaurant is best described as timeless Italian in an upscale fine dining environment. If you're looking to celebrate a special occasion or enjoy a romantic dinner for two, Giovanni's is the perfect spot. The dining room is warm and the wine list is long. The highlight is its focus on fresh seafood, which is flown in daily. The veal and beef dishes are also superlative. Try the veal saltimbocca with fresh sage, prosciutto and fontina cheese in a white wine sauce.

Italian. Dinner. Closed Sunday. Reservations recommended. Bar. $36-85

★★★THE GRILL

The Ritz-Carlton, St. Louis, 100 Carondelet Plaza, Clayton, 314-863-6300, 800-241-3333; www.ritzcarlton.com

Located in the Ritz-Carlton, St. Louis hotel, this upscale dining room serves up contemporary interpretations of American classics. Entrées include roasted Cornish hen with chestnut and apricot stuffing, pan-seared diver scallops with linguine pasta, sugar snap peas and tomato caper ragout and cider-glazed pork tenderloin with yams and red cabbage. Desserts include toasted apple ravioli and caramel apple cobbler. The décor includes extensive mahogany paneling and woodwork, overstuffed leather banquettes, dramatic lighting and a marble fireplace. Nightly entertainment is featured (piano or acoustic guitar), and on weekends, there's live music (jazz, blues, or swing) in the hotel lounge.

American. Dinner. Reservations recommended. Bar. $36-85

★★★HACIENDA
9748 Manchester Road, Rock Hill, 314-962-7100;
www.hacienda-stl.com

Built as a residence for a steamboat captain in 1861, this rambling, casual restaurant consistently delivers in its preparation of the Mexican favorites. During warm-weather months, check out the large and festive outdoor patio, where you can kick back with a margarita. It also offers a happy hour every Thursday evening with live music and a $15 all-you-can-drink deal from 6-9 p.m.

Mexican. Lunch, dinner. Outdoor seating. Bar. $16-35

★★★JOHN MINEO'S
13490 Clayton Road, Town and Country, 314-434-5244;
www.johnmineos.com

For decades, this Italian-continental restaurant has lured diners with dishes such as Dover sole and veal chop, as well as daily fresh fish specials and housemade pasta. The Mineos came to St. Louis in 1958 from Sicily and opened this restaurant in 1971 and today, it's still owned and operated by the Mineo family. You'll get formal old-school service: Waiters are dressed in tuxedos and the owners regularly check on customers.

Italian. Dinner. Jacket required. Bar. $36-85

★★★KEMOLL'S
1 Metropolitan Square, St. Louis, 314-421-0555;
www.kemolls.com

Since 1927, this downtown landmark restaurant has served classic specialties in an elegant atmosphere. It's lured in diners such as Hillary Clinton and Lauren Bacall. The restaurant is run by fourth-generation family members. With its location on the 42nd floor of Metropolitan Square, the Kemoll's offers amazing views of St. Louis. Dishes include broiled lobster tails, veal piccata, manicotti and more.

Italian. Dinner. Closed Sunday. Reservations recommended. $36-85

★★★KREIS'S
535 S. Lindbergh Blvd., St. Louis, 314-993-0735;
www.kreisrestaurant.com

This German-influenced steakhouse (think meat and potatoes) has been at the same location more than 50 years. It sits in a renovated 1930s brick house with beamed ceilings. Enjoy prime rib, filet mignon, pork chops, schnitzel and more.

Steak. Dinner. Bar. $36-85

WHAT ARE THE BEST ITALIAN RESTAURANTS IN ST. LOUIS?

Giovanni's on the Hill: If you are looking to romance your sweetie, this is the place to bring her. The dining room is warm and cozy and the food is delicious, especially the fresh seafood dishes.

John Mineo's: The Mineos came from Sicily and opened this eatery in 1971—and the family still runs it today. The restaurant stays true to the Old World dining experience with a tuxedoed waitstaff and top-notch food.

Kemoll's Celebrities like John Goodman and politicos like Al Gore visit this elegant 42nd-floor restaurant for dishes like housemade toasted ravioli and gorgeous city views.

Tony's: Tony's executes excellent authentic fare, but it also gives typical Italian food a dose of sophistication.

★★★LOMBARDO'S TRATTORIA
201 S. 20th St., St. Louis, 314-621-0666;
www.lombardosrestaurants.com

Family-owned and operated for three generations, this restaurant is in a converted hotel. The menu lists family classics as well as creative seasonal entrées. Try one of the popular dishes, such as the toasted ravioli, flash-fried spinach, and housemade cannelloni filled with meat in a marinara sauce.

Italian. Lunch, dinner. Closed Sunday. Reservations recommended. Bar. $16-35

★★★SCHNEITHORST'S HOFAMBERG INN
1600 S. Lindbergh Blvd., Ladue, 314-993-4100; www.schneithorst.com

Run by the third generation of Schneithorsts, unusual ethnic influences give traditional German cuisine an unexpected new face on this menu. Atlantic salmon with rain forest fruit relish and seafood strudel are a few examples. In true German fashion, 33 specialty beers are also available on tap and can be enjoyed in the Bierkeller, where you can sit at the bar and see the family's large stein collection.

German, American. Breakfast, lunch, dinner. Outdoor seating. Children's menu. Bar. $16-35

★★★★TONY'S
410 Market St., St. Louis, 314-231-7007; www.tonysstlouis.com

Italian food may bring to mind images of pasta with red sauce, but at Tony's you'll find a menu of authentic fare prepared with a measured and sophisticated hand. Expect appetizers like smoked salmon with mascarpone cheese and entrées like beef tenderloin with foie gras in a port wine demi-glace. The room has an urban, postmodern style, with sleek low lighting, linen-topped tables and glossy, wood-paneled walls. The chef's tasting menu is a nice choice for gourmands with healthy appetites.

Italian. Dinner. Closed Sunday; also first week of January and first week of July. Reservations recommended. Jacket required. Bar. $36-85

CENTRAL MISSOURI

Central Missouri offers a little bit of everything for travelers. There are great outdoorsy activities, historic sites and quaint little towns where you can get away from it all. Take Rolla, a scenic area with several streams nearby and the headquarters of Mark Twain National Forest. There's also the resort community of Lake Ozark, which rests on the huge, man-made reservoir called Lake of the Ozarks. In summer the area is packed with tourists who come to boat and float on the lake or stay in its many resorts. If you want a more historic place, visit Jefferson City, the state's capital and government base.

WHAT TO SEE

COLUMBIA
MUSEUM OF ART AND ARCHAEOLOGY
University of Missouri, 1 Pickard Hall, Columbia, 573-882-3591; www.missouri.edu

This museum has a comprehensive collection including more than 13,000 objects from around the world from the Paleolithic period to the present. The cast gallery has items made from original Greek and Roman sculptures.

Admission: free. Tuesday-Friday 9 a.m.-4 p.m., Saturday-Sunday noon-4 p.m.

SHELTER GARDENS

1817 W. Broadway, Columbia, 573-445-8441

This 5-acre garden features more than 300 varieties of trees and shrubs, with rose gardens, domestic and wild flowers, a pool, streams and more. There is a gazebo to sit back and relax and a small one-room schoolhouse to explore. Free concerts take place here in the summertime.

Admission: free. Daily dawn-dusk.

JEFFERSON CITY

COLE COUNTY HISTORICAL SOCIETY MUSEUM

109 Madison St., Jefferson City, 573-635-1850; www.colecohistsoc.org

One of three four-story row houses built in the Federal style, this museum features Victorian furnishings and household items, plus inaugural gowns from Missouri's first ladies dating from 1877.

Tuesday-Saturday.

GOVERNOR'S MANSION

100 Madison St., Jefferson City, 573-751-7929; www.missourimansion.org

This Renaissance Revival house was designed by George Ingham Barnett and features period furnishings, stenciled ceilings, period wall coverings and late 19th-century chandeliers.

Tours Tuesday and Thursday. Closed August and December.

STATE CAPITOL

High Street and Broadway, Jefferson City, 573-751-2854

On a bluff overlooking the Missouri River, this building of Carthage stone is the third state capitol in Jefferson City; both predecessors burned. A Thomas Hart Benton mural is in the House Lounge, on the third floor of the west wing. Also here are paintings by N. C. Wyeth and Frank Brangwyn.

Tours: Monday-Saturday, every hour, Sunday 10 a.m., 11 a.m., 2 p.m., 3 p.m.

LAKE OZARK

JACOB'S CAVE

23114 Highway TT, Versailles, 573-378-4374; www.jacobscave.com

Jacob's Cave offers visitors a look at depth illusion, reflective pools, prehistoric bones and the world's largest geode. The cave was discovered in 1875 and can be viewed today by taking a tour, where you can learn about what you're seeing.

Tours: adults $12, children 4-12 $6. Memorial Day-Labor Day, daily 9 a.m.-5 p.m.; Labor Day-Memorial Day, daily 9 a.m.-4 p.m.

LAKE OF THE OZARKS

Highway 54, Lake Ozark; www.funlake.com

Completed in 1931, the 2,543-foot-long Bagnell Dam impounds the Osage River to form this 54,000-acre recreational lake, which has an irregular 1,150-mile shoreline. Families from all over Missouri come to this recreational spot for fishing, boating and swimming, which are excellent here. The public

HIGHLIGHT

WHAT ARE THE TOP THINGS TO DO IN CENTRAL MISSOURI?

EXPLORE MARK TWAIN NATIONAL FOREST

Spread out over 1.5 million acres, this forest has more than 5,000 caves and nearly 3,000 springs that feed into rivers and streams. Enjoy trails for hiking, biking, horseback riding, campgrounds and picnicking areas.

VISIT ST. JAMES WINERY

Stop in at this winery for a wine tasting and pick up a bottle for later. They make more than 200,000 cases of wine a year, from dry and semidry wines to sweet and semi-sweet wines, including a riesling, pink catawba, and more.

RELAX AT LAKE OZARK

Pack a picnic and head to this 54,000-acre recreational lake. Spend the day fishing, boating and swimming at the public beaches, Osage Beach and Lake Ozark beach. There are also water excursions, mini-golf, horseback riding, water parks, and more.

beaches are Osage Beach and Lake Ozark beach. There's also plenty to do in the surrounding lake area including water excursions, mini-golf, horseback riding, water parks, and more.

LAKE OF THE OZARKS STATE PARK

403 Highway 134, Kaiser, 573-348-2694; www.funlake.com

This more than 17,000-acre park, the largest in the state, has 89 miles of shoreline with two public swimming and boat launching areas. On the grounds is a large cave, Ozark Caverns, with streams of water that continuously pour from stalactites, also referred to as "Angel's Shower." There are plenty of campgrounds and trails for biking and hiking.

Dawn-dusk.

ROLLA

MARAMEC SPRING PARK AND REMAINS OF OLD IRONWORKS

21880 Maramec Spring Drive, Rolla, 573-265-7387; www.maramecspringpark.com

The ironworks was first established in 1826 after the hematite mine and spring were discovered. The beautiful spring, a Registered Natural Landmark, discharges an average of 100 million gallons per day and the present furnace was built in 1857. Visit the Maramec Museum and the Agriculture Museum to learn more about the area, the spring and to see farm machinery from the 1800's. Visitors can go camping, fishing and hiking here.

MARK TWAIN NATIONAL FOREST
401 Fairgrounds Road, Rolla, 573-364-4621; www.fs.fed.us

Mark Twain National Forest occupies 1.5 million acres spread across Missouri and parts of northern Arkansas and within the Ozark Highlands. There are more than 5,000 caves, nearly 3,000 springs that feed into rivers and streams, and almost 750 species of native animals and 2,000 species of plants. Enjoy trails for hiking, biking, horseback riding, campgrounds and picnicking areas. There are seven wilderness areas within the forest including the Paddy Creek Wilderness Area, which covers about 8,178 acres with 30 miles of hiking and riding trails.

ST. JAMES WINERY
540 Sidney St., St. James, 573-265-7912, 800-280-9463; www.stjameswinery.com

Opened in 1970 by the Hofherr family, this winery makes more than 200,000 case of wine a year. It makes dry and semidry wines and sweet and semi-sweet wines, including a riesling, pink catawba, and more. Stop in for a tasting.
Monday-Saturday 8 a.m.-7 p.m., Sunday 9 a.m.-7 p.m. Tours: Monday-Saturday 11 a.m.-4 p.m., Saturday-Sunday noon-4 p.m.

WHERE TO STAY

LAKE OZARK
★★★THE LODGE OF FOUR SEASONS
315 Lodge of Four Seasons Drive, Four Seasons, 573-365-3000; www.4seasonsresort.com

Located in the Ozark Hills, this property overlooks the winding shoreline and offers everything you need in a resort. Many of the rooms and two- and three-bedroom condominiums have views of the lake or Japanese garden and pool and many have gas fireplaces. Enjoy a steak at HK's Steakhouse, which also overlooks the lake and the Japanese gardens and for breakfast and lunch, head to Breezes, where you can relax in the sun on their patio. Spend the day relaxing at Spa Shiki, which offers a variety of treatments including massages, body treatments, facials, manicures, pedicures, as well as full salon services. The resort's golf course offers 54 holes of golf on three scenic courses to enjoy during your stay here. The resort also includes a 250-seat movie theater for guests, tennis courts, three outdoor pools, bike paths, a fitness center and more.
350 rooms. Restaurant, bar. Fitness center. Pool. Spa. Golf. Tennis. $151-250

SOUTHWEST MISSOURI

The shining star of Southwest Missouri is the resort town of Branson. It has become a mecca for fans of country music and old-fashioned acts. Variety shows, comedy acts and performers of all ages hit the stages of the many theaters in town nightly.

In the southwest corner of the state and at the northern edge of the Ozark highlands, Springfield, known as Ozark Mountain Country's Big City, is near some of Missouri's most picturesque areas. "Wild Bill" Hickok, later one of the famous frontier marshals, was a scout and spy for Union forces headquartered in Springfield. Perhaps the city's most famous native son is actor Brad Pitt, who grew up here and later attended the University of Missouri in Columbia.

WHAT TO SEE

BRANSON

ANDY WILLIAMS MOON RIVER THEATER

2500 W. Highway 76, Branson, 417-334-4500; www.andywilliams.com

This theater is the domain of 1960s singer Andy Williams. Sometimes he's joined on stage by guest performers, which in the past have included Charo and Glen Campbell.

May-December, show times vary.

BALDKNOBBERS JAMBOREE SHOW

2835 W. 76 Country Blvd., Branson, 417-334-4528, 800-998-8908; www.baldknobbers.com

This country music variety show features comedy, music and skits from the second and third generations of Mabe brothers, otherwise known as the Baldknobbers. The show was started in 1959 and is a favorite in Branson.

March-mid-December, schedule varies.

BRANSON SCENIC RAILWAY

206 E. Main St., Branson, 417-334-6110, 800-287-2462; www.bransontrain.com

Take a 40-mile roundtrip through Ozark Foothills with this railway. While on board, you'll learn about the history of the area and enjoy beautiful views and if you like, you can also get the four-course candlelight meal (reservations are required for dinner).

Admission: regular: adults $24.50, children 312 $14; dinner: adults $54.25, children $54.25. Mid-March-mid-December, schedule varies.

THE DUTTONS

3454 W. Highway 76, Branson, 417-332-2772; www.theduttons.com

This musical variety show features all seven members of the Dutton family and their spouses playing a variety of instruments. The family has appeared on the TV show America's Got Talent.

April-December, schedule varies.

ELVIS AND THE SUPERSTARS TRIBUTE SHOW

206 S. Commercial, Branson, 417-336-2112, 800-358-4795; www.elvisinbranson.com

A musical tribute to Elvis Presley, this show features impersonator Dave Ehlert (who has been featured on Oprah) belting out tunes by the King from his early days through his Vegas years. After Elvis, other impersonators entertain the audience with the likes of Willie Nelson, Johnny Cash, Dean Martin and others.

Year-round, schedule varies.

GRAND COUNTRY MUSIC HALL

1945 W. Highway 76, Branson, 417-335-2484, 888-506-6278; www.grandcountry.com

Shows at this performance space include everything from Amazing Pets to

HIGHLIGHT

WHAT ARE THE BEST SHOWS IN BRANSON?

ANDY WILLIAMS MOON RIVER THEATER
A favorite in Branson, this country music variety show has been entertaining audiences since 1959. It offers comedy, music and skits from the Mabe brothers.

BALDKNOBBERS JAMBOREE SHOW
A favorite in Branson, this country music variety show has been entertaining audiences since 1959. It offers comedy, music and skits from the Mabe brothers.

THE DUTTONS
See this musical variety show to find out why this family of seven musicians made it into the top 10 in the television show America's Got Talent.

ELVIS AND THE SUPERSTARS TRIBUTE SHOW
Fans of the King will want to catch the musical stylings of Dave Ehlert. You'll also see impersonations of Dean Martin, Tom Jones and other crooners.

THE OSMOND BROTHERS
If you love Donnie and Marie, check out this show featuring their siblings. The singing brothers perform a mix of barbershop, pop, country, rock and jazz.

the Ozarks Mountain Jamboree. See the schedules on the website to find the perfect show to see.
February-December, schedule varies.

HUGHES BROTHERS CELEBRITY THEATRE
3425 W. Highway 76, Branson, 417-334-0076; www.hughes-brothers.com
The five Utah-born Hughes brothers, along with their wives and children, entertain six days a week in this musical variety show. The cast includes more than 43 people who sing, dance and entertain.

JIM STAFFORD THEATRE
3440 W. Highway 76, Branson, 417-335-8080; www.jimstafford.com
Novelty singer Jim Stafford, who had several hits in the '70s, performs at this theater. He mixes music and comedy, making for a very entertaining show.
Yearly, schedule varies.

THE OSMOND BROTHERS

Music City Theatre, 1835 W. Highway 76, Branson, 417-336-6100; www.osmondtheatre.com

The Osmond Brothers perform together again at the Music City Theatre. You can see Jay, Merrill and Wayne perform and on occasional dates, Jimmy joins them.

Schedule varies; see website for details.

PRESLEY'S COUNTRY JUBILEE

2920 W. Highway 76, Branson, 417-334-4874, 800-335-4874; www.presleys.com

Four generations of the Presley family perform country music, gospel, comedy and more. They celebrate the holiday season with specialty Christmas shows as well.

March-mid-December.

RIPLEY'S BELIEVE IT OR NOT! MUSEUM

3326 W. Highway 76, Branson, 417-337-5300; www.branson.ripleys.com

This outpost of the curiosities museum has hundreds of exhibits in eight galleries. View unbelievable attractions like a two-headed calf, a genuine shrunken head, an Aboriginal ancestor mask and much more.

Admission: adults $16.95, children 4-12 $8.95, children 3 and under free. Daily 9:30 a.m.-11 p.m.

THE SHEPHERD OF THE HILLS HOMESTEAD

5586 W. Highway 76, Branson, 417-334-4191; www.oldmatt.com

Take a guided jeep-drawn tour through the homestead, which includes a visit to the authentically furnished Old Matt's Cabin, home of the prominent characters in Harold Bell Wright's Ozark novel *The Shepherd of the Hills*. It puts on an outdoor theater production of the book and a chuckwagon dinner show. The homestead also offers shops and crafters, as well as special events.

May-December, schedule varies.

SHOWBOAT BRANSON BELLE

4800 State Highway 165, Branson, 417-336-7171, 800-475-9370; www.showboatbransonbelle.com

Take a lunch or dinner cruise along the Table Rock Lake through the Ozark Mountains on the Showboat *Branson Belle*, which departs from Highway 165 near Table Rock Dam. The dinner show features the musical production *Showstoppers* and a three-course meal.

March-December, daily.

SILVER DOLLAR CITY

399 Silver Dollar City Parkway, Branson, 800-475-9370; www.bransonsilverdollarcity.com

This fun-filled family amusement park features rides, games, shows, restaurants and more. Children will love the steam train that treks through the countryside, a carousel that spins around the park, and a giant swing.

Admission: $55-94. Mid-March-December, schedule varies.

STONE HILL WINERY

601 Highway 165, Branson, 417-334-1897; www.stonehillwinery.com

Visit Stone Hill Winery to taste some of the best wine in the Ozarks. Visitors can also take a free guided tour, watch bottling demonstrations, witness the process of making wine and taste some of the award-winning wines.

Daily, hours vary. Tours: every 15 minutes.

TABLE ROCK DAM AND LAKE
4600 Highway 165, Branson, 417-334-4101; www.swl.usace.army.mil

This 43,100-acre reservoir, formed by impounding waters of White River, offers swimming; waterskiing; scuba diving; fishing; boating; hunting for deer, turkey, rabbit and waterfowl; picnicking; playgrounds and camping.

SPRINGFIELD

BASS PRO SHOPS OUTDOOR WORLD SHOWROOM AND FISH AND WILDLIFE MUSEUM
1935 S. Campbell Ave., Springfield, 417-887-7334; www.outdoor-world.com

This 300,000-square-foot sporting goods store features a four-story waterfall, indoor boat and RV showroom, an art gallery and an indoor firing range. The Wonders of Wildlife facility, located next to the store, features indoor waterfalls, a live alligator and snapping turtle exhibit and much more. The restaurant, Hemingway's Blue Water Café, has a 30,000-gallon saltwater aquarium. It also offers seminars and workshops from fly-fishing to camping to get you ready for your excursions.
Monday-Saturday 7 a.m.-10 p.m., Sunday 9 a.m.-7 p.m.

DICKERSON PARK ZOO
3043 N. Fort, Springfield, 417-864-1800, 417-833-1570; www.dickersonparkzoo.org

Visit the Dickerson Park Zoo, where more than 150 species of animals are housed in naturalistic settings. The zoo is set up with five different geographic regions, including Tropical Asia, Africa, South America, Missouri Habitats, and Australia. It also features an elephant herd and train rides.
Admission: adults $8, seniors and children 3-12 $5. April-September, daily 9 a.m.-5 p.m.; October-March, daily 10 a.m.-4 p.m.

DISCOVERY CENTER
438 St. Louis St., Springfield, 417-862-9910; www.discoverycenter.org

This interactive hands-on museum includes its "Discovery Town Theatre" where kids can be a star on stage, create a newspaper, run a make-believe TV station or dig for dinosaur bones.
Admission: adults $9, seniors $8, children 3-15 $7. Tuesday-Thursday 9 a.m.-5 p.m., Friday 9 a.m.-8 p.m., Saturday 10 a.m.-5 p.m., Sunday 1-5 p.m.

LAURA INGALLS WILDER-ROSE WILDER LANE MUSEUM AND HOME
3068 Highway A, Mansfield, 417-924-3626, 877-924-7126; www.lauraingallswilderhome.com

The house where Laura Ingalls Wilder wrote the Little House books houses artifacts and memorabilia of the author, her husband Almanzo and daughter Rose Wilder Lane. Included are four handwritten manuscripts and many items mentioned in Wilder's books, including Pa's fiddle.
Admission: adults $8, seniors $6, children 6-17 $4, children 5 and under free. March-mid-November, Monday-Saturday 9 a.m.-5 p.m., Sunday 12:30-5 p.m.

WHERE TO STAY

BRANSON

★★★CHATEAU ON THE LAKE
415 N. Highway 265, Branson, 417-334-1161, 888-333-5253; www.chateauonthelake.com

Chateau on the Lake has a mountaintop location overlooking Table Rock Lake.

WHICH BRANSON HOTEL HAS THE BEST VIEW?

You're sure to get a nice view at **Chateau on the Lake**, which sits atop a mountain overlooking Table Rock Lake. Request a mountain or lake-view room to see the majestic Ozark Mountains or the lovely lake.

The resort is located close to town, and features a spa and salon, as well as an old-fashioned soda fountain. Spacious guest rooms feature cherry wood beds with comfortable bedding, flat-screen TVs and Internet access. Some rooms offer lake views or mountain views. Enjoy fine dining at the Chateau Grill, featuring an award-winning wine list and a popular Sunday brunch. For more casual dining, there are a few options from a wine bar to a deli. Spa Chateau offers an array of treatments, along with men's and women's relaxation rooms, indoor and outdoor hot tubs, and a steam room. The outdoor pool looks out at the lake, providing a beautiful setting to take in some sun. There's also a fitness center, tennis courts, a marina with boat rentals and plenty of outdoor activities to keep all members of your family busy.

301 rooms. Restaurant, bar. Business center. Fitness center. Pool. Spa. Tennis. Pets accepted. $151-250

★★★LODGE OF THE OZARKS

3431 W. Highway 76, Branson, 417-334-7535, 877-866-2219; www.lodgeoftheozarks.com

This hotel offers large rooms and is walking distance from theaters, shopping and other attractions. Guest rooms feature Victorian cherry furniture or lodge cedar furniture, flat-screen TVs, cozy robes and some have Jacuzzi tubs. While the rooms are a bit outdated, the property itself has more to offer. The lodge comes with an indoor pool, a hot tub and complimentary wireless Internet.

190 rooms. Restaurant, bar. Complimentary breakfast. Pool. $61-150

★★★THOUSAND HILLS GOLF AND CONFERENCE RESORT

245 S. Wildwood Drive, Branson, 417-336-5873, 877-262-0430; www.thousandhills.com

This sprawling resort has both cabins and condominiums available for rent alongside the Thousand Hills Golf Course. Most have Jacuzzi tubs, fireplaces and fully stocked kitchens. The resort also has a fitness center, indoor and outdoor pools and tennis courts.

Fitness center. Pool. Tennis. Golf. $251-350

SPRINGFIELD

★★★DOUBLETREE HOTEL SPRINGFIELD

2431 N. Glenstone Ave., Springfield, 417-831-3131; www.doubletree.com

Located in the suburban area of Springfield, this hotel offers comfortable and sleek guest rooms not far from fun attractions. Guest rooms offer the cozy Sweet Dreams by Doubletree beds, flat-screen TVs, complimentary Internet access, MP3 radios and a sitting area. There's a Houlihan's onsite as well as Gracie's, which serves breakfast. Amenities include an indoor-outdoor pool, a fitness center and a business center. Of course, you'll get the hotel's signature chocolate chip cookie when you check in.

201 rooms. Restaurant, bar. Business center. Fitness center. Pool. $61-150

RECOMMENDED

BRANSON
HILTON BRANSON CONVENTION CENTER HOTEL

200 E. Main St., Branson, 417-243-3433; www.hilton.com

The hotel's historic downtown Branson location makes it a good base for tourists, but it's also connected to the Branson Convention Center, which is perfect for business travelers as well. The lobby gives off a rustic feel, with a stone fireplace and waterfall, but the bold rooms are more modern, with dark wood, orange walls, and tan and navy linens and furniture. Rooms come with 32-inch LCD televisions, Cuisinart coffee makers, mini-fridges and views of Branson Landing, Lake Taneycomo, downtown and the Ozark Mountains. If you need to kick back, spend some time in the indoor or outdoor pool, or head down to the chic onsite Level 2 Steakhouse.

294 rooms. Restaurant, bar. Business center. Fitness center. Pool. $179-250

WHERE TO EAT

RECOMMENDED
BRANSON
BLEU OLIVE MEDITERRANEAN GRILLE & BAR

204 N. Commercial St., Branson, 417-332-2538; www.bleuolive.com

Situated in historic downtown Branson near Branson Landing, Bleu Olive serves up sophisticated Mediterranean fare. Start off with mezze like shrimp Santorini, sautéed shrimp with plum tomatoes, spinach, olives and feta. Then move on to main courses like baked Chilean salmon stuffed with crab, andouille sausage and Asiago cheese, or chicken Cordon Bleu Olive, the restaurant's take on chicken cordon bleu, with poultry filled with capicola ham, spinach and feta.

WHICH BRANSON RESTAURANTS HAVE THE BEST OUTDOOR DINING?

Candlestick Inn:
When they aren't dining on lobster, couples canoodle on the patio of this romantic restaurant, which sits on a bluff and offers a breathtaking view of the water.

Chateau Grille:
Take your meal in on the veranda, where you'll have an amazing view of Table Rock Lake while you nosh on your grilled duck.

Then end with the sweet and flaky baklava.

Mediterranean, American. Lunch, dinner, Sunday brunch. Closed Monday. Bar. $16-35

CANDLESTICK INN

127 Taney St., Branson, 417-334-3633; www.candlestickinn.com

Perched on a bluff looking out at the water, this restaurant provides a romantic setting for couples. It's especially amorous at night, when you can dine in the patio under the stars. To keep the romance alive through dinner, treat your sweetheart to the French elk rack with ground mustard beurre blank or an Australian lobster tail.

French, American. Dinner. Closed Monday. Outdoor seating. $36-85

CANTINA LAREDO

1001 Branson Landing, Branson, 417-334-6062; www.cantinalaredo.com

Cantina Laredo elevates typical Mexican dishes by using top ingredients, like fresh fish and Angus beef. The guacamole, which is made tableside, is a solid starter. Then try the hearty Fiesta Grill, with shrimp, costillas, quail, carnitas, beef and chicken fajitas, or the Carne Asada y Camarones, grilled steak with bacon-wrapped shrimp filled with Oaxaca cheese and jalapeño. The Mexican apple pie, warmed with Mexican brandy butter and accompanied by cinnamon ice cream, is a comforting meal capper.

Mexican. Lunch, dinner, Sunday brunch. Outdoor seating. Bar. $16-35

CHATEAU GRILLE

Chateau on the Lake, 415 N. Highway 265, Branson, 417-334-1161, 888-333-5253; www.chateauonthelake.com

Whether you sit inside the walnut-filled dining room or out on the veranda, you'll get a view of Table Rock Lake at this restaurant. The menu is a mix of seafood flown in from Hawaii and meat. Go for the olive oil-poached monchong lemon snapper with chorizo fingerling potatoes and béarnaise sauce, or the orange grilled duck breast with duck confit, sweet potato hash and zested foie gras butter. Be sure to take a look at the wine list, which has won awards from Wine Spectator.

American. Breakfast, lunch, dinner, Sunday brunch. Outdoor seating. $36-85

LEVEL 2 STEAKHOUSE

Hilton Branson Convention Center, 200 E. Main St., Branson, 417-243-3433; www.level2steakhouse.com

The chic dining room gives off a warm vibe with red, tan and dark gray walls; black chandeliers; and big photos of Frank Sinatra and other crooners. If you didn't realize that steak is the focus here, you will when the waiter opens a wooden box and lets you choose among five steak knives, which include a pearl-handled French utensil, for your dinner. True carnivores will want to start the meal with steakhouse soup, with smoked potatoes, steak tips, cheddar, green onions and sour cream, though the tomato basil bisque with puff pastry crust is tempting. For the entrée, try the signature 28-day-aged Kansas City strip. Have a sweet ending with the gooey Missouri butter cake with bourbon-caramel sauce, fresh berries and vanilla ice cream.

Steak. Breakfast, lunch, dinner. Reservations recommended. $36-85

KANSAS CITY

Kansas City was founded at the confluence of the historic Santa Fe, California and Oregon trails and other lesser-known ones that opened the U.S. to the west in the early 1800s. Now, almost 200 years later, the city is a world-class metropolis of 2 million residents with sweeping, tree-lined boulevards like those found in Paris, and grand, sparkling fountains reminiscent of Rome. The city features celebrated attractions, including the Nelson-Atkins Museum of Art, with a 2007 Steven Holl addition lauded by architecture and museum critics worldwide; the renowned National WWI Museum at Liberty Memorial; and the Country Club Plaza shopping district, one of 60 of the World's Greatest Places by the Project for Public Places.

Kansas City is known for its world-famous barbecue, but it's also on the forefront of the locavore movement. You'll see that dichotomy throughout the city's culinary landscape. Restaurants can be as casual as tasty Mexican-style street tacos in an old gas station, to as formal as white-glove service in elegant, soaring spaces. Either way, this city has a robust, delicious foodie scene.

Partly due to being the world headquarters of Hallmark Cards Inc. and home of the Kansas City Art Institute, which trained such artists at Robert Rauschenberg and native son Thomas Hart Benton—who later taught Jackson Pollock—the city has a thriving arts community. There are First Fridays gallery openings each month in the Crossroads, an eclectic mix of galleries, lofts, restaurants and shops in a formerly largely industrial area just south of downtown. Likewise, the lively music scene delivers a wide range of offerings, from opera to indie rock, and it will become even bigger with the fall 2011 opening of the Kauffman Center for Performing Arts, which will house the Kansas City Symphony, the Lyric Opera of Kansas City and the Kansas City Ballet.

If you are looking for entertainment, visit the Kansas City Power & Light District. The downtown district is filled with dozens of nightclubs, bars, restaurants and shops centered around an open-air plaza that hosts many events. It's a popular gathering spot after events at the Sprint Center, one of the top concert venues in the world.

WHAT TO SEE

ARABIA STEAMBOAT MUSEUM
400 Grand Blvd., Kansas City, 816-471-4030; www.1856.com

This museum features excavated pioneer artifacts from the steamboat *Arabia*, which went down in 1856. The boat, discovered in 1988, carried 200 tons of cargo. There is a replica of main deck and hands-on displays.
Daily.

COUNTRY CLUB PLAZA
4745 Central St., Kansas City, 816-753-0100

Spend the day strolling the Plaza, one of the most revered and loved outdoor shopping centers in the U.S. with more 150 shops and dozens of restaurants. Retailers range from large national chains such as Restoration Hardware and Tiffany & Co. to locally owned ones, including Tomboy and Tivol. A must-see

is Hall's, one of the country's finest upscale specialty stores. Owned by Kansas City-based Hallmark Cards Inc., the department store sells goods from around the world at price points ranging from the affordable to sky-high. The plaza features tree-lined walks, statues, fountains and murals; re-creations of Spain's Seville Light fountain and Giralda Tower; horse-drawn carriage rides; and free entertainment.
Hours vary.

CROSSROADS ARTS DISTRICT
19 Street and Baltimore Avenue; www.kccrossroads.org

Visit during the first Friday of each month and tour more than four dozen art galleries in the Crossroads Arts District just south of downtown. Many of the galleries offer wine, beer and small appetizers. There are also interesting retailers, including Birdie's for unusual and beautiful lingerie (116 W. 18th St., 816-842-2473), Christopher Elbow Chocolates (1819 McGee, 816-842-1300) and Hudson Home (1500 Grand, 816-421-3629). Visit the website for information, including gallery openings, restaurants and other special events in the district.
Hours vary.

CROWN CENTER
2450 Grand Blvd., Kansas City, 816-274-8444; www.crowncenter.com

Located in downtown Kansas City, this large entertainment complex offers shopping, theaters, restaurants and hotels around a landscaped central square with plenty of fountains, some of which produce dancing water shows. There are also exhibits and ice skating (mid-November-March).
Daily, hours vary.

JOHN WORNALL HOUSE MUSEUM
6115 Wornall Road, Kansas City, 816-444-1858; www.wornallhouse.org

This restored farmhouse interprets the lives of prosperous Missouri farm families from 1830-1865 and includes an herb garden.
Admission: adults $6, seniors and children 5-12 $5, children 4 and under free. Tuesday-Saturday 10 a.m.-4 p.m., Sunday 1-4 p.m.

KALEIDOSCOPE
2450 Grand Blvd., Kansas City, 816-274-8300; www.hallmarkkaleidoscope.com

Kaleidoscope is a free participatory creative art exhibit for children ages 5-12. Kids are prodded to use their imaginations and create their own masterpieces using Hallmark's discarded materials, including melted crayons, markers, watercolor paints and ribbon.
Admission: free. Mid-June-August, Monday-Saturday; September-mid-June, Saturday or by appointment.

KANSAS CITY CHIEFS (NFL)
Arrowhead Stadium, 1 Arrowhead Drive, Kansas City, 816-920-9300, 800-676-5488; www.kcchiefs.com

Kansas City's professional football team calls Arrowhead Stadium home. During pigskin season, you can tour the stadium, press box, Hall of Honor, broadcast booth and more.
Tours: adults $10, seniors $8, children 4-12 $5, children 3 and under free. Thursday-Saturday, 10 a.m., 1 p.m.

HIGHLIGHT

WHAT ARE THE TOP THINGS TO DO IN KANSAS CITY?

SPEND THE DAY AT THE CITY MARKET
Operating since the 1850s, it's one of the oldest U.S. farmer's markets. Besides fresh produce, vendors hawk an eclectic array of baked goods, cheeses, flowers, jewelry and more.

MEANDER THROUGH GALLERIES IN THE CROSSROADS ARTS DISTRICT
Visit the Crossroads Arts District, just south of downtown, the first Friday of each month and tour more than four dozen galleries, many of which offer wine, beer and appetizers.

SHOP UNTIL YOU DROP AT COUNTRY CLUB PLAZA
Spend the day strolling the Plaza, one of the most revered and loved outdoor shopping districts in the U.S. with more than 150 stores and dozens of restaurants.

KANSAS CITY MUSEUM
3218 Gladstone Blvd., Kansas City, 816-483-8300; www.kcmuseum.com

Science, history and technology exhibits are housed in the former estate of lumber millionaire Robert A. Long. There is a re-creation of an 1821 trading post with an 1860 storefront and functioning 1910 drugstore; a planetarium; and a gift shop.

Admission: free. Tuesday-Saturday 9:30 a.m.-4:30 p.m., Sunday noon-4:30 p.m.

KANSAS CITY ROYALS (MLB)
Kauffman Stadium, 1 Royal Way, Kansas City, 816-921-8000; www.kcroyals.com

The Royals, Kansas City's professional baseball team, play ball here. You can take a tour of the ballpark and check out its trademark 322-foot-wide fountain, the home dugout and the visiting team locker room.

Tours: Vary.

KANSAS CITY ZOO
Swope Park, 6800 Zoo Drive, Kansas City, 816-513-5700; www.kansascityzoo.org

Explore 200 acres landscaped to resemble natural animal habitats at the Kansas City Zoo. There are sea lion and wild bird shows; an IMAX theater; and miniature train, pony and camel rides. Visit the newly opened Polar Bear Passage, a $10 million addition showing off the white beauties. Be sure to check out some of the new babies born recently at the zoo, including black-footed kittens, oryx calves, baby porcupines and more.

Admission: adults $11.50, seniors $10.50, children 3-11 $8.50. Monday-Friday 9:30 a.m.-4 p.m., Saturday-Sunday 9:30 a.m.-5 p.m.

KEMPER MUSEUM OF CONTEMPORARY ART

4420 Warwick Blvd., Kansas City, 816-753-5784; www.kemperart.org

The Kemper fits in perfectly in the neighborhood of the Kansas City Art Institute, both in proximity and in mission with its permanent collection featuring artists such as Jasper Johns, Frank Stella, Jackson Pollock, Robert Rauschenberg, Robert Motherwell, Georgia O'Keeffe, Willem de Kooning and Robert Mapplethorpe. The museum opened in 1994 in a striking building designed by Gunnar Birkerts. Louise Bourgeois' huge bronze "Spider"—designed to honor her mother—welcomes visitors on the front lawn.

Admission: free. Tuesday-Thursday, 10 a.m.-4 p.m., Friday-Saturday 10 a.m.-9 p.m., Sunday 11 a.m.-5 p.m.

NATIONAL WORLD WAR I MUSEUM AT LIBERTY MEMORIAL

100 W. 26th St., Kansas City, 816-784-1918; www.theworldwar.org

After the Armistice in 1918, the city soon set about raising funds for a memorial to its veterans, getting an astounding $2.5 million in just 10 days. The site first opened in the 1930s, and then after a $100 million-plus expansion and renovation in 2006, the Ralph Applebaum-designed museum reopened. Visitors enter the museum and cross a glass bridge over a poppy field, where each of the buds represents a thousand combatant deaths to illustrate the 9 million lost soldiers. You can also see what it was like to be in the trenches with re-created scenes, look at artifacts like a 1917 helmet and check out machinery like a French-made Renault FT-17 tank.

Admission: adults $12, seniors $10, students $10, children 6-17 $6, military personnel and children 5 and under free. Tuesday-Sunday 10 a.m.-5 p.m.

NELSON-ATKINS MUSEUM OF ART

4525 Oak St., Kansas City, 816-751-1278; www.nelson-atkins.org

The museum added a Steven Holl-designed series of five glass-lens-topped galleries in 2007, which garnered praise worldwide by art and architecture critics. Collections range from Sumerian art of 3000 B.C. to contemporary paintings and sculpture. The museum is known for its Chinese art collection, and has acclaimed early American and Native American collections and Egyptian galleries; period rooms; and decorative arts. Don't forget to check out the museum's free 22-acre Kansas City Sculpture Park, which contains works from such artists as Henry Spencer Moore and Claes Oldenburg.

Admission: free. Wednesday 10 a.m.-4 p.m., Thursday-Friday 10 a.m.-9 p.m., Saturday 10 a.m.-5 p.m., Sunday noon-5 p.m.

UNION CEMETERY

227 E. 28th St., Kansas City, 816-472-4990; www.uchskc.org

Some notables are buried here, including George Caleb Bingham, an artist who focused on the American West, and Alexander Majors, the founder of the Pony Express. There are also graves of more than 1,000 Civil War soldiers.

UNION STATION

30 Pershing Road, Kansas City, 816-460-2020; www.unionstation.org

The Beaux-Arts 850,000-square-foot train station opened in 1914. It was the second-largest station in the U.S. and saw tens of thousands of people move through its soaring halls, peaking in WWII. The building deteriorated and eventually closed in the 1980s. But in 1996, seven counties straddling the state line of Missouri and Kansas passed a historic bistate tax and $250 million later, the grand station reopened in 1999. Today, Union Station houses Science City, an interactive science museum; a live theater and IMAX movie theater; and Pierpont's at Union Station, a fine dining restaurant that serves steaks and seafood in a beautiful airy space that was formerly the women's waiting room. The station also hosts special traveling exhibits; past ones have included artifacts from the Titanic and the Dead Sea Scrolls. *Daily.*

WESTPORT

Broadway and Westport Road, Kansas City; www.westportkc.com

This renovated 1830s historic district includes galleries and specialty shops such as Lomavista, a skateboarding and clothing store. When you need to grab a bite, head to Blanc Burgers + Bottles, which serves gourmet patties paired with bottles of beer or wine. Take a walk through the small but significant Pioneer Park, which traces Westport's role in the founding of Kansas City. *Daily, hours vary.*

WORLDS OF FUN

4545 N.E. Worlds of Fun Ave., Kansas City, 816-454-4545; www.worldsoffun.com

This 170-acre entertainment complex features amusement rides, live entertainment, a children's area, special events and restaurants. Thrill-seekers will get their fill on the looping steel and wooden roller coasters.

Admission: adults $41.99, seniors and children $19.99. Late May-October, hours vary.

WHERE TO STAY

★★★HOTEL PHILLIPS

106 W. 12th St., Kansas City, 816-221-7000, 800-433-1426; www.hotelphillips.com

This hotel offers convenience and comfort for out-of-towners who want to be in downtown Kansas City. Built as an upscale hotel in 1931, the lobby and adjacent areas retain their Art Deco grandeur with updated guest rooms, albeit most are on the small side. The hotel is within easy walking distance of an upscale AMC movie theater and a wide array of restaurants and nightclubs in the Power & Light entertainment district, which is across the street from the Sprint Center arena. Also nearby are the Bartle Hall Convention Center, the Crown Center, the National World War I Museum at Liberty Memorial and Union Station.

217 rooms. Restaurant, bar. Business center. Fitness center. $151-250

★★★HYATT REGENCY CROWN CENTER

2345 McGee St., Kansas City, 816-421-1234, 888-591-1234; www.crowncenter.hyatt.com

Connected to the Crown Center by an elevated walkway and located near the Truman Sports Complex, an amusement park and the international airport, this hotel is convenient and comfortable. Rooms come with pillow-top mattresses, granite bathrooms and views of the Crown Center or the city skyline. If you are looking to get in a workout while you're at the hotel but forgot your gear at home, consult the fitness concierge. He will outfit you with a GPS watch for your outdoor run or goggles for your laps in the pool.

733 rooms. Restaurant, bar. Business center. Fitness center. Pool. Tennis. $151-250

★★★INTERCONTINENTAL KANSAS CITY AT THE PLAZA

401 Ward Parkway, Kansas City, 816-756-1500, 888-424-6835; www.ichotelsgroup.com

This hotel completed a multimillion-dollar renovation in 2009. Built in the 1970s, many of the rooms face the renowned Country Club Plaza, itself built in the early 1920s as one of the first planned outdoor shopping centers in the U.S. Today the Plaza features an array of shopping and dining options just steps away for those staying at the Intercontinental. The hotel offers an array of rooms, including a two-room, two-bathroom suite with French doors separating the living room from the bedroom. The living room and bedroom both have a flat-screen TV. Many of the rooms have small balconies with a bistro-style table and chairs with a view overlooking the Plaza, which is a particularly beautiful sight when the holiday lights are on each year from Thanksgiving night through mid-January. The hotel features an outdoor area with two pools connected by a Roman-style fountain that creates a relaxing water-crescendo waterfall. Beverage and dining service is available at the pool with live jazz during some evenings and on weekends. Live music is also available many weekends and evenings in the Oak Bar with a fireplace to ward off winter (or spring or autumn) chill. It is adjacent to the elegant Oak Room restaurant.

366 rooms. Restaurant, bar. Business center. Fitness center. Pool. Pets accepted. $151-250

★★★KANSAS CITY MARRIOT COUNTRY CLUB PLAZA

4445 Main St., Kansas City, 816-531-3000, 800-228-9290; www.marriott.com

Situated 10 minutes from downtown, this hotel is within walking distance of the city's top shopping and restaurants. The hotel has updated guest rooms with luxury bedding, including designer duvets and cozy down comforters; flat-screen TVs; and brightly colored furniture. The lobby is sleek and the perfect spot to enjoy coffee with friends or relax and watch TV.

295 rooms. Restaurant, bar. Business center. Fitness center. Pool. $61-150

★★★MARRIOTT KANSAS CITY AIRPORT

775 Brasilia Ave., Kansas City, 816-464-2200, 800-810-2771; www.marriott.com

Located on the Kansas City International Airport's grounds, this hotel is a good choice for those who have an early-morning flight. Red, orange and white rooms have been updated with luxury bedding and Internet access. Guests can enjoy complimentary onsite parking, making it easier and less expensive to get around the city.

384 rooms. Restaurant, bar. Business center. Fitness center. Pool. $151-250

★★★MARRIOTT KANSAS CITY DOWNTOWN

200 W. 12th St., Kansas City, 816-421-6800, 800-228-9290; www.marriott.com

This large hotel is downtown near the City Market, casinos and family attractions. Its enclosed walkway to the Kansas City Convention Center makes it a popular spot for business travelers. Recently renovated guest rooms feature the Revive

SPECIAL EVENTS

WHAT ARE THE KANSAS CITY'S BEST CULTURAL OFFERINGS?

LYRIC OPERA

1029 Central St., Kansas City, 816-471-4933; www.kcopera.org
Kansas City's Lyric Opera features productions throughout the year such as *Carmen* and *The Marriage of Figaro*.
April-May and mid-September-mid-October, December.

MISSOURI REPERTORY THEATRE

Center for the Performing Arts, 4949 Cherry St., Kansas City, 816-235-2700; www.kcrep.org
This professional equity theater company presents classic and contemporary productions, like *Cabaret* and *Saved*, along with an annual performance of *A Christmas Carol*.
September-May, Tuesday-Sunday.

STARLIGHT THEATER

Swope Park, 4600 Starlight Road, Kansas City, 816-363-7827
This outdoor amphitheater features Broadway musicals and concerts.
Early June-August.

ST. PATRICK'S DAY PARADE

Broadway between 31st Street and Westport Road, Kansas City, 816-931-7373, 816-373-5405; www.kcirishparade.com
One of the nation's largest, this St. Patrick's Day parade is approximately one mile long and features a variety of themed floats, bands and performers.
March.

bedding, granite bathrooms, flat-screen TVs and wireless Internet. Three onsite restaurants, a pub and a coffee bar add to the convenience factor for visitors.
983 rooms. Restaurant, bar. Business center. Fitness center. Pool. Pets accepted. $151-250

★★★THE RAPHAEL HOTEL

325 Ward Parkway, Kansas City, 816-756-3800, 800-821-5343; www.raphaelkc.com
This charming boutique hotel overlooking the renowned Country Club Plaza underwent a top-to-bottom multimillion dollar renovation in 2009. The result is an elegant but updated hotel that has a comfortable, Old World feel and a staff that's eager to please. The property was built in the 1920s as an upscale apartment residence and many of the 120-plus rooms are unique and cater

to different desires, including a dining suite and a Jacuzzi suite that also has a separate glass-wall, walk-in shower with two large rain-style showerheads, one of which is mounted on the ceiling. The rooms are spacious and have an elegant, understated atmosphere with comfortable seating areas, flat-screen TVs, luxurious linens and down pillows. The bathrooms feature black marble and cherry wood vanities and extra-deep soaking tubs. The European toiletries include bath salts. The Chaz Restaurant and Lounge has also been completely renovated and offers a cool respite for those weary from a day of shopping and sightseeing. The Raphael is steps away from the shops and restaurants of the Plaza and is especially popular during the holidays, when more than 80 miles of holiday lights are set ablaze on Thanksgiving night.

123 rooms. Restaurant, bar. Business center. $151-250

★★★SHERATON SUITES COUNTRY CLUB PLAZA

770 W. 47th St., Kansas City, 816-931-4400, 800-325-3535; www.sheraton.com

This all-suite hotel just underwent an extensive renovation featuring refreshed guest rooms with the Sweet Sleeper Bed, neutral-toned and modern décor and flat-screen TVs. The lobby was also transformed to a sleek new spot where you can use the hotel's work centers with complimentary Internet. There are also indoor and outdoor heated pools, a whirlpool and fitness center. The hotel is near sports, cultural and family attractions.

257 rooms. Restaurant, bar. Business center. Fitness center. Pool. Pets accepted. $61-150

★★★THE WESTIN CROWN CENTER, KANSAS CITY

1 E. Pershing Road, Kansas City, 816-474-4400, 800-228-3000; www.westin.com

Located in the downtown area within Hallmark's Crown Center, where visitors will find shops, restaurants and theaters, this hotel is also near the Liberty Memorial and the Bartle Convention Center. The guest rooms recently completed a $10 million renovation and were updated with signature Heavenly Beds with pillow-top mattresses, Internet access and more modern, sleek décor. Enjoy amenities outside of your room, including the beautiful and large outdoor swimming pool, the outdoor track, tennis courts, a sauna, tanning beds and more.

724 rooms. Restaurant, bar. Business center. Fitness center. Pool. Tennis. Pets accepted. $151-250

RECOMMENDED

THE Q HOTEL & SPA

560 Westport Road, Kansas City, 816-931-0001, 800-942-4233; www.theqhotel.com

This friendly, fun-spirited, eco-conscious boutique hotel is in the Westport entertainment district with an interesting array of nightclubs, restaurants and shops within walking distance. The Q Hotel hosts a manager's happy hour each evening in the Quench bar off the lobby. Each morning, guests can head to the downstairs dining room for breakfast, which includes a waffle bar and made-to-order omelets. The property underwent a renovation in 2009 that outfitted all 123 rooms with an eye toward sustainability and minimized the footprint of the hotel itself and that of its guests, including using energy-efficient lighting and water-saving shower heads. The bathrooms come with Aveda products and refillable bath gel, shampoo and conditioner in the showers. The coffee and tea service uses cups made from recycled paper. If you want to stick to your exercise routine, get passes to the Gold's Gym across the street, though if you are looking to get pampered, the Q does manicures, pedicures and massages onsite. The hotel offers free shuttle services and bicycles. The comfy rooms are a tad on the small side, but the large framed mirrors on the walls help make them feel bigger. The beds have fun, round decorative pillows; soft, comfortable linens; and a light cotton throw to ward off any nighttime chills.

130 rooms. Bar. Business center. Pets accepted. $61-150

WHERE TO EAT

★★★★THE AMERICAN RESTAURANT

200 E. 25th St., Kansas City, 816-545-8001; www.theamericankc.com

The flagship restaurant of the Crown Center, the American has attracted Kansas City diners for 40 years. With a concept designed by the legendary James Beard, the father of American cooking, and Joe Baum, the restaurateur of the former Windows on the World in New York City, the restaurant is as elegant as ever, with downtown views, polished service and one of the city's best wine lists. The kitchen staff, led by James Beard Award-winning executive chef Debbie Gold, prepares American fare using local seasonal produce, like applewood-grilled Piedmontese côte de boeuf with candied yams and smoked mushrooms.

American. Lunch, dinner. Closed Sunday. Reservations recommended. Children's menu. Bar. $36-85

★★★ANDRE'S TEAROOM

5018 Main St., Kansas City, 816-561-6484, 800-892-1234; www.andreschocolates.com

An offshoot of legendary Swiss chocolate maker Andres Bollier's candy shop, this tearoom serves continental favorites such as leek and Gruyère pie and vol-au-vent in a quaint setting. After lunch, stock up on truffles or a linzer torte to take home.

Continental. Lunch. Closed Sunday-Monday. $16-35

★★★BLUESTEM

900 Westport Road, Kansas City, 816-561-1101; www.bluestemkc.com

Bluestem is the product of two acclaimed chefs, Colby and Megan Garrelts, who worked at such restaurants as Aureole in Las Vegas and TRU in Chicago. The space is divided into a 40-seat restaurant, with cobalt blue walls and warm candlelight. Three-, five- and seven-course prix menus are available, as is a 12-course tasting menu. Entrées might include a torchon of foie gras, wild Tasmanian salmon with oxtail or LaBelle duck with sweet potato gnocchi and apple emulsion. Desserts are outstanding, simplistic in their approach but full of intense flavors. Try the tempting vanilla-marinated nectarines with peach nectar, cinnamon-toasted feuille de brick, sweet corn ice cream, fresh sheep cheese, popcorn dust and caramel. For more casual fare, head to the adjacent wine bar.

American. Dinner, Sunday brunch. Bar. Reservations recommended. $36-85

★★★GRAND STREET CAFÉ

4740 Grand St., Kansas City, 816-561-8000; www.eatpbj.com

A stylish and modern botanical theme runs through this dining room. Double-cut pork chops with cinnamon apples and brown sugar jus, caramelized sea scallops with Maine lobster butter and a crispy potato pancake, and grilled filet mignon with a veal demi-cabernet sauce and French green beans are among the menu items. Sunday brunch is quite popular, so don't be surprised if you're kept waiting. A small, cozy patio with eight tables offers alfresco dining.

American. Lunch, dinner, Sunday brunch. Reservations recommended. Outdoor seating. Children's menu. Bar. $36-85

★★★JJ'S

910 W. 48th St., Kansas City, 816-561-7136; www.jjs-restaurant.com

Upscale mostly Continental cuisine is served at this European-inspired cafe just off the Country Club Plaza. Classics like osso buco, chicken Marsala and bouillabaisse are served alongside various cuts of beef famous in this part of the country. Entrées spotlight fresh, local ingredients, including salads that offer pears and Stilton and blackberry quail. JJ's is well-known for its eclectic and interesting wine list and über-friendly service.

American, European. Lunch, dinner. Reservations recommended. Bar. $36-85

★★★LE FOU FROG

400 E. Fifth St., Kansas City, 816-474-6060; www.lefoufrog.com

You don't even need to squint your eyes to feel like you're in France at this bistro, which is lively with locals and European expats. Fare is traditional French and presentation is excellent, from the escargot to the steak au poivre.

French. Lunch, dinner. Closed Monday. Reservations recommended. Outdoor seating. Bar. $36-85

★★★LIDIA'S KANSAS CITY

101 W. 22nd St., Kansas City, 816-221-3722; www.lidiasitaly.com

Created by the acclaimed New York restaurateur Lidia Bastianich, this restaurant offers a rustic atmosphere, with rough brick walls and exposed wooden beams. In winter months, a fire roars in the fireplace behind the stone bar. The menu focuses on Bastianich's love of myriad regional Italian cuisines. Particularly popular is the daily offering of three freshly made pastas, which changes each day depending on availability of what's fresh from the garden. But you can also find items on the menu like wild boar ravioli in a rosemary-infused sauce and lobster risotto with heirloom tomatoes.

Italian. Lunch, dinner, Sunday brunch. Reservations recommended. Outdoor seating. Children's menu. Bar. $16-35

★★★THE MAJESTIC STEAKHOUSE

931 Broadway, Kansas City, 816-471-8484; www.majestickc.com

The historic Fitzpatrick Saloon building in downtown Kansas City is home to one of the best, most entertaining steak houses in town. It's also a great place to indulge in a cigar. The restaurant features turn-of-the-century décor with stained-glass windows and an ornate tin ceiling. Go there to hear live jazz on Thursdays to Saturdays and to tear into cuts like the dry-aged French bone-in rib-eye, a favorite among diners.

Steak. Lunch, dinner. Reservations recommended. Bar. $36-8

★★★PLAZA III STEAKHOUSE

4749 Pennsylvania Ave., Kansas City, 816-753-0000;
www.plazaiiisteakhouse.com

The epitome of the Kansas City steak house, this restaurant serves USDA prime aged cuts of Midwestern beef, chops, fresh fish and lobster. Don't miss the restaurant's famous steak soup.

Steak. Lunch, dinner. Reservations recommended. Children's menu. Bar. $36-85

RECOMMENDED

BLANC BURGERS + BOTTLES

4710 Jefferson St., Kansas City, 816-931-6200;
www.blancburgers.com

This is an upscale burger joint, as evidenced by its take on surf 'n turf, a Kobe burger topped with a lobster tail. All the condiments, including ketchup and aioli, are made in-house. The cool modern Blanc Burger space offers hand-cut regular and sweet potato fries, and also has an extensive and eclectic beer menu, hence the "bottles." The proprietors favor local purveyors, including Boulevard Brewing Co. and Shatto Farms, so you can get a real taste of Kansas City.

American. Lunch, dinner. $15 and under

CAFÉ SEBASTIENNE AT THE KEMPER MUSEUM

4420 Warwick Blvd., Kansas City; 816-561-7740;
www.kemperart.org

The Kemper Museum gets additional works of art with chef Jennifer Maloney's upscale, eclectic cuisine. Depending on the season, the menu—which is ever-changing—might feature grilled East Coast halibut, chicken under a brick or Moroccan-spiced rack of lamb. Openers include salads made from greens and cheeses from local farms, including Green Dirt Farms.

American. Lunch, dinner, Sunday brunch. Reservations recommended. $16-35

CHAZ RESTAURANT

The Raphael Hotel, 325 Ward Parkway, Kansas City,
816-756-3800, 800-821-5343; www.raphaelkc.com

Housed in the Raphael Hotel, this restaurant has an

WHAT ARE THE BEST OVERALL RESTAURANTS IN KANSAS CITY?

The American Restaurant:
The legendary James Beard designed this restaurant concept, so you know you're in for a treat. Expect American fare with seasonal local produce, like applewood-grilled Piedmontese côte de boeuf.

Bluestem:
Try one of the prix fixe menus at this American eatery for some delicious fare, but don't forget the amazing desserts, like vanilla-marinated nectarines with feuille de brick, sweet corn ice cream, sheep cheese, popcorn dust and caramel.

elegant dining room and refined service. The Kansas City strip steak with port wine sauce and melted gorgonzola is a menu standout.

International. Breakfast, lunch, dinner. Reservations recommended. Bar. $36-85

EXTRA VIRGIN

1900 Main St., Kansas City, 816-842-2205; www.extravirginkc.com

The menu at this small-plates, Spanish- and Euro-inspired restaurant changes frequently but might include dishes such as Honduran yellowtail ceviche, stuffed pequillo peppers, chorizo-and-fig-filled chicken thighs or gratin of Spanish bacalao. The restaurant—which features an open kitchen; a large, central bar; and an original billboard from the 1960 classic *La Dolce Vita*—focuses on interesting cheeses and meat such as boar sopressata, Italian testa, Fiscalini white cheddar and Spanish manchego. The cocktail and wine menus change to reflect on what goes best in any given season. A daily cocktails-and-small-plates happy hour until 6 p.m. attracts an early crowd, some of whom are still lingering when the post-concert and art gallery crowd come in for a snack and a nightcap. Extra Virgin's menu is meant for grazing in a laid-back, lazy way.

Mediterranean. Lunch, dinner. Reservations recommended. Outdoor seating. $16-35.

WHERE TO SHOP

CITY MARKET

Fifth and Grand streets, Kansas City, 816-842-1274; www.thecitymarket.org

You could easily spend the day at the City Market. In operation since the 1850s, it is one of the nation's oldest farmer's markets. Vendors offer an eclectic array of baked goods, fresh produce, cheeses, flowers, jewelry and more. If you get hungry while you shop, there are plenty of dining options, from barbecue to Vietnamese to Mediterranean.

Saturday 6 a.m.-3 p.m., Sunday 7 a.m.-3 p.m.

COUNTRY CLUB PLAZA

4745 Central St., Kansas City, 816-753-0100; www.countryclubplaza.com

Built by J.C. Nichols in the early 1920s, partly on the site of an old pig farm, the Plaza—as it's known by the locals—was inspired by Nichols' travels through Europe, Mexico and Central America and South America. Today, the Plaza is home to 150 upscale retailers, like Gap, Tiffany & Co., Ann Taylor Loft, Cole Haan, Burberry, Betsey Johnson, and several dozen restaurants that should have something for everyone. The Plaza becomes even more magical during the Christmas season when the switch is flipped on 80 miles of colored lights outlining the facades of buildings, block after block.

Hours vary.

GARMENT DISTRICT BOUTIQUE

1350 Main St., Kansas City, 816-221-4387; www.garmentdistrictboutique.com

This designers' collective boutique offers a wide range of one-of-a-kind pieces from both local designers as well as those from the West and East coasts. You'll find items for men and women from Rebel Spirit, Ben Sherman, English Laundry and Jordan Craig. There is also a bar, which on Sundays offers complimentary Bloody Marys and mimosas so you can take a break while shopping.

Monday-Thursday 11 a.m.- 7 p.m., Friday-Saturday 10 a.m.-8 p.m., Sunday noon-6 p.m

WELCOME TO MONTANA

THIS MAGNIFICENT STATE TOOK ITS NAME FROM

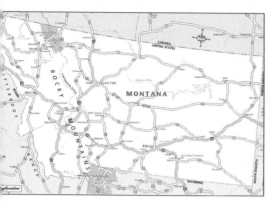

the Spanish word montaña, which means "mountain." The altitude of about half the state is more than 5,000 feet, and the sprawling ranges of the Continental Divide rise more than two miles into air that is so clear, photographers must use filters to avoid overexposure. The names of many towns, though, indicate that Montana has more than mountains. Grass Range, Roundup and Buffalo tell of vast prairie regions, where tawny oceans of wheat stretch to the horizon and a cattle ranch may be 30 miles from front gate to front porch. Big Timber and Highwood suggest Montana's 22 million acres of forests; Gold Creek and Silver Gate speak of the roaring mining days (the roaring is mostly over, but you can still pan for gold in almost any stream). Of special interest to visitors are Antelope, Lame Deer and Trout creeks, which offer excellent hunting and fishing.

The Treasure State's natural resources are enormous. Its hydroelectric potential is the greatest in the world—annual flow of the four major rivers is enough to cover the whole state with six inches of water. The 25 major dams include Fort Peck, one of the world's largest hydraulic earth-fill dams. Near Great Springs, one of the world's largest freshwater springs, pours out nearly 400 million gallons of water every day. In more than 1,500 lakes and 16,000 miles of fishing streams, the water is so clear, you may wonder if it's there at all.

Along with the bounty of its resources, Montana's history has given us Custer's Last Stand (June 25, 1876); the last spike in the Northern Pacific Railroad (September 8, 1883); the country's first Congresswoman (Jeannette Rankin of Missoula, in 1916); the Dempsey-Gibbons fight (July 4, 1923) and a state constitution originally prefaced by the Magna Carta, the Declaration of Independence, the Articles of Confederation and the United States Constitution.

BEST ATTRACTIONS

MONTANA'S BEST ATTRACTIONS

BILLINGS
You'll want to make the trek out to this city. Billings offers the state's only zoo, ZooMontana, and Pictograph Cave State Park, where caves have painted images from prehistoric hunters.

GLACIER COUNTRY
Outdoors enthusiasts will have a field day here, whether they go fishing in Swan Lake or explore Glacier National Park's 730 miles of hiking trails.

GOLD WEST COUNTRY/RUSSELL COUNTRY
In this region, you can see more than 2,000 works from one of the original Western artists who depicted life in the open range and learn about famous explorers Lewis and Clark.

GLACIER COUNTRY

Located on Montana's western region, Glacier Country is composed of small towns, beautiful mountains and natural landscapes. It's the perfect place to take part in outdoor activities and adventures. Surrounded by lakes, a river and a dam, Bigfork's businesses are electric power and catering to tourists who visit the east shore of Flathead Lake, the largest freshwater lake west of the Mississippi. The quaint downtown offers art galleries, specialty shops and an array of restaurants. Since the days of the Lewis and Clark Expedition, Missoula has been a trading and transportation crossroads. It is a lumber and paper manufacturing center, the hub of large reserves of timber, and the regional headquarters of the U.S. Forest Service and Montana State Forest Service.

Not long ago, West Yellowstone was abandoned and snowbound in the winter. Today, winter sports and attractions keep the town busy year-round. Located on the shore of Whitefish Lake, this community headquarters a four-state summer vacation area and is a winter ski center, as well.

WHAT TO SEE

BIGFORK
SWAN LAKE
200 Ranger Station Road, Bigfork, 406-837-7500; www.fs.fed.us
A slender finger of water 20 miles long and a mile wide, Swan Lake is one of a

chain of lakes on the Clearwater River. It's known as a fishing destination—in the spring, northern pike are the prime catch, and in the summer and fall it's Kokanee salmon and bull trout. Swan Lake is also popular with boaters; there are campsites and hiking trails near its shores, as well as in the village of the same name on its southern tip.

MISSOULA

LOLO NATIONAL FOREST
Missoula, 406-329-3750; www.fs.fed.us

Located in West Central Montana, Lolo National Forest is a popular recreation destination in both summer and winter, with hiking and cross-country skiing. Foot trails to 100 lakes and peaks are available in the more than 2 million acres of forest, which include the Welcome Creek Wilderness and Rattlesnake National Recreation Area and Wilderness, part of Scapegoat Wilderness and Selway-Bitterroot Wilderness. Fishing is another big draw here, with four excellent rivers and their myriad tributaries running through the Lolo. The historic Lolo Trail and Lewis and Clark Highway (Highway 12) over the Bitterroot Mountains take visitors along the route of famed exploration. In the town of Huson, the Forest Service operates the unique Nine Mile Wildlands Training Center, where visitors can enroll in classes covering such skills as horsemanship, backcountry survival and historic preservation.

MONTANA SNOWBOWL
Snow Bowl Road, Missoula, 406-549-9777; www.montanasnowbowl.com

Spread over two mountains linked by a skiable saddle, Montana Snowbowl includes an impressive 2,600-foot vertical drop. There are plenty of close-in runs for experienced skiers on Snowbowl's 950 acres (20 percent beginner, 40 percent intermediate and 40 percent expert). The backside Lavelle Creek Area is ideal for families, with runs for all ski levels in close proximity. There is a restaurant and a ski school, and in-mountain accommodations are available at a European-style lodge (with both shared and private bathrooms).
Late November-April, Monday, Wednesday-Sunday.

WEST GLACIER

GLACIER NATIONAL PARK
West Glacier, 406-888-7800; www.nps.gov

In 1910, Glacier National Park became the 10th national park in the United States. There are more than 730 miles of hiking trails, 13 campgrounds and the Sperry and Grinnell glaciers are the largest in the park (and can be found at Going-to-the-Sun road and Highland Trail). Many people head to the park during off-season, at the end of October through winter for the tranquility that the winter brings, along with cross-country skiing. The park provides shuttle buses in the case that visitors don't want to deal with the hassle of driving, and you can pick up the shuttles at many different stops throughout the park (there is no fee and schedules are listed online). There are also guided horseback trips (www.swanmountainoutfitters.com), ranger-led walks and hikes (see website for schedule) and boat cruises (call Glacier Park Boat Co. to set up a cruise 406-257-2426).
Admission: 7-day Vehicle Permit May-November: $25; December-April: $15. Daily.

HIGHLIGHT

WHAT ARE THE BEST THINGS TO SEE IN BILLINGS?

On the west bank of the Yellowstone River, Billings, the seat of Yellowstone County, was built by the Northern Pacific Railway and took the name of the railroad president Frederick K. Billings. Today, Billings is a major distribution point for Montana's and Wyoming's vast strip-mining operations.

GEYSER PARK FUN CENTER
4910 Southgate Drive, Billings, 406-254-2510; www.geyserpark.net

Fun for the whole family, Geyser Park offers plenty to do for a full day of activities. Start with some miniature golf and then head to the go-carts and bumper boats, grab a bite to eat and then play some games in the arcade. After that, spend some time at the playground, have some pizza from the full-service pizza place and then end your day with some laser tag. After a day here, the kids will sleep a good eight hours.
Admission: May-September, daily 11 a.m.-10 p.m.

PICTOGRAPH CAVE STATE PARK
2300 Lake Elmo Drive, Billings, 406-247-2940; www.pictographcave.org

This significant archaeological site consists of sandstone cliffs and three caves, two of which have evidence of prehistoric life from more than 4,500 years ago. The caves—pictograph, middle and ghost—are simply amazing to view. Walk through the largest of the three, pictograph, and view visible pictographs (rock paintings), which tell stories of what life was like then.
Admission: free. Mid-April-Memorial Day, daily 10 a.m-7 p.m., Memorial Day-Labor Day, daily 8 a.m.-8 p.m.; Labor Day-mid-October, daily 10 a.m.-7 p.m.

YELLOWSTONE ART MUSEUM
401 N. 27th St., Billings, 406-256-6804; www.yellowstone.artmuseum.org

The standout attraction in Billings, the one-time Yellowstone County Jail was renovated in the 1960s into this museum. After a significant expansion in the late 1990s, it emerged as the top art museum in Montana and is among the best in the Rocky Mountain region. The focus is on works by Montana artists with a strong emphasis on contemporary art. Temporary exhibitions tend toward the edgy and modern, but not exclusively: a recent exhibition showcased art depicting Montana as seen by Lewis and Clark.
Tuesday, Wednesday, Saturday 11 a.m.-6 p.m., Thursday-Friday 11 a.m.-8 p.m., Sunday 11 a.m.-4 p.m.

ZOOMONTANA
2100 S. Shiloh Road, Billings, 406-652-8100; www.zoomontana.org

This is the state's only zoo, which covers 70 acres of natural habitats, a botanical garden and a homestead petting zoo. Animals range from those native to the northern Rockies and the high plains as well as more exotic locations. Check out Siberian tigers, red pandas, grizzly bears, bald eagles, wolves and more.
Admission: adults $6.25, seniors $4.25, children 3-15 $3.25. May 1-September 24, May-late-September, daily 10 a.m.-5 p.m.; late-September-April, daily 10 a.m.-4 p.m.

WEST YELLOWSTONE
XANTERRA PARKS & RESORTS
West Yellowstone, 307-344-7311; www.xanterra.com

Xanterra offers guided snow coach tours and cross-country ski trips through Yellowstone National Park departing from West Yellowstone and other locations surrounding the park (Mid-December-early March). Summer season offers full-day bus tours, boat tours and horseback rides in the park (June-August). Reservations are recommended.

See website for schedule and pricing.

YELLOWSTONE IMAX THEATRE
101 S. Canyon St., West Yellowstone, 406-646-4100, 888-854-5862; www.yellowstoneimax.com

A six-story-high screen shows *Yellowstone*, a film interpreting the history, wildlife, geothermal activity and grandeur of America's first national park. Exhibits include wildlife photography, props used in the film and The Yellowstone Hot Spot display. Other films are shown, such as *Bears* and *Journey Into Amazing Caves,* among others.

Daily, shows hourly.

WHITEFISH
WHITEFISH MOUNTAIN RESORT
County 487, Flathead National Forest, Whitefish, 800-858-4152; www.skiwhitefish.com

Head to this 3,000-acre resort featuring Big Mountain and spend the day skiing. This ski resort has a double, four triple, two high-speed quad chairlifts, two T-bars, platter lift and ski patrol. The longest run is 3 1/2 miles, and the vertical drop is 2,500 feet. If skiing is not your thing, there are plenty of activities to keep you busy in both the winter and the summer including dog sled adventures, snowmobile tours, sleigh rides, mountain biking, hiking, scenic lift rides and an alpine slide.

WHERE TO STAY

RECOMMENDED
BIGFORK
MARINA CAY RESORT
180 Vista Lane, Bigfork, 406-837-5861, 800-433-6516; www.marinacay.com

This resort features five different buildings with a variety of accommodations from suites with kitchenettes to two- and three-bedroom condos, which feature full kitchens. Some buildings feature beautiful views of the Bigfork Bay. There are also recently renovated deluxe rooms that features updated amenities. Located on property are the Piano Lounge, where guests can enjoy live music and cocktails, and the Champs Sports Pub Grill, which serves lunch and dinner in a casual setting. The Tiki Bar at the pool is the perfect place to grab some lunch or cocktails before or after lounging by the pool.

180 rooms. Restaurant, bar. Pool. $251-350

AVERILL'S FLATHEAD LAKE LODGE
150 Flathead Lake Lodge Road, Bigfork, 406-837-4391; www.flatheadlakelodge.com

Resting on 2,000 acres on the eastern shores of Montana's largest freshwater

HIGHLIGHT

WHAT ARE THE TOP THINGS TO DO OUTDOORS IN GLACIER COUNTRY?

GO FISHING IN SWAN LAKE

Anglers plant themselves at this 20-mile-long lake to catch northern pike, Kokanee salmon and bull trout. It's also a popular spot for boaters.

EXPLORE LOLO NATIONAL FOREST

The 2 million acres that make up this forest are great for hiking and cross-country skiing, making it a year-round outdoors destination.

VISIT GLACIER NATIONAL PARK

It's easy to get around this park. You can hike along 730 miles of trails, hop on the shuttle bus or go on guided horseback trips. Don't leave without seeing the glaciers.

lake, this lodge is a paradise for outdoor enthusiasts. Anglers can fly fish, and the lake is perfect for sailing and canoeing, but the focus is on horseback riding at this authentic dude ranch. From riding instruction and horse competition to team roping and guest rodeos, this resort gives city slickers a taste of cowboy culture. Young riders learn about horse care and barn duties as part of the Junior Wranglers program. The log lodges capture the essence of the Old West with buffalo-hide couches and river-rock fireplaces, and the family-style meals feature roasted meats and other classic Western dishes.

38 rooms. Restaurant, bar. Pool. Tennis. Closed early September-early June. $351 and up

RED LODGE
ROCK CREEK RESORT

Highway 212, Red Lodge, 406-446-1111, 800-667-1119; www.rockcreekresort.com

You'll find this beautiful resort at the base of the Beartooth Mountains, which provides stunning landscapes and views. The resort provides various types of accommodations from lodges with regular rooms or apartments with kitchenettes or townhomes with kitchen and dining areas, three bedrooms, balconies and two and half baths. The Stoney Cabin is perfect if you're looking for privacy with a fireplace and Jacuzzi. Each building has its own theme with different décor from Native American and Southwestern to Western and Mexican themes. Enjoy a charming dinner at the Old Piney Dell restaurant and bar or a more relaxed lunch on the patio at Kiva restaurant. There's plenty to do onsite with the amenities that Rock Creek Resort provides from a pool and Jacuzzi to a soccer field, volleyball court, playground, catch and release fishing pond and tennis courts.

Restaurant, bar. Fitness center. Pool. Tennis. $151-250

WHITEFISH
GROUSE MOUNTAIN LODGE

2 Fairway Drive, Whitefish, 406-862-3000, 800-321-8822;
www.grousemountainlodge.com

With a convenient location, near Glacier National Park and Whitefish Mountain Resort, Grouse Mountain Lodge is a perfect spot for adventure-seekers. While guest rooms are more rustic than luxurious, they are clean and comfortable. And when you're not in your room there's plenty to do onsite: an indoor pool overlooks a golf course, a fitness center, outdoor Jacuzzis, and an outdoor fire pit where you can make s'mores. Enjoy a glass of wine or a cocktail at the Lounge at the Grill and then head to the Grill's dining room; with rustic touches like distressed pine flooring and a large rock fireplace, it's a cozy place to enjoy a delicious steak on a cold winter night. The large outdoor deck and patio are a perfect retreat in the spring and summer.

153 rooms. Restaurant, bar. Business Center. Fitness center. Pool. $151-250

KANDAHAR THE LODGE AT WHITEFISH MOUNTAIN RESORT

3824 Big Mountain Road, Whitefish, 406-862-6098,
800-862-6094; www.kandaharlodge.com

Located just an hour from Glacier National Park, Kandahar Lodge is at the Whitefish Mountain Resort. This resort is perfect for those planning on doing a lot of skiing, thanks to the ski-in access. The intimate resort offers rooms featuring down comfort-ers, sleeper sofas and pine and leather furniture. There are also studios with kitchens and living areas for those wanting something more for a longer stay. Families will love the loft rooms and kitchen lofts, which are spacious and feature pine ceilings, bathrooms with deep soaking tubs and granite coun-tertops. Enjoy dinner at Café Kandahar or a cocktail in the cozy Snug Bar.

50 rooms. Restaurant, bar. Complimentary breakfast. Fitness center. Closed mid-April-May and October-late November. $151-250

GOOD MEDICINE LODGE

537 Wisconsin Ave., Whitefish, 406-862-5488, 800-860-5488;
www.goodmedicinelodge.com

This small, cozy bed and breakfast has rooms

WHICH HOTEL HAS THE BEST VIEW IN GLACIER COUNTRY?

Rock Creek Resort sits at the base of the Beartooth Mountains and offers beautiful landscape views. Most of the rooms have balconies or patios that overlook the mountains.

decorated with rustic furnishings and Native American-influenced fabrics. Some rooms have balconies and all rooms feature custom-made beds and robes for each guest. Amenities include a Jacuzzi, a guest laundry room, a ski room equipped with dryers and a shared TV room/library where guests can relax with complimentary cookies, drinks and appetizers each evening. Guests are served a full breakfast each morning in the dining room.
9 rooms. Complimentary breakfast. $61-150

WHERE TO EAT

BIGFORK
★★★COYOTE ROADHOUSE
602 Three Eagle Lane, Bigfork, 406-837-4250, 406-837-1233; www.coyoteroadhouse.com

This restaurant, located just outside of Bigfork and inside the Coyote Roadhouse Inn, offers an elegant dining experience. The menu reflects chef-owner Gary Hastings' travels, with internationally influenced fare that features Southwestern, Tuscan, Cajun and Mexican flavors in dishes like jambalaya with scampi and petrale sole with red peppers, pea pods, yellow squash and a five-citrus sauce.
International. Dinner. Closed Monday-Tuesday; closed fall-winter. Outdoor seating. Children's menu. $61-150

★★★SHOWTHYME
548 Electric Ave., Bigfork, 406-837-0707; www.showthyme.com

Located in an old bank building, this restaurant has original brick walls and molded tin ceilings. The menu includes steak, fresh seafood and chicken, and the desserts are homemade. Start with the mushroom caps sautéed in white truffle oil and move along to the roasted rack of lamb with a sundried blueberry and rosemary sauce with potatoes. For dessert, try the huckleberry ice cream crêpe.
American. Dinner. Closed January. Reservations recommended. Outdoor seating. Children's menu. Bar. $36-85

RECOMMENDED

MISSOULA
POMP
The Resort at Paws Up, 40060 Paws Up Road, Greenough, 406-244-5200; www.pawsup.com

Located at the Resort at Paws Up, in Greenough, about 30 miles north of Missoula, this fine dining restaurant is named after Sacagawea's son, Jean Baptiste Charbonneau, or Pomp, the nickname given to him by William Clark. The menu from executive chef Wes Coffel features eclectic American cuisine focusing on seasonal ingredients so the menu is always changing. Choose either the chef's six-course tasting menu or the à la carte menu, which features dishes such as the grilled elk loin with pumpernickel-Gruyère spaetzle, kale and mustard demi-glace, pan-roasted chicken breast with Serrano ham mashed potatoes and braised Brussels sprouts and horseradish vinaigrette. The warm and sophisticated dining room reflects the charm of the surrounding area.

American. Dinner. Closed November-March (except certain holidays). $36-85

WHITEFISH

BUFFALO CAFE

514 Third St., Whitefish, 406-862-2833; www.buffalocafewhitefish.com

This family-run café is where the locals head for a hearty breakfast. From the pancakes and cinnamon French toast to the dozen-plus excellent egg dishes, the menu covers all the bases. Try the first-rate homemade biscuits and gravy for a bit of traditional comfort food.

American. Breakfast, lunch. $15 and under

CAFÉ KANDAHAR

3824 Big Mountain Road, Whitefish, 406-862-6247; www.cafekandahar.com

A 22-year-old fine dining tradition in Whitefish, this creative contemporary restaurant draws locals and return tourists alike. This is a place that's great for special occasions—or turning any night into one. A meal here could start with the Glacier salad, a marinated Flathead Valley pork tenderloin, Terrapin Farms arugula and field greens, local goat cheese and toasted pine nuts tossed with a huckleberry vinaigrette, before moving on to the grilled beef tournedos with an oyster-mushroom and smoked-shallot bordelaise alongside tasso-maytag-bleu grits and string beans. The sommelier's wine choices don't disappoint, either.

Contemporary American. Breakfast, dinner. Closed mid-April to mid-June, mid-September to Thanksgiving. $16-35

TUPELO GRILLE

17 Central Ave., Whitefish, 406-862-6136; www.tupelogrille.com

This warm and welcoming little eatery has garnered accolades from all over the country for its inventive take on Cajun cuisine. Visitors who can get a table might enjoy something like cumin grilled sea scallops on chorizo black lentils with ancho crème fraîche to start, followed by grilled shrimp served on a garlic-cheddar grit cake with a tasso cream sauce and, of course, complemented by a wine from Tupelo's commended and extensive wine list.

Cajun, Italian, seafood. Dinner. $16-35

GOLD WEST COUNTRY/RUSSELL COUNTRY

The state capital and Montana's fourth-largest city, Helena was the site of one of the state's largest gold rushes. In 1864, a party of discouraged prospectors decided to explore a gulch—now Helena's Main Street—as their "last chance" at striking it rich. This gulch and the area surrounding produced more than $20 million in gold.

A hundred cabins soon appeared. The mining camp, known as "Last Chance," was renamed Helena, after a town in Minnesota. Besides being the governmental center for Montana, today's Helena hosts agriculture and industry. To the north in Russell Country lies Great Falls, whose growth has been powered by thriving industry, agriculture and livestock, construction, and the nearby Malmstrom Air Force Base. It's also home to the Lewis and Clark National Forest, where you can enjoy the 1.8 million acres of canyons, mountains, meadows and wilderness.

WHAT TO SEE

ANACONDA

COPPER VILLAGE MUSEUM AND ARTS CENTER
401 E. Commercial St., Anaconda, 406-563-2422; www.coppervillageartcenter.com

Located in the Anaconda City Hall Cultural Center, this museum and arts center features local and traveling art exhibitions, theater, music, films and a museum of local pioneer and industrial history. The building is on the National Register of Historic Places.

Tuesday-Saturday 10 a.m.-4 p.m.

ANACONDA VISITOR CENTER
306 E. Park St., Anaconda, 406-563-5458; www.anacondamt.org

Housed in a replica of a turn-of-the-century railroad station, Anaconda's visitor center has a display of smelter works photographs, an outdoor railroad exhibit and a video presentation highlighting area attractions.

Mid-May-mid-September, Monday-Saturday 9 a.m.-5 p.m.; October-April, Monday-Friday 9 a.m.-5 p.m.

GREAT FALLS

C. M. RUSSELL MUSEUM COMPLEX AND ORIGINAL LOG CABIN STUDIO
400 13th St. N., Great Falls, 406-727-8787; www.cmrussell.org

Born in St. Louis, Charles Marion Russell (1864-1926) worked as a wrangler in Montana's Judith Basin before he found his true calling: painting the inhabitants and landscapes of the West. He was the first well-known western artist to live in the West, and his life's work includes more than 4,000 pieces. On the site of Russell's former home (and adjacent log studio), an impressive museum houses 2,000 of Russell's artworks, personal possessions and other relevant artifacts.

Admission: adults $9, seniors and military personnel $7, students $4, children 5 and under free. Memorial Day-Labor Day, Monday-Sunday 9 a.m.-6 p.m.; Labor Day-Memorial Day, Tuesday-Saturday 10 a.m.-5 p.m.

LEWIS AND CLARK NATIONAL FOREST
1101 15th St. N., Great Falls, 406-791-7700; www.fs.fed.us

More than 1.8 million acres of canyons, mountains, meadows and wilderness can be enjoyed here. Activities include scenic drives, stream and lake fishing, big-game hunting, hiking, camping, picnicking and winter sports.

LEWIS AND CLARK NATIONAL HISTORICAL TRAIL INTERPRETIVE CENTER
4201 Giant Springs Road, Great Falls, 406-727-8733; www.nps.gov

No facility better tells the story of Meriwether Lewis and William Clark's

HIGHLIGHT

WHAT ARE THE TOP THINGS TO DO IN GOLD WEST COUNTRY/RUSSELL COUNTRY?

VISIT THE C. M. RUSSELL MUSEUM COMPLEX AND ORIGINAL LOG CABIN STUDIO

This museum houses more than 2,000 of painter Russell's Western-themed works. Check out the studio where he crafted his noted artwork.

EXPLORE THE LEWIS AND CLARK NATIONAL HISTORICAL TRAIL INTERPRETIVE CENTER

Learn more about explorers Meriwether Lewis' and William Clark's famous journey at this informative center, which provides interactive displays and costumed actors.

GET A PINT AT BLACKFOOT RIVER BREWING COMPANY

To get a real taste of Montana, stop by this brewery. There, you can sample its handcrafted beers; four are always on tap and ready for your tasting pleasure.

legendary journey than this attractive structure perched on a bluff above the banks of the Missouri River. What is now Great Falls was in 1805 the site of the most arduous leg of the expedition, where the waterfalls (which have since been subdued by hydroelectric projects) forced the Corps of Discovery to portage their riverboats and other supplies across 18 miles of often-rugged terrain. A variety of interactive exhibits tell this story and others, tracing the fascinating history of Lewis and Clark, chronologically and from both the explorers' perspectives and that of the Native Americans they encountered. Throughout the day, interpreters lecture on topics ranging from the medical techniques used on the expedition to the ecology of the land in the early 19th century. There are also costumed actors demonstrating skills of the era and a theater with regular screenings of an excellent documentary.

Admission: adults $8, children 15 and under free. Memorial Day-Labor Day, daily 9 a.m.-6 p.m.; Labor Day-Memorial Day, Tuesday-Saturday 9 a.m.-5 p.m., Sunday noon-5 p.m.

HELENA

BLACKFOOT RIVER BREWING COMPANY

66 South Park Ave., Helena, 406-449-3005; www.blackfootriverbrewing.com

Blackfoot River Brewing Company has been providing Montana with delicious handcrafted beers since it was founded in 1998. Stop by the Tap Room to get a free taste some of its beers. Or purchase beers by the half-pint or pint to enjoy there or get a growler of your favorite to take home with you. Beers range from

malt IPA, to organic pale ales, wheat, amber ale, pilsner and more.
Daily 2-8 p.m.

EXPLORATION WORKS
995 Carousel Way, Helena, 406-457-1800; www.explorationworks.org

This interactive science museum allows children and adults alike through hands-on exhibits to learn and explore together. Exhibits have included a Knowledge Station from NASA and MIT featuring activities about space, Mars and one of Jupiter's moons. A "Conservation and Sustainable Choices" exhibit focuses on hands-on activities to teach people about conserving water and energy on a daily basis. This museum also features events and educational programs throughout the year.

Admission: adults $8, seniors and students $6.50, children under 18 $5.50, children under 2 free. Tuesday 10 a.m.-8 p.m., Wednesday-Saturday 10 a.m.-5 p.m. Free first Tuesday of every month.

GATES OF THE MOUNTAINS
Highway 15, Helena, 406-458-5241; www.gatesofthemountains.com

This 12-mile, two-hour Missouri River cruise explores the deep gorge in Helena National Forest, discovered and named by Lewis and Clark.

Memorial Day weekend-mid-September, daily.

MONTANA HISTORICAL SOCIETY MUSEUM
225 N. Roberts St., Helena, 406-444-2694; www.montanahistoricalsociety.org

Adjacent to the Montana State Capitol, this museum's exhibits cover the last 12,000 years of the area's history. On display are artifacts relating to everything from agriculture to transportation, as well as a collection of art by Montana's own Charles Russell and a special display about Big Medicine, a rare albino buffalo who lived in the National Bison Range in northwest Montana. His mounted hide is the centerpiece of the exhibit.

Memorial Day-Labor Day, daily; rest of year, Monday-Saturday 9 a.m.-5 p.m., Thursday until 8 p.m.

SPOKANE BAR SAPPHIRE MINE AND GOLD FEVER ROCK SHOP
5360 Castles Road, Helena, 406-227-8989; www.sapphiremine.com

For anyone interested in gold mines, or hunting for gemstones, this is a must-do activity while in Helena. Located on the banks of Hauser Lake along the Missouri River, visitors can dig for sapphires at this gravel bar on a historic site. Even if you can't make it to Montana, you can still purchase a bucket of sapphire gravel to dig through at home. Considering you will find sapphires of all different sizes and carats, the cheapest dig option here costs $60.

Daily 9 a.m.-5 p.m.

WHERE TO STAY

ANACONDA
★★★FAIRMONT HOT SPRINGS RESORT
1500 Fairmont Road, Anaconda, 406-797-3241, 800-332-3272; www.fairmontmontana.com

Standard guest rooms here are comfortable, although a bit outdated. The suites take it up a notch with more modern amenities, like flat-screen TVs and more contemporary furniture. But the amenities onsite make up for it. The four hot springs-fed swimming and soaking pools are the pride of this resort. Filled with 155-degree naturally hot spring water and cooled to varying comfortable temperatures, the pools (open 24 hours to guests) also include a 350-foot enclosed water slide. Conference and convention facilities accommodate groups of up to 500—making this a popular place for events.

153 rooms. Restaurant, bar. Fitness center. Pool. Golf. Tennis. $151-250

★★★TRIPLE CREEK RANCH

5551 W. Fork Road, Darby, 406-821-4600, 800-654-2943; www.triplecreekranch.com

With the mountains of Montana as a backdrop, this ranch allows guests to experience the wilderness in its natural setting. Log cabins, trout-filled lakes, horseback riding and hiking trails provide diversions, as does the fresh mountain air and relaxing atmosphere. These aren't your typical cabins; they are luxurious, offering amenities such as wood-burning fireplaces, wet bars stocked with snacks and spirits, wireless Internet, satellite TV, DVD and CD players, nightly turndown and most have private hot tubs, among other things. There are 12 different options to choose from, such as the Paradise cabin, which features vaulted ceilings, a large living room with a fireplace, bathrooms with double steam showers and a private hot tub overlooking the forest. Triple Creek Restaurant offers fresh cuisine with global influences in a warm, romantic dining room.

19 rooms. Restaurant, bar. Complimentary breakfast. Fitness center. Pool. No children under 16. Tennis. Pets accepted. $351 and up

WHERE TO EAT

RECOMMENDED
DARBY

TRIPLE CREEK RESTAURANT

Triple Creek Ranch, 5551 W. Fork Road, Darby, 406-821-4600, 800-654-2943; www.triplecreekranch.com

Located within the Triple Creek Ranch, this restaurant is a cozy, romantic place to enjoy dinner amid the mountains and forest. The dining room features a large fireplace exuding warmth as well as candles

---

WHICH HOTEL HAS THE MOST UNUSUAL AMENITY?

Tons of hotels offer swimming pools, but the **Fairmont Hot Springs Resort** one-ups the rest by having four hot springs-fed pools. The natural hot springs are a piping-hot 155 degrees, but the water's cooled down so you can soak comfortably.

on white table-clothed tables, high-vaulted ceilings and floor-to-ceiling windows to look out at the beautiful natural surroundings. The international menu features dishes made with meat and seafood flown in from all over the world along with local ingredients from local farms. The four-course prix fixe menu includes wine and features items such as citrus-marinated mahi mahi ceviche, beef short rib salad, orange-braised fowl and organic chicken with summer squash and yellow rice, and for dessert, honey mousse covered with a caramel and almond topping. The wine cellar offers more than 400 wines so you're pretty much guaranteed a great glass of wine with your meal. If you're looking for a more private affair, choose to dine at the chef's table located within the beautiful kitchen.

International. Breakfast, lunch, dinner. $36-85

HELENA
LUCCA'S
56 N. Last Chance Gulch, Helena, 406-457-8311; www.luccasitalian.com

Lucca's emanates a romantic vibe, thanks to the dim lighting and dark-wood-filled dining room. Among the pastas, try the pappardelle, which comes with a variety of mushrooms sautéed with garlic and shallots and a topping of black-truffle-laced pecorino cheese. Or opt for a meaty dish, like the veal scallopini with lemon and Marsala wine sauce.

Italian. Dinner. $36-85

SILVER STAR STEAK COMPANY
833 Great Northern Blvd., Helena, 406-495-0677; www.silverstarsteakco.com

The dish that gets a silver star on the menu is the prime rib, an Angus roast that's served au jus with housemade horseradish. Other meaty main courses include the burgundy-glazed bison rib-eye and the Hawaiian-style pork tenderloin doused with a pineapple-coconut-rum sauce. Pair your steak with one of the selection from the 500-plus wine list, the largest in town.

Steak. Lunch (Monday-Saturday), dinner. Outdoor seating. $36-85

WELCOME TO NEBRASKA

IN LITTLE MORE THAN A CENTURY, NEBRASKA—PART

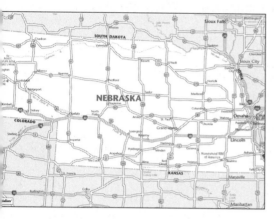

of what was once called the "great American desert"— has evolved from a vast prairie occupied by Native Americans and buffalo to a farming, ranching and manufacturing mainstay of America, with an enticing array of recreational and cultural attractions.

Today, Nebraska is a "breadbasket" state, with an economy rooted in agriculture. But for the visitor, there is much more than corn, wheat and cows. As with Kansas to the south and South Dakota to the north, to traverse Nebraska from east to west is to trace a transition of terrain, climate and culture—from the tidy farms, sticky summers and small towns, along with the occasional big city, to a more unbridled landscape. Cattle graze on vast tracts of rangeland patrolled by actual cowboys, counties are bigger than some Northeastern states, the air dries out and the wind is almost always blowing as the land gradually slopes upward and becomes the high country stretching to the Rocky Mountains and the West.

At the eastern edge, by the Missouri River, is Omaha, the state's largest city. As one might expect in cattle country, it's a place to find a good steak, but if you're hunting for more adventurous cuisine, you'll find it. Home to a number of Fortune 500 companies as well as a major branch of the state university and the highly regarded Creighton University, Omaha offers its share of big-city sophistication.

Heading west on the interstate, you'll come to Lincoln, the state capital and site of the University of Nebraska main campus and the fabled Cornhuskers football team. A rabid army of red-clad fans chews over the fortunes of the squad year-round.

Farther out, if you are traveling by Kearney on Interstate 80, one attraction you literally can't miss is the Great Platte River Road Archway, a structure that spans 300 feet over the highway and houses a multimedia exhibit that salutes Nebraska's pioneer spirit along with the state's progression into modern times. In the movie *As Good as It Gets*, Jack Nicholson's character pays a visit here.

BEST ATTRACTIONS

NEBRASKA'S BEST ATTRACTIONS

LINCOLN
It may be the state's second-largest city, but Lincoln has a number of attractions that make it stand out, including the kid favorite Folsom Children's Zoo and the unusual National Museum of Roller Skating.

OMAHA
In Nebraska's biggest city, tourists and locals shop in the Old Market district's art galleries, antique stores and boutiques; visit the Joslyn Art Museum, the state's best; and eat those famous Omaha steaks.

METROPOLITAN AREA

The largest city in Nebraska, Omaha is named for the Native Americans who lived here until they signed a treaty with the federal government on June 24, 1854. Opportunists across the Missouri River in Council Bluffs, Iowa, who had been waiting for the new territory to open, rushed to stake out property, triggering a real estate boom.

Today, Omaha continues to be a major transportation and agribusiness center but is also a recognized leader in telecommunications, insurance and manufacturing as well as the home of five Fortune 500 companies. Omaha is also the headquarters of STRATCOM, the Strategic Air Command, one of the vital links in the national defense chain.

The second-largest city in Nebraska, Lincoln feuded with Omaha, the territorial seat of government, for the honor of being capital of the new state. When the argument was settled in Lincoln's favor in 1867, books, documents and office furniture were moved in covered wagons late one night to escape the armed band of Omaha boosters. As a young lawyer in the 1890s, William Jennings Bryan went to Congress from Lincoln; in 1896, 1900 and 1908, he ran unsuccessfully for president.

The unicameral (one-house legislature) form of government in Nebraska, which was set up by an amendment to the state constitution in 1934 (mostly by the efforts of Nebraska's famous senator, George W. Norris), is of great interest to students of political science. Supporters say it works efficiently and avoids delays and deadlocks common to two-house legislatures.

WHAT TO SEE

LINCOLN

EXECUTIVE MANSION

1135 M St., Lincoln, 402-434-5335; www.lincoln.org

The state governor's mansion, built in 1957, features Georgian Colonial architecture. Take a tour to see a doll collection of the state's first ladies as well as other items from over the years.

Tours: Thursday 1-4 p.m.

FOLSOM CHILDREN'S ZOO

1222 S. 27th St., Lincoln, 402-475-6741; www.lincolnzoo.org

This zoo features exotic animals, contact areas, botanical gardens and more. Animals here include the red panda, crocodiles, otters, monkeys, bobcats, Shetland ponies, kangaroos and many others. The children's zoo offers a petting farm, a butterfly pavilion where butterflies fly all around you, an area where children can interact with small animals and more. Kids will love the train and pony rides offered here. To learn more about the animal residents, attend one of the hands-on Keeper Talks, where the zookeeper gives a lecture and demonstration.

Admission: adults $6.50, seniors $5.50, children 2-13 $5.50, children under 2 free. Mid-April-mid-October, daily 10 a.m.-5 p.m.; June-August, Wednesday until 8 p.m. Keeper Talks: daily 11 a.m., 1:30 p.m., 3 p.m.

GREAT PLAINS ART MUSEUM

1155 Q St., Lincoln, 402-472-6220; www.unl.edu

Works by Frederic Remington, Charles M. Russell, Norman Rockwell, Jackson Pollock, and other artists are among the nearly 700 pieces in this collection. The library also houses more than 4,000 books related to the Great Plains and Western Americana.

Tuesday-Saturday 10 a.m.-5 p.m., Sunday 1:30-5 p.m.

LINCOLN CHILDREN'S MUSEUM

1420 P St., Lincoln, 402-477-4000; www.lincolnchildrensmuseum.org

A variety of cultural and scientific exhibits invite children to explore and involve their senses at this museum, which covers three floors.

Admission: adults and children 2-18 $6.50, seniors $6, children 1 and under free. Monday-Wednesday, Friday-Saturday 9:30 a.m.-5 p.m., Thursday 9:30 a.m.-7:30 p.m., Sunday 1-5 p.m.

LINCOLN MONUMENT

201 N. Seventh St., Lincoln, 402-434-5348

This standing figure of Abraham Lincoln was designed by sculptor Daniel Chester French, who also produced the seated statue for Henry Bacon's Lincoln Memorial in Washington, D.C.

NEBRASKA HISTORY MUSEUM

15th and P streets, Lincoln, 402-471-4754; www.nebraskahistory.org

The history of Nebraska is summarized in exhibits covering events from prehistoric times through the 1950s. Exhibits included are "The First Nebraskans,"

HIGHLIGHT

WHAT ARE THE TOP THINGS TO DO OUTDOORS?

HANG WITH THE ANIMALS AT THE FOLSOM CHILDREN'S ZOO
You'll see red pandas, crocodiles, Shetland ponies and more at this zoo. The petting zoo, butterfly pavilion and train and pony rides will tire your tykes out.

TAKE IN WORKS AT THE JOSLYN ART MUSEUM
This pink marble Art Deco museum is the state's best spot for visual arts. Check out the works of Karl Bodmer, a German watercolorist who was inspired by Missouri's landscape and people.

ROLL OUT AND HEAD TO THE NATIONAL MUSEUM OF ROLLER SKATING
The only place of its kind in the country, this museum documents the rise of roller skating from 1700 to today. It's a must-visit for fans of roller derbies and the sport.

SHOP TILL YOU DROP AT OLD MARKET
The Old Market district's brick-paved streets are lined with art galleries, antique shops, boutiques and restaurants. In the center, there's a Saturday farmer's market.

which takes a look at Native American life in Nebraska and in the Plains.
Admission: $2. Monday-Friday 9 a.m.-4:30 p.m., Saturday-Sunday 1-4:30 p.m.

NATIONAL MUSEUM OF ROLLER SKATING
4730 South St., Lincoln, 402-483-7551; www.rollerskatingmuseum.com
This unique museum—the only museum in the world devoted solely to roller skating— features skates, costumes and photographs documenting the sport of roller skating and the industry from 1700 to the present. There are also archives dealing with world and national competitions since 1910.
Admission: free. Monday-Friday 9 a.m.-5 p.m.

PIONEERS PARK
2740 A St., Lincoln, 402-441-7895; www.lincoln.ne.gov
If you're looking for a little outdoor fun, this park features hiking, bike trails, bridle path, volleyball courts, a golf course, picnicking areas, playgrounds and an outdoor amphitheater. There is also a nature preserve here that covers 668

acres of woods, prairie and wetlands where visitors can hike through exhibits with bison, elk and white-tailed deer.
Daily, dawn-dusk.

STATE CAPITOL

1445 K St., Lincoln, 402-471-0448; www.capitol.org

Designed by Bertram Goodhue, the most dominant feature of this building is the central tower, which rises 400 feet. Ground was broken in 1922 for this third capitol building in Lincoln and was completed 10 years later. Sculpture by Lee Lawrie includes reliefs and friezes depicting the history of law and justice, great philosophers, symbols of the state and a bronze statue of the Sower (32 feet) atop the tower dome. The great hall, rotunda and legislative chambers are decorated in tile and marble murals, tapestries and wood-inlaid panels.
Monday-Friday 8 a.m.-5 p.m., Saturday 10 a.m.-5 p.m., Sunday 1-5 p.m.

STATEHOOD MEMORIAL—THOMAS P. KENNARD HOUSE

1627 H St., Lincoln, 402-471-4764; www.nebraskahistory.org

This 1869 house is the restored residence of Nebraska's first secretary of state and it is the oldest structure still standing in Lincoln.
Admission: $3, children free. Monday-Friday, by appointment.

STRATEGIC AIR & SPACE MUSEUM

28210 W. Park Highway, Ashland, 402-944-3100; www.strategicairandspace.com

This museum features a permanent collection of 33 aircraft and six missiles relating to the history of Strategic Air Command and its importance in the preservation of world peace. There's also an interactive children's gallery, a theater and a museum store.
Admission: adults $10, seniors and military personnel $9, children 4-12 $5. Memorial Day-Labor Day, daily 10 a.m.-5 p.m.; Labor Day-Memorial Day, Thursday-Tuesday 10 a.m.-5 p.m.

UNIVERSITY OF NEBRASKA STATE MUSEUM

307 Morrill Hall, 402-472-2642; www.museum.unl.edu

This museum features displays of fossils (dinosaurs and mounted elephants), rocks and minerals, and Nebraska plants and animals. There are also Native American exhibits as well as changing exhibits.
Admission: adults $5 children 5-18 $3, children 4 and under free; with planetarium: adults $8, children 5-18 $5.50, children 4 and under $2.50. Monday-Saturday 9:30 a.m.-4:30 p.m., Thursday until 8 p.m., Sunday 1:30-4:30 p.m.

OMAHA

AK-SAR-BEN AQUARIUM

21502 W. Highway 31, Gretna, 402-332-3901

This modern facility features more than 50 species of fish native to Nebraska, as well as a terrarium, the World Herald Auditorium, a natural history classroom and orientation and display areas.
Admission: adults $1, children $.50. December-March, Wednesday-Sunday 10 a.m.-4:30 p.m.; April-late May, Wednesday-Monday 10 a.m.-4:30 p.m.; Memorial Day-Labor Day, Monday-Friday 10 a.m.-4:30 p.m., Saturday-Sunday 10 a.m.-5 p.m.; Labor Day-November, Wednesday-Monday 10 a.m.-4:30 p.m.

DURHAM WESTERN HERITAGE MUSEUM

Omaha Union Station, 801 S. 10th St., Omaha, 402-444-5071; www.durhammuseum.org

This restored Art Deco railroad depot is now a history museum, featuring exhibits on Omaha history from 1880 to 1954; a Byron Reed coin collection; and traveling temporary exhibits.

Admission: adults $7, seniors $6, children 3-12 $5, children 2 and under free. June-mid-August, Monday, Wednesday-Saturday 10 a.m.-5 p.m., Tuesday 10 a.m.-8 p.m., Sunday 1-5 p.m.; late August-May, Tuesday 10 a.m.-8 p.m., Wednesday-Saturday 10 a.m.-5 p.m., Sunday 1-5 p.m.

GERALD R. FORD BIRTH SITE AND GARDENS

32nd and Woolworth avenues, Omaha, 402-444-5955; www.nebraskahistory.org

This house is a model of the original house where Gerald Ford was born (the original home was ruined by a fire in 1971). The Betty Ford Memorial Rose Garden is also here.

Daily dawn-dusk.

GREAT PLAINS BLACK HISTORY MUSEUM

2213 Lake St., Omaha, 402-345-2212

Housed in a building designed in 1907 by prominent Nebraska architect Thomas R. Kimball, the museum preserves the history of African-Americans and their part in the heritage of Omaha and Nebraska since the territorial period of the 1850s. Includes rare photographs, relics, historical displays and films.

Admission: free. Tuesday-Friday 10 a.m.-2 p.m.

HEARTLAND OF AMERICA PARK

Eighth and Douglas streets, Omaha, 402-444-5920; www.cityofomaha.org

This 31-acre site features picnic facilities, arbors and waterfalls. The park's 15-acre lake has a computer-driven fountain that has a colored light show at night.

Daily dawn-dusk. Fountain: Mid-April-November, Monday-Friday 11 a.m.-1 p.m. and 7 p.m.-midnight, Saturday-Sunday 10 a.m.-midnight.

HENRY DOORLY ZOO

3701 S. 10th St., Omaha, 402-733-8401; www.omahazoo.org

More than 18,500 animals, many rare, are on display in a 110-acre park. Exhibits include an aquarium, an indoor rainforest, an indoor desert and a walk-through aviary. There is also an IMAX Theater, a Skyfari where you can ride in ski-lift like chairs over the zoo, a mini-train, a carousel and more.

Admission: adults $11.50, seniors $10, children 3-11 $7.75, children 2 and under free. Memorial Day-Labor Day, daily 8:30 a.m.-5 p.m.; Labor Day-Memorial Day, daily 9:30 a.m.-5 p.m.

JOSLYN ART MUSEUM

2200 Dodge St., Omaha, 402-342-3300; www.joslyn.org

This museum's Art Deco building houses collections of art, ancient to modern, including European and American paintings and sculpture; art of the Western frontier; Native American art; and traveling exhibitions.

Admission: adult $8, seniors $6, children 5-17 $5, children 4 and under free. Free Saturday 10 a.m.-noon. Tuesday-Saturday 10 a.m.-4 p.m., Sunday noon-4 p.m.

HIGHLIGHT

OMAHA'S OLD MARKET

One of the few downtown areas that preserves Omaha's original Victorian-era architecture, the Old Market Area is a five-square-block shopping, dining and gallery district that's the heart and soul of the city center. Window-shop, stop for coffee, pop into art-filled boutiques—this neighborhood is made for strolling. Bounded by Farnam and Jones streets and 10th and 13th streets, the Old Market Area was originally the food-processing center for the region: Swanson Food, Anheuser-Busch and other stalwarts of the food and beverage industry once occupied these buildings. Food is still one of the finest reasons to visit the Old Market Area. Find provisions for a picnic at La Buvette Wine and Grocery (511 S. 11th St.), where you can pick up cheese and wine. On Saturdays in summer and fall, stop for fresh local produce at the farmer's market, held on 11th Street between Jackson and Howard. Directly south of the Old Market Area is the Durham Western Heritage Museum (801 S. 10th St.), housed in the architecturally stunning Union Station, an Art Deco gem from Omaha's past. The museum has vintage cars and railroad equipment, and a period soda fountain is still in operation. Walk north on 10th Street five blocks to reach Gene Leahy Mall, a 10-acre park with a lake that serves as a reflecting pond for the modern high-rise architecture of Omaha. Trails wind through the park, linking formal flower gardens, a playground for children, a bandstand and public art displays. To the east, the Leahy Mall connects to Heartland of America Park and Fountain, which is bounded by Eighth Street and the Missouri River. The highlight of the park is its lake, with a fountain that shoots streams of water 300 feet into the air. The General Marion tour boat navigates the lake to take visitors closer to the fountain. At night, the water display is accompanied by pulsing lights. Return to the Leahy Mall along Douglas Street, which leads into the modern city center. At 24th Street, turn north one block to the Joslyn Art Museum (2200 Dodge St.), Nebraska's premier center for the visual arts. The museum building is itself a work of art, a fanciful Art Deco structure faced with shimmering pink marble. The permanent collection consists of American and European art from the 19th and 20th centuries. A highlight is the cache of works from Karl Bodmer, a German watercolorist who traveled up the Missouri River in the 1830s, capturing the pristine landscapes, Native Americans and wildlife before white pioneer settlement.

OLD MARKET

11th and Howard streets, extending to 10th St. and west to 13th, Omaha, 402-341-1877; www.oldmarket.com

Art galleries, antique shops, boutiques, bars and restaurants fill this area revitalizing an old warehouse district. Some of Omaha's oldest commercial buildings line the market's brick-paved streets. There is also a farmer's market in the center of the Old Market every Saturday from May through October.

Hours vary. Farmer's Market: May-early October, Saturday 8 a.m.-12:30 p.m.

OMAHA CHILDREN'S MUSEUM

500 S. 20th St., Omaha, 402-342-6163; www.ocm.org

Head to this children's museum, where you'll find self-directed exploration and play for children and families. There is a constantly changing series of hands-on exhibits in science, the arts and humanities, health and creative play.

Admission: adults and children 2-15 $8, seniors $7, children 2 and under free. Memorial Day-Labor Day, Tuesday-Saturday 10 a.m.-5 p.m., Thursday 10 a.m.-8 p.m., Sunday 1-5 p.m.; Labor Day-Memorial Day, Tuesday-Friday 10 a.m.-4 p.m., Saturday 10 a.m.-5 p.m., Sunday 1-5 p.m.

WHERE TO STAY

OMAHA

★★★OMAHA MARRIOTT

10220 Regency Circle, Omaha, 402-399-9000; www.marriott.com

This hotel offers two restaurants, a lounge, an indoor and outdoor pool, a health club, and many more amenities. It is located near the Joslyn Art Museum, Old Market, golf courses and tennis facilities. In 2009, guest rooms were renovated and now feature the comfortable Marriott Revive bedding with 300-thread-count sheets, floor-to-ceiling windows or sliding glass doors, flat-screen TVs, and more modern décor. Enjoy a meal at the onsite Omaha Chophouse.

300 rooms. Restaurant, bar. Fitness center. Pool. $61-150

RECOMMENDED

LINCOLN

THE CORNHUSKER, A MARRIOTT HOTEL

333 S. 13th St., Lincoln, 402-474-7474, 800-793-7474; www.thecornhusker.com

Continental style meets Midwestern friendliness at Lincoln's Cornhusker Hotel. A Nebraska landmark since 1926, today's Cornhusker has sophisticated décor, fine dining, exceptional amenities and dedicated service. Guest rooms feature plush bedding, complimentary Internet access and granite countertops and flooring in the bathrooms. The 10th-floor Executive Level offers an upgraded experience. Hand-painted murals and fiber-optic starlight help make the Terrace Grille a pleasant setting for continental cuisine.

297 rooms. Restaurant, bar. Business center. Fitness center. Pool. $61-150

OMAHA

OMAHA MAGNOLIA HOTEL

1615 Howard St., Omaha, 402-341-2500, 888-915-1110; www.magnoliahotelomaha.com

When you enter Omaha's first boutique hotel—which is listed on the National Register of Historic Places—you're greeted with elegant Italianate décor, including travertine walls and Roman columns. But the lobby gets an update with elliptical-shaped chandeliers, leather ottomans and a mahogany check-in desk. The chic rooms are decked out with chocolate-colored leather headboards; a brown, tan and cerulean color scheme; and framed pictures of magnolias hanging on the walls. There's a complimentary breakfast buffet and nightly wine and beer reception, but don't miss the free bedtime cookies and milk buffet.

145 rooms. Restaurant, bar. Complimentary breakfast. Business center. Fitness center. $61-150

HILTON OMAHA
1001 Cass St., Omaha, 402-998-3400; www.hilton.com

The Hilton has a sweet location; a sky bridge connects the hotel to the Qwest Center, and it's only blocks from the hopping Old Market area. The stylish lobby, with brick, warm reds and a waterfall, is a nice place to hang out. The rooms have a more classic feel, with a muted palette of tan, brown and cream; two-poster beds; and 32-inch televisions. If you need to unwind, head to the onsite spa and choose one of the locally inspired treatments, like the Nebraska Rub and Scrub or the Heartland Hydration.

450 rooms. Restaurant, bar. Business center. Fitness center. Spa. Pool. $151-250

WHICH IS THE MOST HISTORIC HOTEL?

Although the **Omaha Magnolia Hotel** is one of the newer properties in town, its building was built in the 1920s. Listed on the National Register of Historic Places, the hotel was modeled after a palace in Florence, and you'll still see those Italian influences today.

WHERE TO EAT

OMAHA

★★★FRENCH CAFÉ
1017 Howard St., Omaha, 402-341-3547; www.frenchcafe.com

Elegant French dishes, continually refreshed with contemporary ingredients, have earned this restaurant a good reputation. Pepper steak is a signature dish, and the roasted rack of pork is popular. The wine cellar is substantial, and the dining room is quite cozy and charming.

American, French. Dinner, Sunday brunch. Bar. $36-85

★★★GORAT'S STEAK HOUSE
4917 Center St., Omaha, 402-551-3733; www.goratsomaha.com

An Omaha landmark for more than 60 years, this steak house specializes in classics with thick cuts of filet mignon and more. Enhance the old-school experience with a traditional side dish such as escargot doused in butter or chilled shrimp cocktail.

Steak. Lunch, dinner. Closed Sunday. Reservations recommended. Children's menu. Bar. $36-85

★★★SIGNATURES
Doubletree Hotel & Executive Meeting Center Omaha-Downtown, 1616 Dodge St., Omaha, 402-346-7600; www.doubletree.com

Located at the top of the Doubletree Hotel, this restaurant offers a panoramic view of the city's skyline. A continental concept, the menu draws on influences from all over the world, but seafood is the specialty.

Seafood. Breakfast, lunch, dinner, late-night. Bar. $16-35

WHICH
RESTAURANTS
HAVE THE BEST
STEAKS?

French Café:
This restaurant is known
for its elegant French
cuisine. But it also serves
up a mean pepper steak,
which also happens to be
the café's signature dish.

Gorat's Steak House:
The steak house special-
izes in thick, juicy cuts
of filet mignon, bone-in
strip sirloin, prime rib
and more.

★★★V. MERTZ

1022 Howard St., Omaha, 402-345-8980; www.vmertz.com

Located just off the brick-walled Old Market Passageway, this cozy, upscale restaurant offers a quiet atmosphere. The menu, consisting of continental dishes, changes weekly. Entrées include Oregon natural lamb chops with apricots, dates, cauliflower and gnocchi, and a sweet corn tart with vegetables. There are also three-course prix fixe menus and five- and eight-course tasting menus different days of the week. An extensive global wine list accompanies the menu. Men should don a jacket and tie at this restaurant.

American. Lunch, dinner. Closed Sunday-Monday. Bar. $16-35

RECOMMENDED

LINCOLN

BILLY'S RESTAURANT

1301 H St., Lincoln, 402-474-0084; www.billysrestaurant.com

Located near the State Capitol in a historic home from 1887, Billy's offers a fine dining experience in a beautiful and historic setting. The restaurant is named after William Jennings Bryan, the politician and secretary of state, and with its proximity to the Capitol, don't be surprised to see politicos here. Dinner entrées include pork chops, pomegranate duck, filet mignon and sea scallops. Lunch is a little less formal, with salads and sandwiches on the menu. It's also a popular spot for special events.

American. Lunch, dinner. Closed Sunday. Outdoor seating. $36-85

LAZLO'S BREWERY & GRILL

210 N. 7th St., Lincoln, 402-434-5636;
www.lazlosbreweryandgrill.com

Lazlo's Brewery & Grill is in the historic Haymarket neighborhood, and it was the first brewpub to appear in Lincoln in 1991. Kick back and enjoy homemade meals and handcrafted beers with family and friends. Food is cooked on a hickory wood grill and made with fresh produce and meats. The menu features burgers (made fresh daily), sandwiches, steaks, seafood and more. Enjoy specials on food and drinks at the Monday-to-Friday (3-6 p.m.) happy hour. There's a second location in South Lincoln, a third in Omaha and FireWorks, a sister restaurant also in Lincoln.

American. Lunch, dinner. Outdoor seating. $16-35

WELCOME TO NORTH DAKOTA

IN BISMARCK THERE IS A STATUARY GROUP, PIONEER

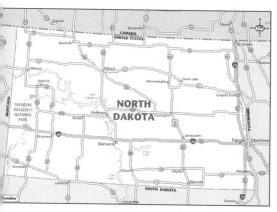

family, and behind it gleamingwhite against the sky, towers the famous skyscraper capitol. One symbolizes the North Dakota of wagon trains and Gen. Custer. The other symbolizes modern North Dakota: a place where a thousand oil wells have sprouted, dams harness erratic rivers and vast natural resources have been found.

This is a fascinating land of prairies, rich river valleys, small cities, huge ranches and vast stretches of wheat. Bordering Canada for 320 miles to the north, North Dakota shares straight-line borders with Montana to the west and South Dakota to the south. The Red River of the North forms its eastern boundary with Minnesota. The Garrison Dam has changed much of the internal geography of the state's western region, converting the Missouri River, known as "Big Muddy," into a broad waterway with splendid recreation areas bordering the reservoir Lake Sakakawea. To the southwest stretch the Badlands in all their natural grandeur, and the open range about which Theodore Roosevelt wrote so eloquently in his Ranch Life and the Hunting Trail.

At various times, Spain, France and England claimed what is now North Dakota as part of their empires. French Canadian fur trappers were the first Europeans to explore the land. After the Louisiana Purchase, explorers Lewis and Clark crossed Dakota, establishing Fort Mandan. The Dakota Territory was organized on March 2, 1861, but major settlement of what later became North Dakota followed after the entry of the Northern Pacific Railroad in the early 1870s.

This is the state in which to trace 19th-century frontier history, to stand at the center of the continent, to see Native American dances and outdoor dramas or to watch the 10 million migratory waterfowl that soar across the sky each spring and fall.

BEST ATTRACTIONS

NORTH DAKOTA'S BEST ATTRACTIONS

FARGO
The town's biggest claim to fame may be the Coen brothers' film *Fargo*, but you may want to stop here solely to check out the hip Plains Art Museum's Beatles exhibit, contemporary Native American art and Pop artist James Rosenquist's work.

LITTLE MISSOURI BADLANDS
The extraordinary Badlands is home to various prairie wildlife, including pronghorn antelope, coyotes, white-tailed deer, prairie dogs and rattlesnakes.

THEODORE ROOSEVELT NATIONAL PARK
The lovely park landscape looks just as it did when Theodore Roosevelt visited it, with unusual sculptured formations, buttes, canyons and rugged hills.

WESTERN NORTH DAKOTA

Located on the east bank of the Missouri, near the geographic center of the state and within 150 miles of the geographic center of the continent, North Dakota's capitol, Bismarck, flourished as a steamboat port called the Crossing. As the terminus of the Northern Pacific Railway, Bismarck gained new importance and was named for the Chancellor of Germany to attract German capital for building transcontinental railroads. Gen. Custer came to Bismarck to take command of the nearby newly constructed Fort Abraham Lincoln and in 1876 rode out to his fatal rendezvous with Sitting Bull. In 1883, Bismarck became the capital of the Dakota Territory, and in 1889, the seat of the new state. The Mandan tribe originally farmed this area, and today the agricultural tradition persists in the dairy and dry farms that surround the city.

WHAT TO SEE

BISMARCK
CHATEAU DE MORES STATE HISTORIC SITE
612 E. Boulevard Ave., Bismarck, 701-623-4355
This site commemorates the life of Antoine de Vallombrosa, the Marquis de Mores. The Marquis dabbled with a stagecoach line, an experiment with refrigerated railroad cars, and a beef-packing plant. Remaining are the ruins of a packing

HIGHLIGHT

WHAT IS THERE TO DO IN FARGO?

Fargo, the largest city in North Dakota, has taken the lead in promoting its gaming tables. There are approximately 30 casinos in the city, making it a major tourist attraction in the three-state region, including Minnesota and South Dakota. Charities and nonprofit organizations run the casinos and collect all profits above expenses. The 1996 dark comedy Fargo took its name from the city, gently poking fun at the residents' thick northern accents, dontcha know, and Scandinavian heritage, but most of the movie actually takes place in Minnesota. While here, be sure to visit the Plains Art Museum (*704 First Ave. N., Fargo, 701-232-3821; www.plainsart.org*).

This hip museum located within an old warehouse building features a variety of different exhibits, including The White Album: The Beatles Meet the Plains, which takes a look at the popular Beatles album and the artwork it inspired from a variety of artists. The museum also features a permanent collection of 3,000 pieces, special events, a gift shop, and children's activities. In addition, it hosts the Plain Food Farmer's Market on Thursdays in the summer and fall where visitors can find local produce, flowers and more. (*Admission: adults $5, seniors $4, students and children free. Tuesday-Wednesday, Friday 11 a.m.-5 p.m., Thursday 11 a.m.-8 p.m., Saturday 10 a.m.-5 p.m., Sunday 1-5 p.m.*)

plant; a 26-room, two-story frame mansion filled with French furnishings; a library; servants' quarters; and a relic room displaying the Marquis's saddles, guns, boots, coats and other possessions. An interpretive center is on the grounds. *Guided tours: mid-May-mid-September, daily; mid-September-mid-May, by appointment.*

NORTH DAKOTA STATE CAPITOL

600 E. Boulevard Ave., Bismarck, 701-328-2480; www.nd.gov

Constructed in 1933 on a $2 million budget after the original building burned in 1930, this state capitol stands out from its traditionally domed peers. The 19-story Art Deco limestone tower is one of only four vertically oriented capitols in the United States (along with those in Nebraska, Louisiana and Florida). Beyond its distinctive exterior, the Skyscraper of the Prairies is capped with an observation deck, features lavish interiors fashioned from wood, stone and metal from all over the globe and has a cavernous Great Hall running to the legislative quarters. Tours are available on weekdays in the summer. Also on the grounds are the former Governors' Mansion, now restored and featuring historic displays, and the North Dakota Heritage Center, a regional history museum with an impressive collection of Plains Native American artifacts. Two notable outdoor sculptures include one of Lewis and Clark guide Sacagawea, and another dubbed *The Pioneer Family* by Avard Fairbanks.

WARD EARTHLODGE VILLAGE HISTORIC SITE

4480 Fort Lincoln Road, Bismarck, 701-222-6455

Mandan Native Americans once occupied this bluff above the Missouri River, living in dome-shaped homes built of logs and earth. By the time Lewis and

HIGHLIGHTS

WHAT ARE THE BEST PLACES FOR OUTDOOR FUN IN WESTERN NORTH DAKOTA?

LEWIS AND CLARK STATE PARK
This park may have gotten its moniker for being near a stop-off point for the Lewis and Clark Expedition, but now it's a popular spot for boaters and anglers.

LITTLE MISSOURI BADLANDS
The colorful striations in this deeply eroded gorge make for incredible scenery. Prairie wildlife like pronghorn antelope and coyotes only add to the picturesque landscape.

THEODORE ROOSEVELT NATIONAL PARK
You'll find lots of animals at this national park. Elk and bison are common sights, but keep an eye out for wild horses, white-tailed deer, hawks, falcons and eagles.

Clark passed through the region, the village was deserted. Depressions remain where the houses once stood, and the site is now part of the city park system. Interpretive signs explain how the village was constructed and relate elements of Mandan cultural life. Take in the spectacular views from the bluff.

MANDAN
FORT ABRAHAM LINCOLN STATE PARK
4480 Fort Lincoln Road, Mandan, 701-667-6340; www.ndparks.com

This historic site marks the fort that General George Custer commanded prior to his famous last stand. There are reconstructed fort buildings and a Mandan earth lodge village along with a visitor center, an amphitheater and a museum, which features interpretive programs in the summer. You can go fishing, hiking, cross-country skiing, snowmobiling and picnicking here. There is a playground, concession stand and camping sites.

Tours: Memorial Day-Labor Day.

WILLISTON
FORT BUFORD STATE HISTORIC SITE
15349 39th Lane NW, Williston, 701-572-9034; www.nd.gov

Established in 1866 near the merging point of the Missouri and Yellowstone rivers, Fort Buford served as the distribution point for government annuities to peaceful natives in the vicinity. The fort also was the site of the surrender of Sitting Bull in 1881. Original features include a stone powder magazine, the post cemetery and a museum.

Mid-May-mid-September, daily; mid-September-mid-May, by appointment.

FORT UNION TRADING POST NATIONAL HISTORIC SITE

15550 Highway 1804, Williston, 701-572-9083; www.nps.gov

The American Fur Company built this fort in 1829 at the junction of the Yellowstone and Missouri rivers. During the next three decades, it was one of the most important trading depots on the Western frontier. In 1867, the government bought the fort, dismantled it and used the materials to build Fort Buford two miles away. Much of the fort has been reconstructed. A National Park Service visitor center is located in the Bourgeois House. Guided tours and interpretive programs are available in the summer.

Daily.

LEWIS AND CLARK STATE PARK

4904 119th Road N.W., Williston, 701-859-3071; www.ndparks.com

Situated on a northern bay in Lake Sakakawea—a man-made body of water created by damming the Missouri River—this state park is so named because the Lewis and Clark expedition camped nearby twice, on the 1805 westward journey in search of the fabled Northwest Passage and on the return trip east the next year. Today, the park is popular because of its marina, a jumping-off point for boaters and anglers. Of the fish lurking below, the most remarkable are immense paddlefish, prehistoric-looking beasts once thought to be extinct, and endangered pallid sturgeon, which grow up to six feet long. A good trail system allows for hiking and cross-country skiing.

LEWIS AND CLARK TRAIL MUSEUM

Highway 85, Alexander, 701-828-3595

Located on the first leg of the Corps of Discovery's westward route (south of Williston and the Missouri River in Alexander), this museum covers not only Lewis and Clark but also early homesteaders in North Dakota. The most notable exhibit is a scale model of Fort Mandan, where the party stayed during the winter of 1804-1805.

Memorial Day-Labor Day, daily.

WHERE TO STAY

RECOMMENDED
DICKINSON

COMFORT INN

493 Elk Drive, Dickinson, 701-264-7300, 877-424-6423;
www.comfortinn.com

Families with kids will appreciate the large indoor water park that includes a two-story spiral slide and hot tub, as well as the suite-style accommodations. Rooms are well priced, and the hotel's side street location—less than an hour from the heart of Theodore Roosevelt park's South Unit—makes for a good night's sleep.

115 rooms. Complimentary breakfast. Fitness center. Pool. Pets accepted. $61-150

HIGHLIGHT

THE LITTLE MISSOURI BADLANDS

Medora sits at the base of the dramatic Little Missouri Badlands, a deeply eroded gorge that exposes millions of years of sedimentary deposits in colorful horizontal striations. Medora itself is a fascinating historical town—Teddy Roosevelt lived near here in the 1880s, as did the flamboyant Marquis de Mores, a French nobleman who journeyed to the Dakota Territory to live out his cowboy fantasies. Before setting out to explore bluffs that rise behind the town, be sure to visit the Chateau de Mores, the luxurious frontier home built by the Marquis. When it was constructed in 1883, this 26-room mansion was the finest and most modern private home for hundreds of miles. Then head out to the Maah Daah Hey Trail, which is 100 miles long and connects the northern and southern sections of the Theodore Roosevelt National Park, passing through the Little Missouri National Grassland. The hike covers four miles at the trail's southern extreme and explores the scenic badlands above Medora, passing through the fascinating and ruggedly beautiful badlands ecosystem. The area is home to prairie wildlife, including pronghorn antelope, coyotes, white-tailed deer, prairie dogs and rattlesnakes. Begin at Sully Creek State Park, two miles south of Medora (the Maah Daah Hey Trail is also popular with mountain bikers, so you'll share the path). The trail crosses the Little Missouri River, which is ankle-deep and easily waded in summer, and follows the river valley through stands of cottonwood, willow and silver sage. The path then begins to climb up the face of a badland mesa, eventually reaching a plateau. From a rocky escarpment, enjoy a magnificent overlook onto Medora and the Little Missouri River breaks. Continue north on the trail through prairie grassland to a side path, the Canyon Trail, which drops steeply down a rugged canyon wall to a prairie dog town. Follow the trail north, through a self-closing gate, to where the Canyon Trail rejoins the Maah Daah Hey. From here, hikers can return to Medora along a gravel road or continue north through more badlands landscape to the South Unit of the Theodore Roosevelt National Park headquarters.

DAYS INN-GRAND DAKOTA LODGE

532 W. 15th St. Dickinson, 701-483-5600, 800-329-7466;
www.daysinn.com

With its welcoming lobby fireplace and onsite Red
Pheasant Restaurant, the hotel promises a true
"lodge" experience with spacious rooms. The Grand
Dakota Lodge is convenient for nighttime dining
after a day exploring Roosevelt park's South Unit
just 35 miles to the west.

*149 rooms. Restaurant. Complimentary breakfast. Business
center. Fitness center. Pool. Pets accepted. $61-150*

MEDORA
AMERICINN MEDORA

75 E. River Road S., Medora, 701-623-4800, 800-396-5007;
www.americinn.com

Conveniently located just a mile from Roosevelt
park in the restored cattle town of Medora, this
affordable chain hotel offers spacious rooms, some
with microwaves and refrigerators.

54 rooms. Complimentary breakfast. Pool. $61-150

ROUGH RIDERS HOTEL

301 Third Ave., Medora, 701-623-4444, 800-633-6721

Antique furnishings outfit the small rooms at this
hotel near Theodore Roosevelt National Park, but
there's more to its history than just tables and chairs.
Originally built in 1884, the structure now housing
the hotel was frequented by Theodore Roosevelt
and served as a stop on his 1900 campaign trail.
Since then, the building has served as a restaurant,
café and bar before being refurbished in 1962 into
its current Rough Riders Hotel state.

9 rooms. Open mid-April to early September. $61-150

WATERFORD CITY
ROOSEVELT INN

600 Second Ave. SW (Highway 85 West), Watford City,
701-842-3686, 800-887-9170; www.rooseveltinn.com

Just 15 minutes from Theodore Roosevelt National
Park, the Roosevelt Inn has a number of affordable
room options, including a suite suitable for families
featuring three double beds and two bathrooms. For
more deluxe accommodations, request one of the
two suites with a Jacuzzi, fireplace and large-screen
TV. The inn also has an indoor pool.

50 rooms. Pool. $61-150

WHICH IS THE
MOST HISTORIC
HOTEL?

Built in 1884, the **Rough
Riders Hotel** isn't just a
nod to former president
Theodore Roosevelt,
he was a frequent
guest there. The hotel
was even a stop on his
campaign trail in 1900.

HIGHLIGHT

THEODORE ROOSEVELT NATIONAL PARK

This national park is a monument to 26th president Theodore Roosevelt, who was the nation's champion of the conservation of natural resources. Roosevelt came to the Badlands in September 1883 to hunt buffalo and other big game. This park preserves the magnificent badlands landscape just as the former president knew it. Wind and water have carved curiously sculptured formations, tablelands, buttes, canyons and rugged hills from a thick series of flat-lying sedimentary rocks. Thick, dark layers of lignite coal, which are sometimes fired by lightning and burn slowly for many years, are exposed in eroded hillsides. The fires often bake adjacent clay layers into a red, brick-like substance called scoria or clinker. Elk and bison have been reintroduced and thrive here; you can see them throughout the park. There are several large prairie dog towns, and mule and whitetail deer are abundant. Wild horses can be seen in the South Unit, and the area is populated with hawks, falcons, eagles and other more common species. The park is divided into three units. The South Unit is accessible from Interstate 94 (I-94) at Medora, where there is a visitor center and Roosevelt's Maltese Cross cabin. The Elkhorn Ranch Site on the Little Missouri River can be reached only by rough dirt roads, and you should check in with rangers at the Medora Visitor Center before venturing out (*701-623-4466*). The North Unit is accessible from U.S. 85, near Watford City and has a visitor center. An additional visitor center is at the Painted Canyon Scenic Overlook on I-94 (April-October, daily). The park is open all year; visitor centers are closed on holidays. Park headquarters: *701-623-4466; www.nps.gov*

WHAT TO EAT

RECOMMENDED
MEDORA
THE COWBOY CAFÉ

215 Fourth St., Medora, 701-623-4343

A line of American flags wave outside the two-story rustic wooden building that houses the Cowboy Café. On the inside, cowboy pictures and old-fashioned tin cups, plates and utensils line the walls. The service is friendly, and the pies—including ground cherry, sour cream raisin and peach—are always a treat for dessert.

American. Breakfast, lunch, dinner. $15 and under

LITTLE MISSOURI SALOON & DINING

440 Third St., Medora, 701-623-4404

Enjoy the friendly service and great bar food at this local favorite. When you're through with your meal, head downstairs and sidle up to the bar to enjoy the live music during weekends in the summer.

American. Breakfast, lunch, dinner. Bar. $15 and under

PITCHFORK STEAK FONDUE

Tjaden Terrace, Medora

At this popular restaurant, steaks are cooked on pitchfork skewers and come with fondue dipping sauces, such as horseradish, curry and mustard crème. The meaty skewers are served with homemade potato chips and fresh salads. Lemon bars are the perfect way to end the heavy meal.

Steak. Dinner. Closed early September-May. Children's menu. $15 and under

ROUGH RIDERS DINING ROOM

301 Third Ave., Medora, 701-623-4444

In the historic restored Rough Riders Hotel built circa 1880, dining in this restaurant, with its antique furnishings and Western-style food, is like stepping back to the turn of the century. The restaurant also has an impressive past: Theodore Roosevelt used to dine here on his frequent trips through Medora. It's also one of the only fine-dining establishments in town. The menu features such dishes as butternut squash pasta with venison medallions, walleye pike with lemon-cream sauce and prime rib.

American. Breakfast, lunch, dinner. Closed Labor Day-Memorial Day. Bar. $16-35

WHAT IS THE BEST OVERALL RESTAURANT?

Since this is park country, you won't find lots of fine dining. But the **Rough Riders Dining Room**, with brown leather booths and a fireplace, is the exception, dishing out upscale fare like butternut squash pasta with veal medallions.

WELCOME TO OKLAHOMA

PROBABLY EVERY STATE IS MISUNDERSTOOD IN ITS OWN

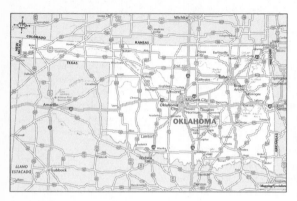

way. But Oklahoma may have a special claim. Is it the vast dusty terrain from which impoverished farmers fled during the Great Depression? Is it the good-ol'-boy land of Okie from Muskogee that Merle Haggard celebrated in song, or the romantic land of the stylized cowboy culture as sung about in the musical *Oklahoma!*? Is it Southern—bordered, as it is, by Arkansas on the east? Is it a northern annex of Texas? (The twang of the Lone Star state is certainly audible here.) Or does it belong to the West, with its neatly rectangular panhandle touching New Mexico and Colorado?

The area that was to become the state of Oklahoma was practically unknown to Americans at the time of the Louisiana Purchase of 1803. Believing those unsettled lands to be of little value, the government set them aside as "Indian Territory" in 1830, assigning a portion to each of the Five Civilized Tribes. Thousands of Creeks, Choctaws, Chickasaws, Seminoles and Cherokees were forced to leave the Southeastern U.S. and move to Oklahoma. About one-fourth of those forced west over this Trail of Tears died on the way of hunger, disease, cold and exhaustion. Today Oklahoma has the largest Native American population in the United States.

Oklahoma produces millions of barrels of oil a year, and you might see churning derricks almost anywhere, including beside runways of the Oklahoma City airport. The state has vast expanses of lightly settled country forests and green fields in the eastern part, ranchland and prairie in the drier west. Some people would be surprised to learn that Oklahoma has mountains, but in the southeastern corner of the state, there are seven ranges. Northeast Oklahoma has both rolling hills and flat prairies, along with several large lakes and plenty of state parks. The southwestern part of the state is true Great Plains and Chisholm Trail territory and has several major museums that explore the region's heritage and history, which started with the Kiowa, Comanche and Apache, the original inhabitants, and then saw the impact of settlers and clashes between newcomers and natives.

BEST ATTRACTIONS

WHAT ARE OKLAHOMA'S BEST ATTRACTIONS?

BARTLESVILLE
Who knew this town was a hotbed of great modern architecture? You'll find Frank Lloyd Wright's only completed skyscraper among the eye-pleasing offerings.

OKLAHOMA CITY
The city may be best known for its national memorial to honor those who died in the 1995 bombing, but it also offers a slew of other attractions, like the Oklahoma City Museum of Art and National Cowboy & Western Museum.

TULSA
Tulsa may be the second-largest city in the state, but it is the No. 1 museum spot. Check out the Philbrook Museum of Art and Sherwin Miller Museum of Jewish Art.

NORTHEAST/GREEN COUNTRY

This region offers rivers, lakes, tallgrass prairie and rolling hills, but you'll also find culture among all the scenery. The Bartlesville area is proud of its Western and Native American heritage, which involves three tribes: the Cherokee, Delaware and Osage. Bartlesville also has become internationally known for its distinguished, modern architecture, a building trend initiated by the H. C. Price family, which made its fortune in oil. The town boasts a number of both public and private buildings by Frank Lloyd Wright and Bruce Goff.

Claremore is most famous for being the birthplace of Will Rogers. He was actually born about halfway between this city and Oologah but claimed Claremore as his home because, he said, "nobody but an Indian could pronounce Oologah."

The cosmopolitan cultural center of the region is Tulsa. The second-largest city in Oklahoma offers a number of museums, theater and more. But if you do want to experience some of the region's scenic spots, visit Muskogee. Located near the confluence of the Verdigris, Grand and Arkansas rivers, Muskogee is dotted with 32 small parks and serves as the gateway to the eastern lakes area.

WHAT TO SEE

BARTLESVILLE
FRANK PHILLIPS MANSION
1107 S. Cherokee Ave., Bartlesville, 918-336-2491; www.frankphillipshome.org
Built in 1909 by the founder of the Phillips Petroleum Company, this

HIGHLIGHTS

WHAT ARE THE TOP THINGS TO DO IN NORTHEAST/GREEN COUNTRY?

CHECK OUT THE ARCHITECTURE OF PRICE TOWER
A National Historic Landmark, this 19-story building has the distinct honor of being Frank Lloyd Wright's only completed skyscraper.

VISIT THE WILL ROGERS MEMORIAL
Fans of the famous cowboy, movie star and humorist will want to make a stop at this memorial, which contains his personal belongings, a saddle collection and more.

SEE OKLAHOMA! AT DISCOVERYLAND! OUTDOOR THEATER
Oklahoma! is practically required viewing in these parts. Watch the foot-tapping musical in this outdoor 2,000-seat theater, which puts on the play all summer long.

LOOK AT ART IN THE GILCREASE MUSEUM
This museum carries a collection of Native American art that dates back 12,000 years ago. It also offers a vast reserve of art inspired by the American West.

TAKE A TRIP TO THE PHILBROOK MUSEUM OF ART
A beautiful Italian villa houses an eclectic art collection, from Renaissance works to Native American baskets and pottery. Be sure to walk in the sculpture gardens.

PERUSE JUDAICA AT THE SHERWIN MILLER MUSEUM OF JEWISH ART
The museum offers the largest Judaica collection in the Southwest. It examines the Oklahoma Jewish experience and the Holocaust, with artifacts from the concentration camps.

neoclassical house has been restored to the 1930s period. The interior includes imported woods, marble, Oriental rugs and original furnishings. This mansion is listed on the National Register of Historic Places.

Wednesday-Saturday 10 a.m.-5 p.m.; second Sunday of the month 1-5 p.m.

PRICE TOWER

510 Dewey Ave., Bartlesville, 918-336-4949; www.pricetower.org

Designed by Frank Lloyd Wright, this 221-foot office building was built for pipeline construction pioneer H. C. Price as headquarters for his company. The building design is based on a diamond module of 30/60-degree triangles. Although Wright designed many skyscrapers, Price Tower was his only tall building to be completed.

Guided tours: Tuesday-Saturday.

WOOLAROC

Highway 123, Bartlesville, 918-336-0307; www.woolaroc.org

This complex covers 3,600 acres with a wildlife preserve for herds of American bison, longhorn cattle, Scottish Highland cattle, elk, deer and other native wildlife. A museum features paintings by Russell, Remington and other great Western artists; exhibits on the development of America; and artifacts of several Native American tribes, pioneers and cowboys. The Native American Heritage Center has multimedia shows, authentic crafts, art displays, a picnic area and a nature trail.

Memorial Day-Labor Day, Tuesday-Sunday; Labor Day-Memorial Day, Wednesday-Sunday 10 a.m.-5 p.m.

CLAREMORE

LYNN RIGGS MEMORIAL

121 N. Chickasaw Ave., Claremore

The memorial showcases the *Oklahoma!* author's personal belongings, a sculpture of Riggs, original manuscripts and the original "surrey with the fringe on top" from the famous musical.

Admission: free. Monday-Friday 9 a.m.-noon and 1-4 p.m.

WILL ROGERS BIRTHPLACE AND DOG IRON RANCH

9501 E. 380 Road, Oologah, 918-275-4201; www.willrogers.com

This is the home where the actor and cowboy, Will Rogers, was born on November 4, 1879.

Daily 8 a.m.-5 p.m.

WILL ROGERS MEMORIAL

1720 W. Will Rogers Blvd., Claremore, 918-341-0719, 800-324-9455; www.willrogers.com

Located at this memorial, you'll find mementos, murals, a saddle collection, dioramas, theater, films, tapes and a research library. Jo Davidson's statue of Rogers stands in the foyer. The memorial sits on 20 acres once owned by the humorist.

Daily 8 a.m.-5 p.m.

GROVE

HAR-BER VILLAGE

4404 W. 20th St., Grove, 918-786-3488; www.har-bervillage.com

This reconstructed village with 90 buildings and shops is a typical pioneer town.

March-November, Monday-Saturday 9 a.m.-6 p.m., Sunday 12:30-5 p.m.

LENDONWOOD GARDENS

1308 W. 13th St., Grove, 918-786-2938; www.lendonwood.com

The gardens hold one of the largest collections of chamaecyparis in the United States as well as rhododendrons, day lilies and azaleas. The grounds also include the Display Garden, English Terrace Garden and Japanese Garden.

Admission: adults $5, children 12 and under free. Daily dawn-dusk.

MUSKOGEE

FIVE CIVILIZED TRIBES MUSEUM

Honor Heights Park, 1101 Honor Heights Drive, Muskogee, 918-683-1701; www.fivetribes.org

The museum highlights art and artifacts of the Cherokees, Chickasaws, Choctaws, Creeks and Seminoles. Check out displays relating to their history and culture.

March-December: daily; January-February, Tuesday-Saturday.

FORT GIBSON HISTORIC SITE

907 N. Garrison St., Fort Gibson, 918-478-4088; www.fortgibson.com

Established as the state's first military post in 1824, the park includes 12 reconstructed or restored buildings on a 55-acre site; period rooms depict army life in the 1830s and 1870s. Fort Gibson National Cemetery is about a mile east.

Mid-April-mid-October, Tuesday-Sunday 10 a.m.-5 p.m.; mid-October-mid-April, Thursday-Sunday 10 a.m.-5 p.m.

HONOR HEIGHTS PARK

North Honor Heights Drive, Muskogee, 918-684-6302; www.muskogeeparks.com

This 120-acre park features azalea, rose and chrysanthemum gardens. There also are nature walks, lakes, waterfalls and picnicking areas.

Daily.

TULSA

ARKANSAS RIVER HISTORICAL SOCIETY MUSEUM

Tulsa Port of Catoosa, 5350 Cimarron Road, Catoosa, 918-266-2291; www.tulsaweb.com

Located in the Port Authority Building, this museum has pictorial displays and operating models that trace the history of the 1,450-mile Arkansas River and McClellan-Kerr Navigation System.

Monday-Friday 8 a.m.-4:30 p.m.

BOSTON AVENUE UNITED METHODIST CHURCH

1301 S. Boston Ave., Tulsa, 918-583-5181; www.bostonavenue.org

Designed and built in 1929 by Adah Robinson, this structure was the first large-scale Art Deco church. It features a 225-foot tower and many lesser towers decorated with bas-relief pioneer figures. The sanctuary is ornamented with Italian mosaic reredos.

Tours after 11 a.m. Sunday services.

CREEK COUNCIL OAK TREE

18th Street and Cheyenne Avenue, Tulsa

A landscaped plot housing the Council Oak, this burr oak tree stands as a memorial to the Lochapokas Creek tribe.

DISCOVERYLAND! OUTDOOR THEATER

19501 W. 41st St., Tulsa, 918-245-6552; discoverylandusa.com

This theater calls itself the national home of Rodgers and Hammerstein's *Oklahoma!* because during the summer, the musical runs six nights a week. You can catch one of the shows in a 2,000-seat outdoor theater complex with a Western theme. There's authentic Native American dancing, a Western musical revue and a barbecue dinner prior to performance.

Mid-June-late August, Monday-Friday.

GILCREASE MUSEUM

1400 Gilcrease Museum Road, Tulsa, 918-596-2700; www.gilcrease.org

Founded by Thomas Gilcrease, an oil man of Creek descent, this museum has a collection of Native American art and artifacts that date as far back as 12,000 years ago. The library houses about 90,000 items, including the earliest known letter sent to Europe from the New World.

Tuesday-Sunday 10 a.m.-5 p.m.

PHILBROOK MUSEUM OF ART

2727 S. Rockford Road, Tulsa, 918-749-7941, 800-324-7941; www.philbrook.org

Exhibits here include Italian Renaissance, 19th-century English, American and Native American paintings; Native American baskets and pottery; Chinese jade and decorative material; Southeast Asian tradeware; and African sculpture. Housed in an Italian Renaissance Revival villa on 23 acres, the museum also has a formal and sculpture gardens.

Tuesday-Sunday 10 a.m.-5 p.m., Thursday 10 a.m.-8 p.m.

SHERWIN MILLER MUSEUM OF JEWISH ART

2021 E. 71st St., Tulsa, 918-492-1818; www.jewishmuseum.net

The Southwest's largest collection of Judaica contains objects representative of Jewish history, art, ceremonial events and daily life from around the world.

Monday-Friday 10 a.m.-5 p.m., Sunday 1-5 p.m.

THE TULSA ZOO

6421 E. 36th St., Tulsa, 918-669-6600; www.tulsazoo.com

More than 200 varieties of animals are housed within 68 acres of landscaped grounds. The zoo features Native American artifacts, geological specimens, dinosaur replicas, live plants and, of course, animals.

Daily 9 a.m.-5 p.m.

WHERE TO STAY

BARTLESVILLE

★★★INN AT PRICE TOWER

510 Dewey Ave., Bartlesville, 918-336-1000, 877-424-2424;
www.innatpricetower.com

This contemporary hotel is in the Frank Lloyd Wright-designed Price Tower. The tower suites, decorated in mid-century modern style, are two stories and offer views of the prairie.

19 rooms. Restaurant, bar. Complimentary breakfast. Business center. $251-350

TULSA

★★★CROWNE PLAZA

100 E. Second St., Tulsa, 918-582-9000, 800-227-6963; www.crowneplaza.com

This hotel caters to business travelers with its central Tulsa location. A full-service spa, a restaurant, a lounge, a business center, an indoor and outdoor pool, a fitness room, and conference facilities are among the services.

460 rooms. Pets accepted. Restaurant, bar. Business center. Fitness center. Pool. Spa. $61-150

★★★HILTON TULSA SOUTHERN HILLS

7902 S. Lewis St., Tulsa, 918-492-5000, 800-774-1500; www.hilton.com

Located in the Southern Hills area of Tulsa and across the street from Oral Roberts University, this hotel features spacious guest rooms with comfortable beds and Crabtree and Evelyn bath products. There's also complimentary wireless Internet access and a full fitness center.

282 rooms. Restaurant, bar. Business center. Fitness center. Pool. Pets accepted. $61-150

★★★MARRIOTT TULSA SOUTHERN HILLS

1902 E. 71st St., Tulsa, 918-493-7000, 866-530-3760; www.marriott.com

Rising 11 stories in two connected wings, the Marriott Tulsa Southern Hills offers well-appointed guest rooms with full amenities. It is located near golf courses, tennis facilities, the Tulsa Zoo and other area attractions.

383 rooms. Restaurant, bar. Business center. Fitness center. Spa. Pool. $61-150

★★★RADISSON HOTEL TULSA

10918 E. 41st St., Tulsa, 918-627-5000, 800-325-3535;
www.radissontulsa.com

An indoor water park is tucked inside this hotel, making it a good choice for families. Located in the heart of southeast Tulsa, near the Tulsa International Airport and the Philbrook Museum, the hotel has rooms that are comfortable and spacious.

325 rooms. Restaurant, bar. Business center. Fitness center. Pool. Pets accepted. $61-150

RECOMMENDED

TULSA

HOTEL AMBASSADOR

1324 S. Main St., Tulsa, 918-587-8200, 888-408-8282; www.hotelambassador-tulsa.com

Located away from the downtown bustle in Tulsa's uptown neighborhood, this hotel is a good pick if you want a quiet respite in the city. Spacious rooms are bathed in ivory, red and brown and come with luxe Gilchrist & Soames toiletries, complimentary wireless Internet access, pillow-top mattresses and iPod docking stations. To kick back, visit the library and curl up with a book in the velvety oversized armchairs or have a glass of wine at Chalkboard restaurant's bar.

55 rooms. Restaurant, bar. Business center. Fitness center. Pets accepted. $151-250

THE MAYO HOTEL

115 W. Fifth St., Tulsa, 918-582-6296;
www.themayohotel.com

Listed on the National Register of Historic Places, this all-suite hotel opened in 1925. But you wouldn't be able to tell from the sleek suites, which sport wood floors, roman blinds, oversized studded black headboards, and a black and tan color scheme with bursts of red. Most of the kitchens come with granite countertops and stainless-steel appliances. Charlie Chaplin, Babe Ruth and President John F. Kennedy have all stayed here; if you want to learn more, visit the Mayo Museum, which displays articles and artifacts detailing the hotel's storied past.

102 rooms. Restaurant, bar. Business center. Fitness center. $151-250

WHERE TO EAT

★★★BODEAN SEAFOOD

3323 E. 51st St., Tulsa, 918-749-1407;
www.bodean.net

This popular restaurant serves creative seafood dishes, like sesame-crusted Gulf yellowfin tuna with a chilled soba noodle salad, soy reduction and wasabi vinaigrette. And the seafood is fresh; items are flown in twice daily. The dining room provides a comfortable atmosphere that includes white-linen-topped tables. A three-course prix fixe menu is available, and Tuesdays feature a four-course menu with three wines to match.

Seafood. Lunch, dinner. Bar. $16-35

★★★POLO GRILL

2038 Utica Square, Tulsa, 918-744-4280;
www.pologrill.com

The inventive American cuisine served at this restaurant draws from French, Southern and Southwest influences. Signature dishes include oven-roasted tomato bisque, tender leaf spinach and strawberry

---

WHICH HOTEL HAS THE MOST UNIQUE DESIGN?

The one thing that sets **Inn at Price Tower** apart from the pack is that its building was designed by no other than the legendary Frank Lloyd Wright. The structure is the only Wright-designed skyscraper to ever be built.

WHAT IS THE BEST OVERALL RESTAURANT?

Hailed as one of the "Rising Chefs of American Cuisine," Robert Merrifield cooks up imaginative takes on French, Southern and Southwestern fare at **Polo Grill.**

salad, crispy grit cakes, grilled steaks and baked fudge. There is a nine-course prix fixe tasting menu and an extensive wine list.

American. Lunch, dinner. Closed Sunday. Reservations recommended. Outdoor seating. Children's menu. Bar. $36-85

★★★WARREN DUCK CLUB
6110 S. Yale Ave., Tulsa, 918-495-1000; www.doubletree.com

This fine-dining restaurant is inside the Doubletree Hotel. The menu features American classics such as grilled steaks, seafood and more.

American. Breakfast, lunch, dinner, late-night. Children's menu. Bar. $36-85

RECOMMENDED

TULSA
THE CHALKBOARD
Hotel Ambassador, 1324 S. Main St., Tulsa, 918-587-8200, 888-408-8282; www.hotelambassador-tulsa.com

Hidden away in the lower level of the Hotel Ambassador, this restaurant serves European-inspired seasonal cuisine. A must on the menu is the signature beef Wellington, but vegetarians can opt for the artichoke hearts and leek lasagna smothered with a garlic-béchamel sauce. For dessert, go for the white chocolate bread pudding; it's a real palate-pleaser.

Continental. Breakfast, lunch, dinner. $36-85

WHERE TO SHOP

TULSA
UTICA SQUARE
21st and Utica streets, Tulsa, 918-742-5531; www.uticasquare.com

This upscale shopping district includes Saks Fifth Avenue, Coach and Williams-Sonoma. Set in a peaceful landscape that features manicured gardens, the area also contains many restaurants and cafés.

OKLAHOMA CITY

What is now the site of Oklahoma's capital was barren prairie on the morning of April 22, 1889. Unassigned land was opened to settlement that day, and by nightfall the population numbered 10,000. No city was ever settled faster. The city sits atop one of the nation's largest oil fields—there are even wells on the lawn of the Capitol. First discovered in 1928, the field was rapidly developed throughout the city. It still produces large quantities of high-gravity oil. Oil well equipment manufacturing became one of the city's major industries.

WHAT TO SEE

45TH INFANTRY DIVISION MUSEUM
2145 N.E. 36th St., Oklahoma City, 405-424-5313; www.45thdivisionmuseum.com
Exhibits showcase state military history from its beginnings in the early Oklahoma Territory through World War II and Korea to the present National Guard, including a Desert Storm exhibit; uniforms, vehicles, aircraft, artillery and an extensive military firearms collection with pieces dating from the American Revolution; and memorabilia and original cartoons by Bill Mauldin.
Admission: Free. Tuesday-Friday 9 a.m.-4:15 p.m., Saturday 10 a.m.-4:15 p.m., Sunday 1-4:15 p.m.

AQUATICUS
2101 N.E. 50th St., Oklahoma City, 405-424-3344
This marine life science facility contains a comprehensive collection of aquatic life; a shark tank; adaptations and habitat exhibits; and underwater viewing.
Daily.

CIVIC CENTER MUSIC HALL
201 N. Walker Ave., Oklahoma City, 405-297-2584; www.okcciviccenter.org
The hall is home to the Oklahoma City Philharmonic, Canterbury Choral Society, Ballet Oklahoma and Lyric Theatre of Oklahoma. Other entertainment choices include Broadway shows and popular concerts.

FRONTIER CITY
11501 N.E. Expressway, Oklahoma City, 405-478-2412; www.frontiercity.com
This 65-acre Western theme park includes more than 75 rides, shows and attractions; entertainment; and shops and restaurants.
Memorial Day-late August, daily; late March-Memorial Day and late August-October, Saturday-Sunday.

GARDEN EXHIBITION BUILDING AND HORTICULTURE GARDENS
3400 N.W. 36th St., Oklahoma City, 405-943-0827
These gardens feature azalea trails; a butterfly garden; rose, peony and iris gardens; and an arboretum. The conservatory has one of the country's largest cactus and succulent collections.
Admission: free. Gardens: April-September, daily 8 a.m.-8 p.m.; October-March, daily 8 a.m.-5 p.m.

HIGHLIGHTS

WHAT ARE THE TOP THINGS TO DO IN OKLAHOMA CITY?

ESCAPE TO THE MYRIAD BOTANICAL GARDENS

When you need a break, visit these calming gardens. The centerpiece is the Crystal Bridge Tropical Conservatory, a 224-foot-long circular jungle with palm trees, waterfalls and animals.

VISIT THE NATIONAL COWBOY & WESTERN MUSEUM AT HIGH NOON

It isn't all 10-gallon hats and lassos at this museum. It celebrates cowboys and the American West with a collection of fine art and John Wayne memorabilia.

EXAMINE THE COLLECTIONS AT THE OKLAHOMA CITY MUSEUM OF ART

Among the museum's many great exhibits, don't miss the vast collection of artist Dale Chihuly's magnificent glass sculptures.

REMEMBER THE FALLEN AT THE OKLAHOMA CITY NATIONAL MEMORIAL

A series of monuments pays tribute to those who died during the April 1995 bombing. Field of Empty Chairs is a sobering reminder of the 168 lives lost.

INTERNATIONAL PHOTOGRAPHY HALL OF FAME AND MUSEUM

2100 N.E. 52nd St., Oklahoma City, 405-424-4055; www.iphf.org

This museum, located within the Science Museum of Oklahoma, features permanent and traveling exhibits of photographic equipment and photographs from such noted shutterbugs as Ansel Adams and Dorothea Lange. The museum also displays one of world's largest photographic murals.

Admission: adults $10.95, seniors and children 4-12 $8.95 (includes admission to Science Museum). Monday-Friday 10 a.m.-5 p.m., Saturday 10 a.m.-6 p.m., Sunday 11 a.m.-6 p.m.

KIRKPATRICK SCIENCE AND AIR SPACE MUSEUM

2100 N.E. 52nd St., Oklahoma City, 405-602-6664, 800-532-7652; www.omniplex.org

This hands-on museum features an Air Space Museum, Kirkpatrick Galleries, a gardens/greenhouse and the Kirkpatrick Planetarium (shows change quarterly).

Admission: adults $10.95, seniors and children 4-12 $8.95. Monday-Friday 9 a.m.-5 p.m., Saturday 9 a.m.-6 p.m., Sunday 11 a.m.-6 p.m.

HIGHLIGHT

OKLAHOMA CITY THEN AND NOW

Single-day events have shaped both the past and present of this settlement in the American heartland. Oklahoma City was born on April 22, 1889, when the area known as the Unassigned Lands in Oklahoma Territory was opened for settlement. A cannon was fired at noon that day, signaling a rush of thousands of settlers who raced into the two million acres of land to make their claims on the plains. Just over a century later, the city was the site of the April 19, 1995 bombing of the Alfred P. Murrah Federal Building by American terrorist Timothy McVeigh. Today, this event is memorialized at the Oklahoma City National Memorial. Begin at the Gates of Time, twin monuments that frame the moment of destruction: 9:02 a.m. The east gate represents 9:01 a.m. and the west gate 9:03 a.m. The Field of Empty Chairs consists of 168 bronze-and-stone chairs arranged in nine rows, representing the lives lost and the floor each victim was on at the time of the blast. Smaller chairs memorialize the 19 children killed. The area also includes an orchard and reflecting pool.

MYRIAD BOTANICAL GARDENS

301 W. Reno Ave., Oklahoma City, 405-297-3995; www.myriadgardens.com

This 17-acre botanical garden is in the heart of the city's redeveloping central business district. It features a lake, an amphitheater, botanical gardens and the seven-story Crystal Bridge Tropical Conservatory.

Admission: adults $6, seniors and children 13-18 $5, children 4-12 $3, children 3 and under free. Monday-Saturday 9 a.m.-6 p.m., Sunday noon-6 p.m.

NATIONAL COWBOY & WESTERN MUSEUM

1700 N.E. 63rd St., Oklahoma City, 405-478-2250; www.nationalcowboymuseum.org

This center features major art collections depicting America's Western heritage, a Rodeo Hall of Fame and landscaped gardens.

Admission: adults $12.50, seniors and students $9.75, children 4-12 $5.75, children 3 and under free. Daily 10 a.m.-5 p.m.

OKLAHOMA CITY MUSEUM OF ART

415 Coach Drive, Oklahoma City, 405-236-3100; www.okcmoa.com

This museum holds a permanent collection of 16th- to 20th-century European and American paintings, prints, drawings, photographs, sculpture and decorative arts. Don't miss the 20 stunning installations from glass artist Dale Chihuly.

Admission: adults $12, seniors, students, military personnel and children 6-18 $10, children 5 and under free. Tuesday-Saturday 10 a.m.-5 p.m., Thursday 10 a.m.-9 p.m., Sunday noon-5 p.m.

HIGHLIGHT

MUSIC TO BROADWAY'S EARS: OKLAHOMA!

Oklahoma is lucky to have one of the most popular Broadway musicals celebrating its name in the title. *Oklahoma!*, the first musical collaboration between Richard Rodgers and Oscar Hammerstein II, was different. It had a plot. The songs and dances emerged logically from the plot and the thoughts and emotions of the characters helped carry the storyline, which, atypically for the time, had its share of dark moments and serious themes. The dancing was more folk-ballet style than kick-line. Even the rural setting of the play was unusual, as most musicals were set in urban confines, with sophisticated, affluent characters, not farmhands. When it opened on Broadway in 1943, critics thought *Oklahoma!* wouldn't make it to a second performance. Scouts who saw the show in out-of-town tryouts were said to deliver a verdict along the lines of, "No girls, no gags, no chance." In the tryout stage, the show had a different title: *Away We Go!* Rogers and Hammerstein changed the title to *Oklahoma!* and added the exuberant song of the same name as the show's closing number. The rousing song thrilled the audience, which gave a standing ovation. The next day, the once-doubting critics could not find enough praise for the show, and *Oklahoma!* was on its to theatrical immortality. It set a record of more than 2,000 performances over five years at St. James Theatre and is still performed at theaters across the country.

OKLAHOMA CITY NATIONAL MEMORIAL

N.W. Fifth Street and North Robinson Avenue, Oklahoma City, 405-235-3313, 888-542-4673; www.oklahomacitynationalmemorial.org

A series of monuments honors the men, women and children killed by a bomb at the Murrah Federal Building on April 19, 1995. The Gates of Time memorial represents the moment of the blast; the Field of Empty Chairs pays tribute to the 168 lives lost in the bombing. The Survivor Tree is an American elm that withstood the blast.

Museum: Monday-Saturday 9 a.m.-6 p.m., Sunday 1-6 p.m.

OKLAHOMA CITY ZOO

2101 N.E. 50th St., Oklahoma City, 405-424-3344; www.okczoo.com

This zoo is home to more than 2,000 animals representing 500 species. Don't miss the new $13 million elephant habitat covering 9.5 acres which opens in Spring 2011. It will include an elephant barn, bull yard, a calf yard and a demonstration pavilion.

Admission: adults $7, seniors and children 3-11 $4, children 2 and under free. Daily 9 a.m.-5 p.m.

OKLAHOMA HISTORY CENTER

2401 N. Laird Ave., Oklahoma City, 405-522-5248; www.okhistorycenter.org

Located on 18 acres across from the capitol building, the History Center is a self-guided exploration of Oklahoma from past to present. Outside the museum, the Red River Journey offers visitors a walking tour of the Red River Valley. The grounds also include an outdoor oil field exhibit with drilling derricks, a portable derrick and machinery associated with Oklahoma oil explorations.

Admission: Adults $7, seniors $5, students $4, children 5 and under free. Monday-Saturday 9 a.m.-5 p.m., Sunday noon-5 p.m.

STATE CAPITOL

2300 N. Lincoln Blvd., Oklahoma City, 405-521-3356; www.travelok.com

This Greco-Roman, Neoclassical building was designed by S. A. Layton and Wemyss Smith. It's the only capitol in the world only that's surrounded by working oil wells. Legislature meets annually for 78 days beginning on the first Monday in February.

Tours: daily.

WHERE TO STAY

★★★CROWNE PLAZA HOTEL

2945 N.W. Expressway, Oklahoma City, 405-848-4811, 877-227-6963; www.crowneplaza.com

Located in the business district of Oklahoma City, this hotel offers easy access to city attractions. Granite bathrooms with closets, dark wood furniture and club chairs with ottomans are found in guest rooms. The Spa Select bedding package includes an amenity bag of lavender linen spray, an eye pillow and a CD of soothing music.

215 rooms. Restaurant, bar. Business center. Fitness center. Pool. Pets accepted. $61-150

★★★MARRIOTT WATERFORD

6300 Waterford Blvd., Oklahoma City, 405-848-4782, 800-992-2009; www.marriott.com

Located in Oklahoma City's tony Waterford community, the hotel is 15 minutes from downtown and the airport. Enjoy a drink in the waterfront lounge or take a swim in the outdoor pool. Volleyball and squash facilities are also available. Rooms feature pillow-top mattresses and crisp white linens, and the granite bathrooms have jetted tubs and Bath & Body Works amenities.

197 rooms. Restaurant, bar. Business center. Fitness center. Pool. Spa. $151-250

WHICH HOTEL HAS THE BEST IN-ROOM AMENITIES?

To ensure a good night's sleep, get the **Crowne Plaza Hotel's Spa** Select bedding package. The lavender linen spray, eye pillow and CD of soothing tunes will ease your stresses and help you get some shut-eye.

WHAT IS THE
BEST OVERALL
RESTAURANT?

The Coach House's
chef Kurt Fleischfresser
cooked for former
president George W.
Bush twice. Dubya
must be a fan of
Fleischfresser's seasonal
American cuisine that
employs local produce
and meats.

★★★RENAISSANCE OKLAHOMA CITY CONVENTION CENTER HOTEL

10 N. Broadway, Oklahoma City, 405-228-8000, 800-468-3571;
www.renaissancehotels.com

Located in downtown Oklahoma City, the Renaissance
Oklahoma City is a 15-story tower that is connected to
the adjacent Cox Convention Center by a sky bridge.
It's close to the restored Bricktown area, with its shops,
restaurants, amusements and river walk. A 13-story
atrium dominates the center of the hotel and the lobby
is filled with lush landscaping that includes koi ponds
and a waterfall.

*311 rooms. Restaurant, bar. Business center. Fitness center. Pool.
Spa. $151-250*

★★★THE SHERATON OKLAHOMA CITY

1 N. Broadway, Oklahoma City, 405-235-2780, 800-285-2780;
www.sheraton.com

This downtown hotel is connected to the Cox
Convention Center as well as many shops and businesses by an underground concourse. Contemporary
styling is the theme, from the lobby with its leather sofas
and modern art collection to the oversized guest rooms
with long working desks with ergonomic chairs, black-
and-white photographs and brown and black granite
bathrooms. An outdoor pool, sun deck and fitness
center are available, and pets are welcomed with bowls,
treats and beds.

*396 rooms. Restaurant, bar. Business center. Fitness center. Pool.
Spa. Pets accepted. $151-250*

WHERE TO EAT

★★★BELLINI'S RISTORANTE & GRILL

6305 Waterford Blvd., Oklahoma City, 405-848-1065;
www.bellinis.net

This casual restaurant has the ambience of an Italian
piazza. Modern art hangs on the dark wood-paneled
walls, and tables are set with black cloths. Everything
from pizza to steak, seafood to pasta dishes, is featured
on the extensive menu. It offers a view of the lakeside
sunset.

*American, Italian. Lunch, dinner, Sunday brunch. Reservations
recommended. Outdoor seating. Children's menu. Bar. $16-35*

★★★THE COACH HOUSE

6437 Avondale Drive, Oklahoma City, 405-842-1000;
www.thecoachokc.com

The seasonally changing menu at this restaurant
features local produce and meats, with rack of lamb as

a signature dish. The cuisine is supported by an extensive wine list. Subdued lighting, double-linen tablecloths, fine stemware and flatware and copper chargers give the restaurant an elegant, formal feel.

American. Lunch, dinner. Closed Sunday. Reservations recommended. Children's menu. $36-85

★★★JW'S STEAKHOUSE

3233 N.W. Expressway, Oklahoma City, 405-842-6633; www.marriott.com

This steakhouse in the Oklahoma City Marriott has dark wood paneling and red leather chairs and banquettes. Serving dinner only, JW's has the full steakhouse look and specializes in classics such as filet mignon and prime rib.

Steak. Dinner, late-night. Reservations recommended. Children's menu. $36-85

★★★LA BAGUETTE BISTRO

7408 N. May Ave., Oklahoma City, 405-840-3047; www.labaguettebistro.com

Just northwest of downtown, this bistro offers an authentic experience. The owners/chefs hail from France and serve simple but authentic bistro fare, including baguette sandwiches, in an L-shaped dining room.

French. Breakfast, lunch, dinner, brunch. Bar. $16-35

WELCOME TO SOUTH DAKOTA

THIS IS THE LAND OF THE PROUD AND MIGHTY SIOUX.

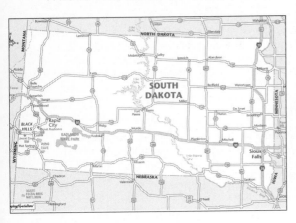

If your only picture of this tribe is from the 1990 film *Dances With Wolves*, a visit to South Dakota will reveal much about the fascinating history of this vast nation that ruled the plains, hunting buffalo by horseback. South Dakota Sioux are generally referred to as Lakota, Dakota or Nakota, and today there are more than 62,000 members of the tribes living in the state.

There are museums and monuments throughout South Dakota where you can learn more about the Sioux, from the Crazy Horse Memorial and Indian Museum of North America in Custer, to the Cultural Heritage Center in the state capital of Pierre. Visit a powwow or tribal gathering with dancing and contests in towns throughout the state. Or soak up the scenery with a drive along the Native American Scenic Byway, which stretches north from Nebraska north through the center of South Dakota.

Beyond its rich Native American history, South Dakota is a quiet, sparsely filled space teeming with natural beauty. Each year, scores of tourists visit Badlands National Park, or trek a little further west to take a look at Mount Rushmore, a granite mountain carved with the visages of George Washington, Thomas Jefferson, Abraham Lincoln and Theodore Roosevelt.

South Dakota offers more than parks and presidential figures. It's one of the nation's richest archaeological dig sites. The largest and most complete Tyrannosaurus rex in the world, Sue (who now lives at Chicago's Field Museum) was discovered here, and mammoths, marine life and other creatures from the earth's past are found regularly. Join in an archeological dig during summer months with Rapid City's Archaeological Research Center, or any of the other organizations digging in the state.

Americana abounds in South Dakota, with roadside delights like the famously kitschy Corn Palace in Mitchell and more diners serving inexpensive, hearty meals and fantastic slices of fruit pie than any appetite can handle.

BEST ATTRACTIONS

SOUTH DAKOTA'S BEST ATTRACTIONS

MOUNT RUSHMORE
The larger-than-life granite sculpture of four of our nation's greatest presidents draws about 3 million visitors each year. See the iconic memorial in person.

SIOUX FALLS
Stop here on your South Dakota tour. See black rhinos and red pandas at the Great Plains Zoo and hop aboard the *USS South Dakota*, a ship instrumental in WWII.

WESTERN SOUTH DAKOTA
See what the Wild West was like in Deadwood, then learn about the area's interesting geology and former dinosaur inhabitants in Rapid City.

WESTERN SOUTH DAKOTA

Deadwood is best known for gold and the famous Wild West characters, such as Calamity Jane, Preacher Smith and Wild Bill Hickock, who lived here. At the height of the 1876 gold rush, 25,000 people swarmed over the hillsides to dig gold. When gold was first struck at Deadwood, nearly the entire population of Custer rushed here. Predictably, at the height of a newer strike, nearly the entire population of Deadwood fled to the town of Lead. Recently, legalized gambling has given Deadwood another boom. In the last few decades, tourism has replaced gold mining as the main industry of Rapid City. Visitors come here to visit nearby Mount Rushmore or to learn about the many dinosaurs that once roamed the area (and even participate in dinosaur digs).

WHAT TO SEE

DEADWOOD
MOUNT MORIAH CEMETERY
Deadwood, 605-578-2600
The graves of Wild Bill Hickock, Calamity Jane, Preacher Smith, Seth Bullock and others reside here.

OLD STYLE SALOON #10
657 Main St., Deadwood, 605-578-3346; www.saloon10.com
You'll find a collection of Western artifacts, pictures and guns here. This is

HIGHLIGHTS

WHAT ARE THE TOP THINGS TO DO IN WESTERN SOUTH DAKOTA?

REVISIT THE WILD WEST AT OLD STYLE SALOON #10
If you really want to see what the Wild West was like, visit this saloon. It was where gunslinger Wild Bill Hickock was shot, and it offers a display of Western artifacts.

VISIT MOUNT RUSHMORE NATIONAL MEMORIAL
About 3 million people come to South Dakota each year to see the iconic Mount Rushmore. The extraordinary granite sculpture took 14 years to build.

STROLL THROUGH THE BLACK HILLS PETRIFIED FOREST
Examine the interesting geology of the region with a walk through this petrified forest. There's also a rock, fossil and mineral museum on the grounds.

SEE THE DINOS THAT ROAMED THE EARTH AT DINOSAUR PARK
You weren't around when dinosaurs inhabited this area, but you can imagine what it was like at this park, which offers life-size steel and cement dinosaur models.

the saloon in which Wild Bill Hickock was shot. There is entertainment (four shows per day, Memorial Day-Labor Day), gambling and a restaurant. *Daily.*

KEYSTONE

MOUNT RUSHMORE NATIONAL MEMORIAL
13000 Highway 244, Keystone, 605-574-2523; www.nps.gov
About 3 million people visit this national memorial every year to see the iconic 5,725-foot-tall faces carved in the granite of the Black Hills. The visages of four presidents were chosen for the hulking sculpture to represent the meaning of America: as the nation's first president, Washington embodies the birth of the country; Jefferson's Louisiana Purchase made him the face of expansion; Lincoln's Civil War struggles made him a symbol for preservation; and as a champion for the construction of the Panama Canal, Theodore Roosevelt represents development. It took 14 years and 400 workers to execute sculptor Gutzon Borglum's beautiful vision.
Admission: $10 parking fee. Daily.

RAPID CITY

BLACK HILLS PETRIFIED FOREST
8220 Elk Creek Road, Rapid City, 605-787-4560; www.elkresort.net

Visit the Black Hills Petrified Forest, which includes an interpretive film on the Black Hills geology and petrifaction process as well as a five-block walkthrough area of logs ranging from five to 100 feet long and up to three to five feet in diameter and stumps three to five feet tall. Self-guided tours are available. There's a rock, fossil and mineral museum, and gift and rock-lapidary shops.

Memorial Day-Labor Day, daily.

DINOSAUR PARK
940 Skyline Drive, Rapid City; www.dinosaurpark.net

This park has life-size steel and cement models of dinosaurs.

Daily 6 a.m.-10 p.m.

MUSEUM OF GEOLOGY
O'Harra Memorial Building, 501 E. St. Joseph, Rapid City, 605-394-2467; www.sdsmt.edu

The museum provides an exceptional display of minerals, fossils, gold samples and other geological material. It also has the first Tyrannosaurus rex skull found in South Dakota.

Admission: free. Memorial Day-Labor Day, Monday-Friday 9 a.m.-5 p.m., Saturday 9 a.m.-6 p.m., Sunday noon-5 p.m.; Labor Day-Memorial Day, Monday-Friday 9 a.m.-4 p.m., Saturday 10 a.m.-4 p.m.

THUNDERHEAD UNDERGROUND FALLS
10940 W. Highway 44, Rapid City, 605-343-0081; www.thunderheadfalls.com

Thunderhead, which dates to 1878, is one of the oldest gold mining tunnels in the Black Hills area. Inside are stalactites and gold-bearing granite formations. Falls are 600 feet inside the mine.

May-October.

WHERE TO STAY

RECOMMENDED
RAPID CITY

ABEND HAUS COTTAGES & AUDRIE'S BED & BREAKFAST
23029 Thunderhead Falls Road, Rapid City, 605-342-7788;www.audriesbb.com

This bed and breakfast's pine-log lodges and cottages sit on 7 forested acres in the Black Hills, about an hour east of the Badlands. Both the cottages and the bed and breakfast itself have great mountain views, and Rapid Creek runs through the property (fishing poles are provided). Crickets and the gurgling brook are the only noise you'll hear from your private patio or hot tub at night, given the no-kids policy.

8 cottages, 2 suites. No children allowed. Complimentary breakfast. $61-150

HOTEL ALEX JOHNSON
523 Sixth St., Rapid City, 605-342-1210, 800-888-2539; www.alexjohnson.com

Two mounted bison heads keep watch over the large lobby in the Alex Johnson, which recently completed a multi-million dollar renovation. Named for the vice

WHAT IS THE MOST HISTORIC HOTEL?

Construction on the **Hotel Alex Johnson** started the day before work started to build Mount Rushmore. Listed on the National Register of Historic Places, the 1928 hotel has played host to a number of presidents and celebrities over the years.

president of the Chicago and Northwestern Railroad who built this hotel in the 1920s as a "showplace of the West," this downtown hotel displays original Native American artwork and old-fashioned photos of the many celebrities—including presidents—who have stayed here. Everything has been restored to resemble how the hotel looked when it was constructed, right down to solid maple furniture in the guest rooms. Guests will find pillow-top beds, plush robes, and large TVs in the guest rooms. There's a newly added coffee shop, salon and spa as well.

143 rooms. Restaurant, bar. Business center. Fitness center. Pets accepted. $61-150

WHERE TO EAT

DEADWOOD

★★★JAKE'S ATOP THE MIDNIGHT STAR

677 Main St., Deadwood, 605-578-1555, 800-999-6482; www.themidnightstar.com

Located on the top floor of the Midnight Star Casino, this elegant dining room serves American favorites. Piano entertainment is provided five nights a week.

American. Dinner. Reservations recommended. Children's menu. Bar. $16-35

ALSO RECOMMENDED
INTERIOR

CEDAR PASS LODGE RESTAURANT

20681 South Dakota Highway 240, Interior, 605-433-5460; www.cedarpasslodge.com

This restaurant right inside the park serves up burgers, sandwiches and steaks but if you're looking to sample a local favorite, bypass those standards and order the Sioux Indian tacos, made with seasoned buffalo.

American. Breakfast, lunch, dinner. Mid-May to early October. $15 and under

RAPID CITY

FIREHOUSE BREWING CO.

610 Main St., Rapid City, 605-348-1915; www.firehousebrewing.com

Giant vats visible behind the bar are brew ales right onsite at this brewpub. Housed in Rapid City's historic first firehouse, the unique setting is the perfect place to sip beer and enjoy the Midwest-meets-English pub grub menu, including a local favorite—the buffalo burger.

American. Lunch, dinner. Outdoor seating. Children's menu. Bar. $16-35

FLYING T CHUCKWAGON SUPPER & SHOW

8971 S. Highway 16, Rapid City, 605-342-1905, 888-256-1905; www.flyingt.com

Buffalo, beef, homemade biscuits with honey and other Western-style meals are served on tin plates at this lively restaurant. After dinner, served at 6:30 p.m., the Flying T Wranglers entertain audiences with old-time favorites ranging from cowboy ballads to country Western and bluegrass music.

American. Dinner. Closed mid-September to mid-May. Reservations recommended. Children's menu. $15 and under

WALL

WALL DRUG STORE

510 Main St., Wall, 605-279-2175; www.walldrug.com

Ted and Dorothy Hustead bought the Wall Drug pharmacy in 1931 during the Great Depression. Business was lukewarm for five years, until Ted put up signs around town advertising free ice water. It worked—and business boomed. Now in the hands of a third Hustead generation, Wall Drug is a sprawling tourist outpost that attracts nearly 20,000 visitors on hot summer days, pouring some 5,000 glasses of ice cold water in the process. Today the Hustead's empire includes not just a drugstore, but a 500-seat restaurant, where hungry campers come for classic hot beef sandwiches, buffalo burgers and homemade doughnuts. The coolest part: Coffee still costs just 5 cents!

American. Breakfast, lunch, dinner. Children's menu. $15 and under

---

WHAT IS THE MOST UNUSUAL DINING EXPERIENCE?

Dinner and a show sounds like a common date night, but the **Flying T Chuckwagon Supper & Show** gives it a Great Plains twist. Have an authentic Western meal, with buffalo and homemade biscuits, and then take in a live country music show.

WELCOME TO WYOMING

FROM THE HIGH WESTERN PLATEAUS OF THE GREAT

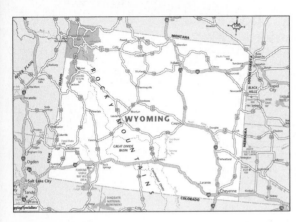

Plains, Wyoming stretches across the Continental Divide and into the Rocky Mountains. This is a land of scenic beauty and geographic diversity; mountain ranges, grasslands and desert can all be found within the state's borders.

The first Europeans to explore this region were French; brothers Louis and Francois Verendrye trapped here in 1743. The first American to enter what is now Yellowstone National Park was John Colter, a member of the Lewis and Clark expedition, during the winter of 1807 to 1808. The 1820s saw a number of trappers and fur traders become established in the area. The territory became the site of important stops along the pioneer trails to the West Coast in the 1840s through the 1860s.

Trails across Wyoming allowed pioneers to cross the rugged spine of the Rocky Mountains on an easy grade, following grass and water over the Continental Divide. Of the approximately 350,000 individuals who made their way along the various westward trails, some 21,000 died en route, claimed by disease, accidents and mountain snow. After 1847, thousands of Mormons came along the Mormon Trail to join Brigham Young's settlement at Salt Lake. The situation improved dramatically for the westward bound when the Union Pacific Railroad pushed across Wyoming during 1867-1869. The "iron horse" made the journey considerably safer and easier, not to mention faster. Permanent settlement of the West then began in earnest.

The hard existence wrought from a sometimes inhospitable land bred a tough, practical people who recognized merit when they saw it. While still a territory, Wyoming in 1869 became the first area in the United States to grant women the right to vote. Subsequently, Wyomingites were the first in the nation to appoint a woman justice of the peace; the first to select women jurors; and the first to elect a woman, Nellie Tayloe Ross, governor in 1924. This reputation has earned Wyoming the nickname "the Equality State."

BEST ATTRACTIONS

WYOMING'S BEST ATTRACTIONS

GRAND TETON NATIONAL PARK
The scenery is breathtaking at this open-year-round national park, where you'll see canyons, craggy peaks and alpine lakes.

HOT SPRINGS STATE PARK
After Yellowstone National Park, this is the second-most-popular tourist attraction in the state. People come out to soak in the mineral-rich hot springs that are supposed to have therapeutic power.

YELLOWSTONE NATIONAL PARK
Yellowstone is the world's oldest national park, and its beauty remains a sight to behold. See vast wildlife, a waterfall twice as tall as Niagara Falls and that famous geyser, Old Faithful.

The civic-mindedness of its citizens spread beyond the political arena with equal vigor. Wyoming introduced the nation's first county library system and instituted a public education system that today ranks among the finest in the country.

Cattle and sheep outnumber people by more than five to one in Wyoming, which is the least-populated state in the country. It is, therefore, easy to see how the cowboy has become such a prominent symbol here. The bucking horse insignia has appeared on Wyoming license plates since 1936. It also appears in various versions on road signs, storefronts and newspapers.

Visitors come for the numerous national parks, forests and monuments. But Wyoming offers a wide range of attractions, from abundant camping to rustic guest ranching, all set among some of the finest natural beauty to be found in the nation.

The country's first national park (Yellowstone), first national monument (Devils Tower) and first national forest (Shoshone) are all in Wyoming.

GRAND TETON NATIONAL PARK AREA

Two of the main towns in the Grand Teton National Park Area are ones that are commonly confused. Jackson, uninhibitedly western but increasingly upscale (former vice president Dick Cheney has a residence here among other notables), is the key town for the mountain-rimmed, 600-square-mile valley of Jackson Hole, which is surrounded by mountain scenery, dude ranches, national parks, big game and other vacation attractions.

Located in the Grand Teton National Park, in Jackson Hole valley, Moose is a neighbor to the resort area of Jackson Hole. Easily Wyoming's highest-profile ski resort, Jackson Hole Mountain Resort, located in Teton Village, is set on the eastern flank of the Teton Range, south of Grand Teton National Park and northwest of Jackson itself. The booming base village buzzes with activity, thanks to a number of charming hotels and time-share complexes, as well as restaurants, stores and a ski school. While not as well known for warm-weather recreation, the resort also is a good base for hiking, golf and horseback riding.

WHAT TO SEE

JACKSON
AERIAL TRAMWAY
Jackson, 307-733-2292; www.tram-formation.com
The tram makes a 2½-mile ride to top of Rendezvous Mountain for spectacular views.
Late May-early October.

BRIDGER-TETON NATIONAL FOREST
Jackson, 307-739-5500; www.fs.fed.us
With more than 3.3 million acres, the forest surrounds the town of Jackson. Bridger-Teton was the site of one of the largest earth slides in U.S. history, the Gros Ventre Slide in 1925, which dammed the Gros Ventre River (to a height of 225 feet and a width of nearly a half mile), forming Slide Lake, which is approximately three miles long. There are scenic drives along the Hoback River Canyon, the Snake River Canyon and in Star Valley. Unspoiled backcountry includes parts of Gros Ventre, Teton and Wind River ranges along the Continental Divide and the Wyoming Range. Teton Wilderness (557,311 acres) and Gros Wilderness (247,000 acres) are accessible on foot or horseback. There are also places for swimming, fishing, rafting, hiking, mountain biking, winter sports and camping. Also in the forest is Bridger Wilderness.

NATIONAL MUSEUM OF WILDLIFE ART
2820 Rungius Road, Jackson, 307-733-5771, 800-313-9553; www.wildlifeart.org
Nearly blending into the hillside across from the National Elk Refuge, this organic-looking structure (made of red sandstone from Arizona) houses an impressive collection of wildlife art: nearly 4,000 works dating from 2000 B.C., the 21st century and just about every artistic era in between. The museum is the largest arts facility committed to the theme of wildlife and includes galleries dedicated to the American bison and legendary wildlife impressionist Carl Rungius.

HIGHLIGHT

WHAT ARE THE BEST THINGS TO SEE IN CENTRAL WYOMING?

Before oil was discovered, Casper was a railroad terminus in the cattle-rich Wyoming hinterlands, where Native Americans and migrants on the Oregon Trail had passed before. Casper was known as an oil town after the first strike in 1890 in the Salt Creek Field, site of the Teapot Dome naval oil reserve that caused a top-level government scandal in the 1920s. The world's largest mineral hot spring is at Thermopolis, which lies in a beautiful section of Big Horn Basin where canyons, tunnels and buttes abound. The town is surrounded by rich irrigated farm and grazing land.

FORT CASPAR MUSEUM AND HISTORIC SITE

4001 Fort Caspar Road, Casper, 307-235-8462; www.fortcasparwyoming.com

A U.S. Army post in the 1860s, Fort Caspar served as a base for soldiers who first sought to protect pioneers, telegraph linemen and mail carriers and later fought Lakota warriors in a series of increasingly violent battles. Abandoned in 1867 after the railroad became the focal point of cross-country travel, Fort Caspar now features a number of replica buildings built in 1936 to depict the fort as it was in 1865. Also onsite is a museum stocked with artifacts of regional historic importance.

May and September, Monday-Sunday 8 a.m.-5 p.m.; June-August, Monday-Sunday 8 a.m.-7 p.m.; October-April, Tuesday-Saturday 8 a.m.-5 p.m.

NATIONAL HISTORIC TRAILS INTERPRETIVE CENTER

1501 N. Poplar St., Casper, 307-261-7700; www.wy.blm.gov

Casper sits on numerous historic trails, including the Oregon, California, Mormon, Pioneer and Pony Express trails, all prime westerly routes of the mid-19th century. To commemorate the region's rich trail legacy, the Bureau of Land Management opened the National Historic Trails Interpretive Center in 2002, with exhibits covering everything from packing for a cross-country journey in a covered wagon to negotiating such a wagon across a raging river. The historic trail route is now marked and runs directly through the center's property.

April-late October, daily 8 a.m.-7 p.m.; November-late March, Tuesday-Saturday 9 a.m.-4:30 p.m.

HOT SPRINGS STATE PARK

538 N. Park St., Thermopolis, 307-864-2176; wyoparks.state.wy.us

The second-most-visited tourist attraction in Wyoming after Yellowstone National Park, Hot Springs State Park in Thermopolis is the result of one of the largest mineral hot springs in the world. It's free to soak in the bathhouse, where the water is maintained at a toasty 104 degrees. The water is supposed to have therapeutic properties.

Admission: free. Bathhouse: Monday-Saturday 8 a.m.-5:30 p.m., Sunday noon-5:30 p.m.

HIGHLIGHTS

WHAT ARE THE BEST OUTDOOR ACTIVITIES IN THE GRAND TETON NATIONAL PARK AREA?

HOP ON THE AERIAL TRAMWAY

Take the tram to the top of Rendezvous Mountain for breathtaking views. There are trailheads at the peak, in case you prefer to get some fresh air and hike back down.

FLOAT DOWN THE RIVER

Admire the park's gorgeous scenery aboard a raft. Several companies offer five- and 10-mile trips at sunrise, in the evening and at dinnertime—with supper included.

RIDE A HORSE

Saddle up and explore Grand Teton National Park on horseback. A number of companies will outfit you with an equine and show you around the park.

Admission: adults $12, seniors $10, children 5-18 $6, children 4 and under free. Monday-Saturday 9 a.m.-5 p.m., Sunday 11 a.m.-5 p.m.

SOLITUDE FLOAT TRIPS
110 E. Karns Ave., Jackson, 307-733-2871, 888-704-2800; www.grand-teton-scenic-floats.com
Take a five- or 10-mile scenic trip on a raft down the river within Grand Teton National Park. Reservations are suggested.

TETON MOUNTAIN BIKE TOURS
Jackson, 307-733-0712, 800-733-0788; www.tetonmtbike.com
This company offers guided mountain bike tours for all ability levels. Mountain bikes, helmets, transportation and local guides are provided; day, multiday and customized group tours are available.

TRIANGLE X FLOAT TRIPS
Two Triangle X Ranch Road, Moose, on the Snake River in Grand Teton National Park, 307-733-2183; www.trianglex.com
Trips include 10-mile floats, sunrise and evening wildlife floats and cookout supper floats. Most trips originate at Triangle X Ranch.
May-October.

JACKSON HOLE
NATIONAL ELK REFUGE
Jackson Hole, 307-733-9212; www.fws.gov

The refuge is 25,000 acres dedicated to elk, and more than 1,000 of these graceful animals spend their winters here. Throughout the year, more than 47 mammals and 147 bird species make the park their home.

MOOSE
GRAND TETON NATIONAL PARK
Moose, 307-739-3300; www.nps.gov

These rugged, block-faulted mountains began to rise about 9 million years ago, making them some of the youngest on the continent. Geologic and glacial forces combined to buckle and sculpt the landscape into a dramatic setting of canyons, cirques and craggy peaks, which cast their reflections across numerous clear alpine lakes. The Snake River winds gracefully through Jackson Hole. French-Canadian trappers in the region thought the peaks resembled breasts and applied the French word teton to them. The park is open year-round (limited in winter), with food and lodging available in the park from mid-May through September and in Jackson. There are three visitor centers with interpretive displays: Moose Visitor Center (daily), Colter Bay Visitor Center & Indian Arts Museum (mid-May-late September, daily), and Jenny Lake Visitor Center (June-Labor Day). Ranger-led hikes are available (mid-June-mid-September, daily; inquire for schedule), and self-guided trails are marked. A 24-hour recorded message gives information about weather: 307-739-3611.

MORAN
HORSEBACK RIDING
If you are looking to tackle the Grand Tetons the old-fashioned way, by horse, you have several options for saddling up. Corrals at Jackson Lake Lodge and Colter Bay have horses accustomed to rocky trails; and pack trips can be easily arranged. Several independent stables offer commercial trips at various lengths and levels: Flagg Ranch Resort (*800-443-3211; www.flaggranch.com*), Grand Teton Lodge Company (*307-543-2811; www.gtlc.com*), Gros Ventre River Ranch (*307-733-4138; www.grosventreriverranch.com*), Triangle X Ranch (*307-733-2183; www.trianglex.com*) and Signal Mountain Lodge (*307-543-2831; www.signalmtnlodge.com*).

WHERE TO STAY

JACKSON
★★★JACKSON LAKE LODGE
North Highways 89 and 1191, Moran, 307-543-3100, 800-628-9988; www.gtlc.com

This full-service resort in Grand Teton National Park offers a view across Jackson Lake and of Mount Moran and the Grand Tetons. The grand lobby has two fireplaces and a 60-foot picture window. Lodge rooms offers views of the forest or mountains.

385 rooms. Closed early October-mid-May. Restaurant, bar. Pool. $161-250

HIGHLIGHT

CHEYENNE FRONTIER DAYS

The rodeo equivalent of the Super Bowl, Cheyenne Frontier Days is not just a sporting event; it's also a rollicking street party, a family-friendly country fair and an annual celebration of the Wyoming capitol city's cowboy heritage.

Frontier Days began in 1897, and its second year saw a performance by Buffalo Bill Cody's Wild West Show. In 1903, President Teddy Roosevelt paid a visit, putting it on the national stage. Today, it attracts about 400,000 people every year, especially impressive in relation to Cheyenne's population of 50,000.

Held over the course of 10 days in late July and early August, Frontier Days features nine rodeos, all of them sanctioned by the Professional Rodeo Cowboys Association. Top cowboys compete in staple events such as bull riding, calf roping, barrel racing and steer wrestling at the CFD Rodeo Arena.

The Frontier Days' pancake breakfasts, held three times over the course of the event, are also legendary. About 30,000 attendees gobble up 100,000 free flapjacks, which are poured on the griddle and flipped by the local Kiwanis club. Chuck wagon cook-offs, also free, are another culinary highlight. Rodeo tickets are available at www.cfdrodeo.com.

★★★RUSTY PARROT LODGE
175 N. Jackson St., Jackson, 307-733-2000, 888-739-1749; www.rustyparrot.com

Just minutes from Grand Teton and Yellowstone national parks and Jackson Hole, the lodge is also just three blocks from Town Square. Rustic rooms are filled with mountain-style touches: antler chandeliers, handmade furniture and goose-down comforters. A hearty breakfast is included in the rates.

31 rooms. Restaurant, bar. Complimentary breakfast. Spa. $251-350

★★★SPRING CREEK RANCH
1800 Spirit Dance Road, Jackson, 307-733-8833, 800-443-6139; www.springcreekranch.com

Offering a view of the Teton Mountain Range and surrounded by two national parks and tons of wildlife, this resort features great accommodations and ways to prepare you for or unwind after a day of hiking or skiing, including yoga classes and personal training at the spa. After you've stretched, relax in front of the wood-burning fireplace in your room.

122 rooms. Restaurant, bar. Fitness center. Pool. Spa. Tennis. $251-350

★★★THE WORT HOTEL
50 N. Glenwood St., Jackson, 307-733-2190, 800-322-2727; www.worthotel.com

Reflecting the history and culture of Jackson Hole, this popular country inn is decorated with fabrics and furnishings of the Old West.

59 rooms. Restaurant, bar. Fitness center. $251-350

JACKSON HOLE

★★★★AMANGANI

1535 N.E. Butte Road, Jackson Hole, 307-734-7333, 877-734-7333; www.amanresorts.com

Perched on the edge of a butte outside one of the country's most popular ski resorts, this American outpost of the acclaimed Aman resort group is a welcoming blend of Eastern minimalism and Western style. With only 40 rooms, the atmosphere is one of relaxation and renewal. Rooms are streamlined and contemporary with fireplaces and deep soaking tubs, while the resort's public spaces take advantage of the impressive mountain views. The culinary staff at The Grill keeps the focus on fresh organic ingredients, and the staff at the onsite health center accommodates every whim, from private yoga sessions to soothing spa treatments.

40 rooms. Restaurant, bar. Fitness center. Pool. Spa. $351 and up

MOOSE

★★★JENNY LAKE LODGE

Inner Loop Road, Moose, 307-733-4647, 800-628-9988; www.gtlc.com

Nestled at the base of the Tetons in Grand Teton National Park, this rustic, all-inclusive retreat is actually a cluster of Western-style cabins outfitted with down comforters and handmade quilts. The pine-shaded property welcomes visitors from June through October for elegantly rustic accommodations and back-to-nature recreation, including the Jackson Hole Golf & Tennis Club, numerous hiking trails and three lakes.

37 rooms. Closed early October-late May. Restaurant. Complimentary breakfast. $351 and up

TETON VILLAGE

★★★★★FOUR SEASONS RESORT JACKSON HOLE

7680 Granite Loop Road, Teton Village, 307-732-5000; www.fourseasons.com

Laidback Western style is paired with big-city attention to detail in this full-service resort set amid the natural beauty of the Teton Mountains. Rooms are warm and welcoming, with gas fireplaces and décor that hints at the area's Native American heritage. Besides ski in/ski out access to the area's famous trails, the resort boasts a ski concierge, who handles lift tickets, advises skiers on trails and assists with equipment selections. Guests can reward themselves after a day of skiing or fly-fishing with a meal at the cozy Westbank Grill, where local specialties such as mustard- and tarragon-crusted Colorado lamb fill the menu. During the winter months, guests can enjoy complimentary hot chocolate and S'mores while soaking in the outdoor hot tubs (heated robes are available to ward off the cold when you're ready to head back to your room). In summer, chilled peppermint-scented face cloths are given out at the pool.

124 rooms. Restaurant, bar. Fitness center. Pool. Spa. Pets accepted. Ski in/ski out. $351 and up

★★★SNAKE RIVER LODGE & SPA

7710 Granite Loop Road, Teton Village, 307-732-6000; www.snakeriverlodge.rockresorts.com

From the 7,000-square-foot spa to the beautiful indoor/outdoor pool with waterfalls, warmed walkways and a hot tub inside a steamy cave, to the five-spiced duck breast in the restaurant, Gamefish, this Teton Village resort delivers upscale relaxation. Work out in the state-of-the-art gym and book the

Sportsman's Relief massage at the spa for when you ski back in after a long day on the slopes.

93 rooms. Restaurant, bar. Complimentary breakfast. Business center. Fitness center. Pool. Spa. $251-350

★★★TETON MOUNTAIN LODGE
3385 Cody Lane, Teton Village, 307-734-7111, 800-631-6271; www.tetonlodge.com

Just steps away from Grand Teton National Park, this lodge spoils skiers with in-room boot dryers and overnight ski storage and tuning. After hitting the slopes, indulge with an aromatherapy or hot-stone massage at Solitude Spa or warm up near the fireplace over a plate of potato and goat cheese ravioli at Cascade Grill House & Spirits.

129 rooms. Restaurant, bar. Fitness center. Pool. Spa. $251-350

RECOMMENDED

DUBOIS
BROOKS LAKE LODGE
458 Brooks Lake Road, Dubois, 307-455-2121; www.brookslake.com

Built as an inn for Yellowstone travelers in 1922, this historic property offers guests accommodations in the spirit of the early west in beautiful surroundings.

14 rooms. Closed mid-April-mid-June and mid-September-early October. Restaurant, bar. Complimentary breakfast. Fitness center. Spa. $251-350

MOOSE
LOST CREEK RANCH
Old Ranch Road, Moose, 307-733-3435; www.lostcreek.com

This guest ranch occupies a spectacular location, bordered by Grand Teton National Park and Bridger-Teton National Forest and just 20 miles south of Jackson. One- and two-bedroom log cabins provide comfortable accommodations, and recreational activities include horseback riding, tennis, hiking, auto tours to nearby Yellowstone National Park and float trips down the Snake River. The spa presents a more sybaritic experience with mineral wraps, sea salt body scrubs and Dead Sea Fango mud massages. Enjoy family-style meals and traditional cookouts, and in the evenings revisit the Old West with swing dancing, cowboy poetry and serenades.

30 rooms. Closed October-late May. Restaurant, bar. Complimentary breakfast. Fitness center. Pool. Spa. Tennis. $351 and up

WHERE TO EAT

JACKSON

★★★BLUE LION

160 N. Millward St., Jackson, 307-733-3912;
www.bluelionrestaurant.com

Housed in a charming old home, this restaurant offers creative preparations of many dishes. Try the jumbo prawns simmered with tomatoes, snow peas, and cilantro in a green curry sauce or the Alaskan halibut coated with buttermilk, shredded potatoes and Asiago cheese, and doused with a roasted red pepper sauce.

American. Dinner. Reservations recommended. Outdoor seating. Children's menu. Bar. $36-85

★★★CADILLAC GRILLE

55 N. Cache Drive, Jackson, 307-733-3279;
www.cadillac-grille.com

Aglow with neon lights, this energetic restaurant on the town square's west side has been open since 1983. Creative dishes, like elk meatloaf with a balsamic glaze, are served in a fun, casual atmosphere.

American. Lunch, dinner. Closed November. Reservations recommended. Outdoor seating. Bar. $36-85

★★★SNAKE RIVER GRILL

84 E. Broadway, Jackson, 307-733-0557;
www.snakerivergrill.com

A cozy stone fireplace is set in the center of this rustic restaurant, where you'll find novel dishes like sake-steamed black cod and wood-fired steak tartar pizza.

American. Dinner. Closed April and November. Reservations recommended. Outdoor seating. Bar. $36-85

MOOSE

★★★JENNY LAKE LODGE DINING ROOM

Inner Loop Road, Moose, 307-733-4647; www.gtlc.com

Located in a restored log cabin, Jenny Lake Lodge Dining Room offers à la carte lunch and five-course prix fixe dinners along with an extensive wine list. Expect dishes like seared duck breast with orange-mint spaetzle, roasted figs and port fig reduction.

American. Breakfast, dinner. Closed early October-May. Jacket required. Reservations recommended. $86 and up

---

WHAT ARE THE BEST OVERALL RESTAURANTS?

The Alpenrose in the Alpenhof Lodge:
This Teton Village restaurant is hailed as the best in the area. You'll taste why when you dine on hearty dishes like caribou steak Diane and a tasty bananas Foster.

Jenny Lake Lodge Dining Room:
The log cabin restaurant offers upscale fare with a Western flair in its five-course prix fixe dinners, like the buffalo osso buco with parsnip puree and root veggies.

TETON VILLAGE
★★★THE ALPENROSE IN THE ALPENHOF LODGE
The Alpenhof Lodge, 3255 W. Village Drive, Teton Village,
307-733-3242, 800-732-3244; www.alpenhoflodge.com

At the base of the Jackson Hole ski area, the restaurant at this Bavarian-style lodge is the best-regarded dining room in the area. Here the emphasis is on hearty dishes of Western-influenced continental cuisine. Variations on classic themes include the tableside preparation of caribou steak Diane and a great bananas Foster. The property's upstairs bistro offers more casual fare.
American. Dinner. Closed Sunday-Monday, November. Bar. $86 and up

SPA

TETON VILLAGE
★★★★THE SPA AT FOUR SEASONS RESORT JACKSON HOLE
Four Seasons Resort Jackson Hole, 7680 Granite Loop Road, Teton Village, 307-732-5200;
www.fourseasons.com

The Four Seasons Resort Jackson Hole marries the rugged style of the West with international elegance, service and style. Therapies, like the mountain clay body wrap, reflect the resort's alpine location and draw from local ingredients. The massage menu offers everything from aromatherapy and deep-tissue treatments to moonlight massages and native stone therapies. Hair and nail care is available in the adjacent salon, while the fitness center and pool complete the well-rounded experience here.

YELLOWSTONE NATIONAL PARK AREA

Yellowstone, the world's first national park, 3,000 square miles of rambling wilderness open to exploration since 1872, welcomes visitors from all over the globe through its five entrances in three states (Wyoming, Montana and Idaho) onto 370 miles of scenic public roads. You'll travel past impressive granite peaks and through lodgepole pine forests that open onto meadows dotted with wildflowers and elk. Beyond the beautiful panorama, Yellowstone boasts a marvelous list of sights and attractions: a big freshwater lake that ranks as the largest in North America at high elevation (7,733 feet); a waterfall almost twice as high as Niagara; a dramatic, 1,200-foot-deep river canyon; and the world's most famous geyser, Old Faithful.

Nearby Cody may not have all of those credentials, but it has its own claim to fame. Old West showman Buffalo Bill Cody founded the town that bears his name. You'll see his mark all over the town.

WHAT TO SEE

CODY
BUFFALO BILL DAM AND VISITOR CENTER
4808 North Fork Highway, east end of reservoir, Cody, 307-527-6076; www.bbdvc.org

Originally called the Shoshone Dam, the 350-foot dam's name was changed in 1946 to honor Buffalo Bill, who helped raise money for its construction. The

HIGHLIGHT

WHAT ARE THE TOP THINGS TO DO IN YELLOW-STONE NATIONAL PARK?

VISIT BUFFALO BILL'S CODY
Buffalo Bill Cody founded this town, gave it his name, and devoted time and money to its development. See his signature all over Cody's attractions.

EXPLORE YELLOWSTONE NATIONAL PARK
The world's first national park is arguably its best. Go to see the world-famous Old Faithful geyser, cascading falls and a number of wildlife.

visitor center has a natural history museum, dam overlook and gift shop.
May and September, Monday-Saturday 8 a.m.-6 p.m., Sunday 10 a.m.-6 p.m.; June-August, Monday-Friday 8 a.m.-8 p.m., Saturday 8 a.m.-6 p.m., Sunday 10 a.m.-6 p.m.; closed, October-April.

BUFFALO BILL MUSEUM
720 Sheridan Ave., Cody, 307-857-4771; www.bbhc.org
Browse personal and historical memorabilia of the great showman and scout, including guns, saddles, clothing, trophies, gifts and posters. Buffalo Bill Cody founded this town, gave it his name, and devoted time and money to its development. He built a hotel and named it after his daughter Irma, arranged for a railroad spur from Montana and, with the help of his friend Theodore Roosevelt, had what was then the world's tallest dam constructed just west of town.

BUFFALO BILL DAM AND VISITOR CENTER
4808 North Fork Highway, east end of reservoir, Cody, 307-527-6076; www.bbdvc.org
Originally called the Shoshone Dam, the 350-foot dam's name was changed in 1946 to honor Buffalo Bill, who helped raise money for its construction. The visitor center has a natural history museum, dam overlook and gift shop.
May and September, Monday-Saturday 8 a.m.-6 p.m., Sunday 10 a.m.-6 p.m.; June-August, Monday-Friday 8 a.m.-8 p.m., Saturday 8 a.m.-6 p.m., Sunday 10 a.m.-6 p.m.; closed, October-April.

SHOSHONE NATIONAL FOREST
808 Meadow Lane, Cody, 307-527-6241; www.fs.fed.us
This nearly 2.5 million-acre area is one of the largest in the national forest system. It includes a magnificent approach route (Buffalo Bill Cody's Scenic Byway) to the east gate of Yellowstone National Park along the north fork of the Shoshone River. The Fitzpatrick, Popo Agie, North Absaroka, Washakie and a portion of the Absaroka-Beartooth wilderness areas all lie within its

boundaries. It includes outstanding lakes, streams, big-game herds, mountains and some of the largest glaciers in the continental United States.

WHITNEY GALLERY OF WESTERN ART

Buffalo Bill Historical Center, 720 Sheridan Ave., Cody, 307-857-4771; www.bbhc.org

A major collection and comprehensive display of Western art by artists from the early 1800s through today, the gallery mostly features painting and sculpture. *Admission: adults $15, seniors and students $13, children 6-17 $10, children 5 and under free. Hours vary per month; check website for schedule.*

YELLOWSTONE NATIONAL PARK

FISHING

Yellowstone National Park

The fishing season in Yellowstone runs from Saturday of Memorial Day weekend through the first Sunday in November. Though no state license is required, fishing in Yellowstone National Park requires a permit; anglers 16 years and older must have a $15 three-day permit, a $20 seven-day permit or a $35 season permit. Rowboats, powerboats and tackle may be rented at Bridge Bay Marina. Only barbless hooks are permitted. The Firehole River, which starts south of Old Faithful and flows northward into the Madison River, is world-famous for its abundance of healthy brown, brook and rainbow trout. The Madison River offers blue-ribbon fly fishing for its healthy stocks of mountain whitefish and brown and rainbow trout.

OLD FAITHFUL

West entrance, Yellowstone National Park

The most popular geyser in the world, Old Faithful has not missed a performance in the more than 100 years since eruptions were first recorded. Eruptions occur on average every 70 to 90 minutes. It takes 10 to 20 seconds for the eruption to reach its maximum height. Make sure the camera is ready; the eruption starts to recede in less than a minute.

UPPER AND LOWER FALLS OF YELLOWSTONE

Yellowstone National Park

The Upper Falls, a 109-foot drop, is upstream from the spectacular Lower Falls. The Lower Falls, which have a 308-foot drop, is more than twice the height of Niagara Falls. You can see the Lower Falls from Lookout Point, Red Rock Point, Artist Point, Brink of the Lower Falls Trail, and from various places along the South Rim Trail.

YELLOWSTONE LAKE

Near the south and east entrances, Yellowstone National Park

Yellowstone Lake is the largest natural freshwater lake at high elevation (about 7,000 feet) in the United States. Early explorers thought that the shape of the lake resembled a hand, with the westernmost bay forming its thumb. A variety of rare species of waterfowl make their home along its 110 miles of shoreline.

HIGHLIGHT

TOURING YELLOWSTONE

The Grand Loop Road, a main access way within the park, winds approximately 140 miles past many major points of interest. Five miles south of the North Entrance is Mammoth Hot Springs, the park headquarters and museum (open year-round). The visitor center provides a general park history. Naturalist-guided walks are conducted on boardwalks over the terraces (summer).

The Norris Geyser Basin is 21 miles south of Mammoth Hot Springs. The hottest thermal basin in the world provides a multitude of displays; springs, geysers, mud pots and steam vents hiss, bubble and erupt in a showcase of thermal forces. The visitor center has self-explanatory exhibits and dioramas and is open daily June-Labor Day. A self-guided trail (2½ miles) offers views of the Porcelain and Back basins from boardwalks. The Museum of the National Park Ranger is also nearby.

At Madison, 14 miles southwest of Norris, West Entrance Road (Highway 20-91 outside the park) joins Grand Loop Road. Heading south of Madison, it is a 16-mile trip to Old Faithful. Along the route are four thermal spring areas; numerous geysers, mud pots and pools provide a prologue to the spectacle ahead. Old Faithful has not missed a performance in the more than 100 years since eruptions were first recorded. Eruptions occur on average every 75 minutes. A nearby visitor center provides information, exhibits and a film.

From Old Faithful, it is 17 miles east to West Thumb. Yellowstone Lake, the highest natural freshwater lake in the United States, is here. Early explorers thought that the shape of the lake resembled a hand, with the westernmost bay forming its thumb. A variety of rare species of waterfowl make their home along its 110 miles of shoreline. The 22-mile road from the South Entrance on the John D. Rockefeller, Jr. Memorial Parkway (Highway 29-287 outside the park) meets the Grand Loop Road here.

Northeast of West Thumb, about 19 miles up the western shore of Yellowstone Lake, the road leads to Lake Village and then to Fishing Bridge. Although fishing is not permitted at Fishing Bridge (extending one mile downstream, to the north, and a quarter mile up-stream, to the south of Fishing Bridge), the numerous lakes and rivers in the park make Yellowstone an angler's paradise. At Fishing Bridge the road splits; 27 miles east is the East Entrance from Highway 14/16/20 and 16 miles north is Canyon Village. Canyon Village is near Upper Falls (a 109-foot drop) and the spectacular Lower Falls (a 308-foot drop). The colorful and awesome Grand Canyon of the Yellowstone River can be viewed from several points; there are self-guided trails along the rim and naturalist-led walks during summer. Groomed cross-country ski trails are open in winter. (Museum: Mid-May-late September, daily.)

Sixteen miles north of Canyon Village is Tower. Just south of Tower Junction is the 132-foot Tower Fall, which can best be observed from a platform at the end of the path leading from the parking lot. The Northeast Entrance on Highway 212 is 29 miles east of Tower; Mammoth Hot Springs is 18 miles west.

WHERE TO STAY

RECOMMENDED
CODY

ABSAROKA MOUNTAIN LODGE
1231 Northfork Highway, Cody, 307-587-3963; www.absarokamtlodge.com

Dating back to 1910, this historic family-friendly lodge is just 12 miles east of Yellowstone's entrance. The Absaroka warmly welcomes guests with espresso, cocktails, board games, nightly movies and home-cooked meals next to crackling fires before they retire to cozy rustic cabins on Gunbarrel Creek. Fishing, a variety of horseback riding options and other family activities are available.

18 cabins. Restaurant, bar. $61-150

HOLIDAY INN
1701 Sheridan Ave., Cody, 307-587-5555, 800-315-2621; www.blairhotels.com, www.holidayinn.com

About 50 miles from Yellowstone's east entrance, this Holiday Inn in downtown Cody offers comfortable accommodations and family-friendly amenities, including a heated outdoor pool, a gym and tickets to local events and attractions.

189 rooms. Restaurant, bar. Fitness center. Pool. $61-150

YELLOWSTONE NATIONAL PARK AREA

LAKE YELLOWSTONE HOTEL
Yellowstone National Park, 307-344-7311, 866-439-7375; www.travelyellowstone.com

This lodge dating back to 1891 on the shore of Yellowstone Lake is listed on the National Register of Historic Places and is the oldest hotel in the park. Refurbished to recapture the grand ambiance of the Roaring '20s, this elegant hotel offers a wide range of accommodations from deluxe suites to simple cabins. Couch potatoes will really rough it in this hotel; the rooms don't have TVs.

158 rooms. Closed mid-October to late May. Restaurant, bar. $151-250

OLD FAITHFUL INN
Yellowstone National Park, 307-344-7311, 866-439-7375; www.travelyellowstone.com

This national historic landmark was designed by architect Robert C. Reamer, who said its asymmetry was intended to reflect the chaos of nature. Built in 1904, the log and wooden shingle exterior conveys an apropos rustic ambiance. With its convenient location near Old Faithful, guests here have countless activities at their fingertips, except for TV viewing, since rooms don't have televisions.

327 rooms. Closed mid-October to early May. Restaurant, bar. $151-250

OLD FAITHFUL SNOW LODGE
Yellowstone National Park, 307-344-7311, 866-439-7375; www.travelyellowstone.com

This lodge is the newest of Yellowstone's hotels, completed in 1999, but was designed to fit harmoniously into its mountain environment and among the historic buildings it joined. A wildlife theme is carried throughout the décor in the inn's TV-less comfortable rooms and furnishings.

95 rooms. Closed mid-October to mid-December and mid-March to early May. Restaurant, bar. $151-250

WHERE TO EAT

RECOMMENDED
CODY

WYOMING'S RIB AND CHOP HOUSE

1367 Sheridan Ave, Cody, 307-527-7731;
www.ribandchophouse.com

Many claim this joint serves up the best baby-back ribs—anywhere. The filet mignon is also highly recommended. The menu isn't limited to satiating carnivore cravings, though. There are also many salads and seafood dishes to choose from, as well as an ample wine list.

American. Dinner. $16-35

YELLOWSTONE NATIONAL PARK

CANYON LODGE DINING ROOM

Grand Canyon of the Yellowstone, Yellowstone National Park

For casual dining at affordable prices, the Canyon Lodge eateries fit the bill. A cafeteria and deli provide visitors with quick meals when they're on the go. The full-service dining room offers both full and continental breakfast menus, a number of burgers and salads for lunch, and a menu ranging from a wild Alaska sockeye salmon burger to chicken-fried steak for dinner.

American. Breakfast, lunch, dinner. Closed mid-September-May. Children's menu. $16-35

GRANT VILLAGE DINING ROOM

Grant Village, southwestern shore of Yellowstone Lake, Yellowstone National Park, 866-439-7375;
www.travelyellowstone.com

Overlooking the lake, guests in this restaurant can enjoy a breakfast buffet, sandwiches and salads in the afternoon and a full dinner menu presenting such Western specialties as a farm-raised bison meatloaf with rosemary gravy, mashed red potatoes and sautéed spinach.

American. Breakfast, lunch, dinner. Closed October-late May. Reservations required. Children's menu. $16-35

LAKE YELLOWSTONE HOTEL DINING ROOM

Highway 89, Yellowstone National Park, 307-344-7311, 866-439-7375; www.travelyellowstone.com

The park's finest dining is presented in its oldest, most elegant hotel. Highlights on its upscale menu are such specialties as farm-raised bison, wild Alaskan salmon and Montana tenderloin, all to be

> ### WHAT IS THE BEST STEAK HOUSE?
>
> **Wyoming's Rib and Chop House** serves the best meat around. The filet mignon is a definite winner, but the locals proclaim that this place turns out the best baby-back ribs in the world.

enjoyed with views of lovely Yellowstone Lake.

American, seafood. Breakfast, lunch, dinner. Closed October-May. Reservations recommended. Children's menu. Bar. $16-35

OBSIDIAN DINING ROOM

Old Faithful Snow Lodge, Old Faithful, Yellowstone National Park, 866-439-7375; www.travelyellowstone.com

This homey dining room offers a full breakfast menu with such specialties as a vegan breakfast burrito and eggs Benedict with wild Alaska salmon. The lunch menu is varied with soups, salads and tasty sandwiches, like a honey mustard chicken sandwich served on a pretzel roll. Evening house specialties include Rocky Mountain farm-raised trout and a unique eggplant "mignon" served with fresh mozzarella, wild mushroom orzo and tomato fondue.

American. Breakfast, lunch, dinner. Closed mid-October-mid-December and March-May. $36-85

Numbers

4 Olives Wine Bar
  Manhattan, KS, **46**
45th Infantry Division
  Museum
  Oklahoma City, OK, **137**
1859 Marshal's Home and
  Jail Museum
  Independence, MO, **56**

A

Abend Haus Cottages & Aud-
  rie's Bed & Breakfast
  Rapid City, SD, **147**
Abilene & Smoky Valley Rail
  Road
  Abilene, KS, **41**
Absaroka Mountain Lodge
  Cody, WY, **164**
Adventureland Park
  Altoona, IA, **24**
Aerial Tramway
  Jackson, WY, **152**
Ak-Sar-Ben Aquarium
  Gretna, NE, **113**
Allen-Lambe House Museum
  and Study Center
  Wichita, KS, **46**
The Alpenrose in the
  Alpenhof Lodge
  Teton Village, WY, **160**
Amangani
  Jackson Hole, WY, **157**
Americinn Medora
  Medora, ND, **125**
Anaconda Visior Center
  Anaconda, MT, **104**
Andre's Tearoom
  Kansas City, MO, **91**
Andy Williams Moon River
  Theater
  Branson, MO, **76**
Anheuser-Busch Brewery
  St. Louis, MO, **60**
Aquaticus
  Oklahoma City, OK, **137**
Arabia Steamboat Museum
  Kansas City, MO, **83**
Arkansas River Historical
  Society Museum
  Catoosa, OK, **132**
Arnolds Park Amusement
  Park
  Arnolds Park, IA, **31**
Averill's Flathead Lake Lodge
  Bigfork, MT, **99**

B

Baldknobbers Jamboree
  Show
  Branson, MO, **76**

Bass Pro Shops Outdoor World Showroom and Fish and Wildlife Museum
Springfield, MO, **79**

Becky Thatcher House
Hannibal, MO, **54**

Bellevue State Park
Dubuque, IA, **17**

Bellini's Ristorante & Grill
Oklahoma City, OK, **142**

Bell's Amusement Park
Tulsa, OK, **132**

Billy's Restaurant
Lincoln, NE, **118**

Bingham-Waggoner Estate
Independence, MO, **56**

Blackfoot River Brewing Company
Helena, MT, **105**

Black Hills Petrified Forest
Rapid City, SD, **147**

Blanc Burgers + Bottles
Kansas City, MO, **93**

Blank Park Zoo
Des Moines, IA, **25**

Bleu Olive Mediterranean Grille & Bar
Branson, MO, **81**

Blue Lion
Jackson, WY, **159**

Bluestem
Kansas City, MO, **91**

Bodean Seafood
Tulsa, OK, **135**

Boston Avenue United Methodist Church
Tulsa, OK, **132**

Botanica, The Wichita Gardens
Wichita, KS, **47**

Branson Scenic Railway
Branson, MO, **76**

Bridger-Teton National Forest
Jackson, WY, **152**

Brooks Lake Lodge
Dubois, WY, **158**

Brown V. Board of Education National Historic Site
Topeka, KS, **36**

Buffalo Bill Cody Homestead
Princeton, IA, **13**

Buffalo Bill Dam and Visitor Center
Cody, WY, **160, 161**

Buffalo Bill Museum
Cody, WY, **161**

Buffalo Cave
Whitefish, MT, **103**

Butterfly House
Chesterfield, MO, **60**

C

Cadillac Grille
Jackson, WY, **159**
Café Kandahar
Whitefish, MT, **103**
Café Sebastienne at the Kemper Museum
Kansas City, MO, **93**
Candlestick Inn
Branson, MO, **82**
Cantina Laredo
Branson, MO, **82**
Canyon Lodge Dining Room
Yellowstone National Park, WY, **165**
Cardwell's at the Plaza
St. Louis, MO, **69**
The Castle Inn at Riverside
Wichita, KS, **49**
Cathedral Basilica of St. Louis
St. Louis, MO, **60**
Cathedral Square
Dubuque, IA, **17**
Cedar Crest Governor's Mansion
Topeka, KS, **36**
Cedar Falls Historical Society Victorian Home Museum
Cedar Falls, IA, **14**

Cedar Pass Lodge Restaurant
Interior, SD, **148**
Cedar Rapids Museum of Art
Cedar Rapids. IA, **14**
Centro
Des Moines, IA, **30**
The Chalkboard
Tulsa, OK, **136**
The Chase Park Plaza
St. Louis, MO, **66**
Chateau de Mores State Historic Site
Bismarck, ND, **120**
Chateau Grille
Branson, MO, **82**
Chateau on the Lake
Branson, MO, **79**
Chaz Restaurant
Kansas City, MO, **93**
Chester's Chophouse & Wine Bar
Wichita, KS, **50**
Christ Church Cathedral
St. Louis, MO, **61**
Christopher's
Des Moines, IA, **29**
City Market
Kansas City, MO, **94**
Civic Center Music Hall
Oklahoma City, OK, **137**
Clear Lake State Park
Clear Lake, IA, **16**

C. M. Russell Museum
    Complex and
    Original Log Cabin
    Studio
  Great Falls, MT, **104**
The Coach House
  Oklahoma City, OK, **142**
Cole County Historical
    Society Museum
  Jefferson City, MO, **73**
Combat Air Museum
  Topeka, KS, **36**
Comfort Inn
  Dickinson, ND, **123**
Copper Village Museum
    and Arts Center
  Anaconda, MT, **104**
Coralville Lake
  Iowa City, IA, **20**
Corbin Education Center
  Wichita, KS, **47**
The Cornhusker,
    A Marriott Hotel
  Lincoln, NE, **116**
Council Oak Shrine
  Council Grove, KS, **43**
Country Club Plaza
  Kansas City, MO, **83**, **94**
Courtyard Salina
  Salina, KS, **45**
Courtyard Wichita
    at Old Town
  Wichita, KS, **50**

The Cowboy Café
  Medora, ND, **126**
Coyote Roadhouse
  Bigfork, MT, **102**
Creek Council Oak Tree
  Tulsa, OK, **133**
Crossroads Arts District
  Kansas City, MO, **84**
Crown Center
  Kansas City, MO, **84**
Crowne Plaza
  Cedar Rapids, IA, **21**
  Tulsa, OK, **134**
Crowne Plaza Hotel
  Oklahoma City, OK, **141**
Crystal Lake Cave
  Dubuque, IA, **17**
Custer's Elm Shrine
  Council Grove, KS, **43**
Czeck Village
  Cedar Rapids, IA, **14**

D

David Traylor Zoo of Em-
    poria
  Emporia, KS, **43**
Days Inn-Grand Dakota
    Lodge
  Dickinson, ND, **125**
Della Voce
  Manhattan, KS, **46**

Des Moines Art Center
  Des Moines, IA, **25**
Des Moines Botanical Center
  Des Moines, IA, **26**
Des Moines Marriott
    Downtown
  Des Moines, IA, **28**
Dickerson Park Zoo
  Springfield, MO, **79**
Dickinson County
    Historical Museu
  Abilene, KS, **41**
Dinosaur Park
  Rapid City, SD, **147**
Discovery Center
  Springfield, MO, **79**
Discoveryland! Outdoor
    Theater
  Tulsa, OK, **133**
Dominic's Restaurant
  St. Louis, MO, **70**
Doubletree Hotel Springfield
  Springfield, MO, **80**
Dubuque Arboretum and
    Botanical Gardens
  Dubuque, IA, **17**
Dubuque County Court-
    house
  Dubuque, IA, **18**
Dubuque Museum of Art/
    Old County Jail
  Dubuque, IA, **19**

Durham Western Heritage
    Museum
  Omaha, NE, **114**
The Duttons
  Branson, MO, **76**

E

Eads Bridge
  St. Louis, MO, **61**
Eagle Point Park
  Dubuque, IA, **19**
Eisenhower Center
  Abilene, KS, **42**
The Eldridge Hotel
  Lawrence, KS, **38**
Elvis and the Superstars
    Tribute Show
  Branson, MO, **76**
Emporia Gazette Building
  Emporia, KS, **43**
The Eugene Field House
    and St. Louis Toy
    Museum
  St. Louis, MO, **61**
Executive Mansion
  Lincoln, NE, **111**
Extra Virgin
  Kansas City, MO, **94**

F

Fairfield Inn Manhattan
  Manhattan, KS, **44**

Fairfield Inn Wichita East
  Wichita, KS, **50**
Fairmont Hot Springs Resort
  Anaconda, MT, **106**
The Faithful Pilot Café
  Le Claire, IA, **23**
Family Museum of Arts
      & Science
  Bettendorf, IA, **14**
Fenelon Place Elevator
  Dubuque, IA, **19**
Field of Dreams Movie Site
  Dyersville, IA, **19**
Figge Art Museum
  Davenport, IA, **16**
Firehouse Brewing Co.
  Rapid City, SD, **148**
Fishing
  Yellowstone National Park,
    WY, **162**
Five Civilized Tribes
      Museum
  Muskogee, OK, **132**
Five Flags Theater
  Dubuque, IA, **19**
Flint Hills National Wildlife
      Refuge
  Hartfort, KS, **43**
Flying T Chuckwagon
      Supper & Show
  Rapid City, SD, **149**

Folsom Children's Zoo
  Lincoln, NE, **111**
Fort Abraham Lincoln State
      Park
  Mandan, ND, **122**
Fort Atkinson State Preserve
  Decorah, IA, **17**
Fort Buford State Historic
      Site
  Williston, ND, **122**
Fort Caspar Museum and
      Historic Site
  Casper, WY, **153**
Fort Gibson Historic Site
  Fort Gibson, OK, **132**
Fort Union Trading Post
      National Historic Site
  Williston, ND, **123**
Four Seasons Hotel St. Louis
  St. Louis, MO, **66**
Four Seasons Resort Jackson
      Hole
  Teton Village, WY, **157**
Frank Phillips Mansion
  Bartlesville, OK, **129**
Fred Maytag Park
  Newton, IA, **27**
Free State Brewing Company
  Lawrence, KS, **39**
French Café
  Omaha, NE, **117**

Frontier City
 Oklahoma City, OK, 137

G

Gage Park
 Topeka, KS, 36
Garden Exhibition Build-
  ing and Horticulture
  Gardens
 Oklahoma City, OK, 137
The Gardens at Malmaison
 St. Albans, MO, 70
Garment District Boutique
 Kansas City, MO, 94
Garth Woodside Mansion
  Bed and Breakfast
 Hannibal, MO, 57
Gates of the Mountains
 Helena, MT, 106
Gateway Arch
 St. Louis, MO, 61
George Wyth House
 Cedar Falls, IA, 14
Gerald R. Ford Birth Site
  and Gardens
 Omaha, NE, 114
Gilcrease Museum
 Tulsa, OK, 133
Giovanni's on the Hill
 St. Louis, MO, 70
Glacier National Park
 West Glacier, MT, 97

Golden Spike Monument
 Council Bluffs, IA, 32
Good Medicine Lodge
 Whitefish, MT, 101
Gorat's Steak House
 Omaha, NE, 117
Governor's Mansion
 Jefferson City, MO, 73
Grand Country Music Hall
 Branson, MO, 76
Grand Opera House
 Dubuque, IA, 19
Grand Street Café
 Kansas City, MO, 91
Grand Teton National Park
 Moose, WY, 155
Grant's Farm
 St. Louis, MO, 61
Grant Village Dining Room
 Yellowstone National Park,
  WY, 165
Grant Wood Murals
 Ames, IA, 24
Great Plains Art Museum
 Lincoln, NE, 111
Great Plains Black History
  Museum
 Omaha, NE, 114
The Grill
 Clayton, MO, 70
Grinnell Historical Museum
 Grinnell, IA, 27

Grouse Mountain Lodge
  Whitefish, MT, **101**

H

Hacienda
  Rock Hill, MO, **71**
Har-ber Village
  Grove, OK, **132**
Harry's
  Manhattan, KS, **45**
Harry S. Truman Courtroom
    and Office Museum
  Independence, MO, **56**
Harry S. Truman Presidential
    Museum and Library
  Independence, MO, **56**
Heartland of America Park
  Omaha, NE, **114**
Henry Doorly Zoo
  Omaha, NE, **114**
Herbert Hoover National
    Historic Site
  West Branch, IA, **20**
Herbert Hoover Presidential
    Library-Museum
  West Branch, IA, **21**
Heritage Trail
  Dubuque, IA, **19**
Hilton Branson Convention
    Center Hotel
  Branson, MO, **81**
Hilton Garden Inn
    Independence

  Independence, MO, **57**
Hilton Omaha
  Omaha, NE, **117**
Hilton St. Louis at the
    Ballpark
  St. Louis, MO, **66**
Hilton St. Louis Downtown
  St. Louis, MO, **67**
Hilton St. Louis Frontenac
  St. Louis, MO, **67**
Hilton Tulsa Southern Hills
  Tulsa, OK, **134**
Historic Pottawattamie
    County Squirrel
    Cage Jail
  Council Bluffs, IA, **32**
Holiday Inn
  Cody, WY, **164**
Honor Heights Park
  Muskogee, OK, **132**
Horseback Riding
  Moran, WY, **155**
Hotel Alex Johnson
  Rapid City, SD, **147**
Hotel Ambassador
  Tulsa, OK, **134**
Hotel Phillips
  Kansas City, MO, **87**
Hotelvetro
  Iowa City, IA, **22**
Hotel Winneshiek
  Decorah, IA, **22**

Hot Springs State Park
  Thermopolis, WY, **153**
Hoyt Sherman Place
  Des Moines, IA, **26**
Hughes Brothers
        Celebrity Theatre
  Branson, MO, **77**
Hyatt Place Topeka
  Topeka, KS, **38**
Hyatt Regency Crown
        Center
  Kansas City, MO, **87**
Hyatt Regency St. Louis at
        the Arch
  St. Louis, MO, **69**
Hyatt Regency Wichita
  Wichita, KS, **49**

I

Indian Creek Nature Center
  Cedar Rapids, IA, **15**
Inn at Price Tower
  Bartlesville, OK, **134**
The Inn on Crescent Lake
  Excelsior Springs, MO, **57**
Intercontinental Kansas
        City at the Plaza
  Kansas City, MO, **88**
International Photography
        Hall of Fame and
        Museum
  Oklahoma City, OK, **138**

Iowa Arboretum
  Madrid, IA, **27**
Iowa Children's Museum
  Coralville, IA, **21**
Iowa Historical Museum
  Des Moines, IA, **26**
Iowa Speedway
  Newton, IA, **28**
Isle of Capri Casino
  Bettendorf, IA, **14**

J

Jackson Lake Lodge
  Moran, WY, **155**
Jacob's Cave
  Versailles, MO, **73**
Jake's Atop the Midnight Star
  Deadwood, SD, **148**
Jasper County Historical
        Museum
  Newton, IA, **28**
Jefferson National
        Expansion Memorial
  St. Louis, MO, **62**
Jenny Lake Lodge
  Moose, WY, **157**
Jenny Lake Lodge
        Dining Room
  Moose, WY, **159**
Jesse James's Farm
  Kearney, MO, **54**

Jim Stafford Theatre
  Branson, MO, **77**
JJ's
  Kansas City, MO, **92**
John M. Clemens Justice
    of the Peace Office
  Hannibal, MO, **54**
John Mineo's
  Town and Country, MO, **71**
John Wornall House
    Museum
  Kansas City, MO, **84**
Joslyn Art Museum
  Omaha, NE, **114**
Julien Dubuque Monument
  Dubuque, IA, **20**
JW's Steakhouse
  Oklahoma City, OK, **143**

K

Kalona Historical Village
  Kalona, IA, **21**
Kandahar the Lodge
    at Whitefish
    Mountain Resort
  Whitefish, MT, **101**
Kansas City Chiefs (NFL)
  Kansas City, MO, **84**
Kansas City Marriott
    Country Club Plaza
  Kansas City, MO, **88**

Kansas City Museum
  Kansas City, MO, **85**
Kansas City Royals (MLB)
  Kansas City, MO, **85**
Kansas City Zoo
  Kansas City, MO, **85**
Kansas State Historical
    Society
  Topeka, KS, **37**
Kemoll's
  St. Louis, MO, **71**
Kemper Museum of
    Contemporary Art
  Kansas City, MO, **86**
Kirby House
  Abilene, KS, **45**
Kirkpatrick Sciencec and Air
    Space Museum
  Oklahoma City, OK, **138**
Kreis's
  St. Louis, MO, **71**

L

La Baguette Bistro
  Oklahoma City, OK, **143**
Laclede's Landing
  St. Louis, MO, **63**
La Corsette Maison Inn
  Newton, IA, **28**, **30**
Lake Afton Public
    Conservatory
  Wichita, KS, **48**

Lake of the Ozarks
  Lake Ozark, MO, **73**
Lake of the Ozarks State Park
  Kaiser, MO, **74**
Lake Yellowstone Hotel
  Yellowstone National Park,
    WY, **164**
Lake Yellowstone Hotel
    Dining Room
  Yellowstone National Park,
    WY, **165**
La Mie
  Des Moines, IA, **30**
Larkspur
  Wichita, KS, **51**
Laura Ingalls Wilder-Rose
    Wilder Lane Museum
    and Home
  Mansfield, MO, **79**
Lawrence Arts Center
  Lawrence, KS, **36**
Lazlo's Brewery & Grill
  Lincoln, NE, **118**
Le Fou Frog
  Kansas City, MO, **92**
Lendonwood Gardens
  Grove, OK, **132**
Level 2 Steakhouse
  Branson, MO, **82**
Lewis and Clark Monument
  Council Bluffs, IA, **32**
Lewis and Clark National
    Forest

Great Falls, MT, **104**
Lewis and Clark National
    Historical Trail
    Interpretive Center
  Great Fall, MT, **104**
Lewis and Clark State Park
  Williston, ND, **123**
Lewis and Clark Trail Mu-
    seum
  Alexander, ND, **123**
Lidia's Kansas City
  Kansas City, MO, **92**
Lincoln Children's Museum
  Lincoln, NE, **111**
Lincoln Monument
  Council Bluffs, IA, **32**
  Lincoln, NE, **111**
Linn St. Café
  Iowa City, IA, **23**
Little Missouri Saloon
    & Dining
  Medora, ND, **126**
Little Red School
  Cedar Falls, IA, **14**
Living History Farms
  Urbandale, IA, **26**
The Lodge of Four Seasons
  Four Seasons, MO, **75**
Lodge of the Ozarks
  Branson, MO, **80**
The Lodge Restaurant
  Bettendorf, IA, **23**

Lolo National Forest
  Missoula, MT, **97**
Lombardo's Trattoria
  St. Louis, MO, **72**
Longhorn Steakhouse
  Independence, MO, **58**
  Topeka, KS, **40**
Lost Creek Ranch
  Moose, WY, **158**
Lucca's
  Helena, MT, **108**
Lynn Riggs Memorial
  Claremore, OK, **131**

M

Madonna of the Trail
    Monument
  Council Grove, KS, **43**
The Majestic Steakhouse
  Kansas City, MO, **92**
Mamie Doud Eisenhower
    Birthplace
  Boone, IA, **24**
Maramec Spring Park and
    Remains of Old
    Ironworks
  Rolla, MO, **74**
Marina Cay Resort
  Bigfork, MT, **99**
Mark Twain Cave
  Hannibal, MO, **54**

Mark Twain Museum and
    Boyhood Home
  Hannibal, MO, **54**
Mark Twain National Forest
  Rolla, MO, **75**
Mark Twain Riverboat Ex-
    cursions
  Hannibal, MO, **54**
Marriott Kansas City Airport
  Kansas City, MO, **88**
Marriott Kansas City
    Downtown
  Kansas City, MO, **88**
Marriott Tulsa Southern
    Hills
  Tulsa, OK, **134**
Marriott Waterford
  Oklahoma City, OK, **141**
Marriott Wichita
  Wichita, KS, **49**
Mathias Ham House
    Historic Site
  Dubuque, IA, **20**
The Mayo Hotel
  Tulsa, OK, **135**
Mid-America All-Indian
    Center Museum
  Wichita, KS, **48**
Missouri Botanical Garden
  St. Louis, MO, **63**
Missouri History Museum-
    Missouri Historical
    Society

St. Louis, MO, **63**
Molly Brown Birthplace and
    Museum
Hannibal, MO, **55**
Montana Historical Society
    Museum
Helena, MT, **106**
Montana Snowbowl
Missoula, MT, **97**
Motley Cow Café
Iowa City, IA, **23**
Mount Moriah Cemetery
Deadwood, SD, **145**
Mount Rushmore National
    Memorial
Keystone, SD, **146**
Museum of Art and
    Archaeology
Columbia, MO, **72**
Museum of Geology
Rapid City, SD, **147**
Museum of Transportation
Kirkwood, MO, **63**
Myriad Botanical Gardens
Oklahoma City, OK, **139**

N

Nascar Speedpark
Hazelwood, MO, **64**
National Cowboy & Western
    Museum
Oklahoma City, OK, **139**

National Elk Refuge
Jackson Hole, WY, **155**
National Frontier Trails
    Center
Independence, MO, **56**
National Historic Trails
    Interpretive Center
Casper, WY, **153**
National Mississippi River
    Museum
    and Aquarium
Dubuque, IA, **20**
National Museum
    of Roller Skating
Lincoln, NE, **112**
National Museum of
    Wildlife Art
Jackson, WY, **152**
National World I Museum at
    Liberty Memorial
Kansas City, MO, **86**
Nebraska History Museum
Lincoln, NE, **111**
Nelson-Atkins Museum
    of Art
Kansas City, MO, **86**
New City Café
Topeka, KS, **40**
North Dakota State Capitol
Bismarck, ND, **121**

O

Obsidian Dining Room
Yellowstone National Park, WY, **166**
Oklahoma City Museum of Art
Oklahoma City, OK, **139**
Oklahoma City National Memorial
Oklahoma City, OK, **140**
Oklahoma City Zoo
Oklahoma City, OK, **140**
Oklahoma History Center
Oklahoma City, OK, **140**
Okoboji Queen II
Arnolds Park, IA, **32**
Old Cathedral
St. Louis, MO, **64**
Old Courthouse
St. Louis, MO, **62**
Old Cowtown Museum
Wichita, KS, **48**
Old Faithful
Yellowstone National Park, WY, **162**
Old Faithful Inn
Yellowstone National Park, WY, **164**
Old Faithful Snow Lodge
Yellowstone National Park, WY, **164**

Old Market
Omaha, NE, **115**
Old Style Saloon #10
Deadwood, SD, **145**
Old West Lawrence Historic District
Lawrence, KS, **36**
Olive Tree
Wichita, KS, **50**
Omaha Children's Museum
Omaha, NE, **116**
Omaha Magnolia Hotel
Omaha, NE, **116**
Omaha Marriott
Omaha, NE, **116**
Omni Majestic Hotel
St. Louis, MO, **68**
Ophelia's Restaurant & Inn
Independence, MO, **58**
The Osmond Brothers
Branson, MO, **78**

P

Palisades-Kepler State Park
Mount Vernon, IA, **16**
Paramount Theatre
Cedar Rapids, IA, **16**
Parkwood Inn & Suites
Manhattan, KS, **45**
Philbrook Museum of Art
Tulsa, OK, **133**

Pictograph Cave State Park
   Billings, MT, **98**
Pilaster House and
         Grant's Drugstore
   Hannibal, MO, **55**
Pioneers Park
   Lincoln, NE, **112**
Pitchfork Steak Fondue
   Medora, ND, **127**
Plaza III Steakhouse
   Kansas City, MO, **93**
Plum Grove Historic Farm
   Iowa City, IA, **21**
Polo Grill
   Tulsa, OK, **135**
Pomp
   Greenough, MT, **102**
Post Office Oak
   Council Grove, KS, **43**
Prairie Meadows Racetrack
         and Casino
   Altoona, IA, **26**
Presley's Country Jubilee
   Branson, MO, **78**
Price Tower
   Bartlesville, OK, **131**
Proof
   Des Moines, IA, **31**
Putnam Museum of History
         & Natural Science
   Davenport, IA, **16**

Q

The Q Hotel & Spa
   Kansas City, MO, **90**

R

Radisson Hotel Tulsa
   Tulsa, OK, **134**
Railswest Railroad Museum
   Council Bluffs, IA, **32**
The Raphael Hotel
   Kansas City, MO, **89**
Renaissance Des Moines
         Savery Hotel
   Des Moines, IA, **28**
Renaissance Oklahoma City
         Convention Center
         Hotel
   Oklahoma City, OK, **142**
Renaissance St. Louis Grand
         Hotel
   St. Louis, MO, **68**
Renaissance St. Louis
         Hotel Airport
   St. Louis, MO, **68**
Ripley's Believe it or Not!
         Museum
   Branson, MO, **78**
The Ritz Carlton, St. Louis
   St. Louis, MO, **68**
Rockcliffe Mansion
   Hannibal, MO, **55**

Rock Creek Resort
  Red Lodge, MT, **100**
Roosevelt Inn
  Waterford City, ND, **125**
Rough Riders Dining Room
  Medora, ND, **127**
Rough Riders Hotel
  Medora, ND, **125**
Rowhouse Restaurant
  Topeka, KS, **40**
Rusty Parrot Lodge
  Jackson, WY, **156**

S

Salina Art Center
  Salina, KS, **44**
Schneithorst's
    Hofamberg Inn
  Ladue, MO, **72**
Science Center of Iowa
  Des Moines, IA, **27**
Science Station
  Cedar Rapids, IA, **16**
Scotch & Sirloin
  Wichita, KS, **51**
Sedgwick County Zoo
  Wichita, KS, **48**
Seed Savers Heritage Farm
  Decorah, IA, **17**
Seelye Mansion and Museum
  Abilene, KS, **42**

The Senate Luxury Suites
  Topeka, KS, **39**
Sergeant Floyd Monument
  Sioux City, IA, **32**
Shelter Gardens
  Columbia, MO, **73**
The Shepherd of The Hills
    Homestead
  Branson, MO, **78**
Sheraton Iowa City Hotel
  Iowa City, IA, **22**
The Sheraton Oklahoma City
  Oklahoma City, OK, **142**
Sheraton St. Louis City Cen-
    ter Hotel and Suites
  St. Louis, MO, **69**
Sheraton Suites Country
    Club Plaza
  Kansas City, MO, **90**
Sherwin Miller Museum of
    Jewish Art
  Tulsa, OK, **133**
Shoshone National Forest
  Cody, WY, **161**
Showboat Branson Belle
  Branson, MO, **78**
Showthyme
  Bigfork, MT, **102**
Signatures
  Omaha, NE, **117**
Silver Dollar City
  Branson, MO, **78**

Silver Star Steak Company
  Helena, MT, **108**
Sioux City Public Museum
  Sioux City, IA, **33**
Six Flags St. Louis
  Eureka, MO, **64**
Smoky Hill Museum
  Salina, KS, **44**
Snake River Grill
  Jackson, WY, **159**
Snake River Lodge & Spa
  Teton Village, WY, **157**
Solitude Float Trips
  Jackson, WY, **154**
The Spa at Four Seasons
        Resort Jackson Hole
  Teton Village, WY, **160**
Spokane Bar Sapphire
        Mine and Gold Fever
        Rock Shop
  Helena, MT, **106**
Spring Creek Ranch
  Jackson, WY, **156**
State Capitol
  Des Moines, IA, **27**
  Jefferson City, MO, **73**
  Lincoln, NE, **113**
  Oklahoma City, OK, **141**
  Topeka, KS, **38**
Statehood Memorial—
        Thomas P. Kennard
        House
  Lincoln, NE, **113**
St. James Winery
  St. James, MO, **75**
St. Louis Airport Marriott
  St. Louis, MO, **67**
St. Louis Art Museum
  St. Louis, MO, **64**
St. Louis Cardinals (MLB)
  St. Louis, MO, **65**
St. Louis Science Center
  St. Louis, MO, **65**
St. Louis Symphony
        Orchestra
  St. Louis, MO, **64**
St. Louis Union Station
  St. Louis, MO, **65**
St. Louis Union Station
        Marriott
  St. Louis, MO, **67**
St. Louis Zoo
  St. Louis, MO, **65**
Stone Hill Winery
  Branson, MO, **78**
Strategic Air & Space
        Museum
  Ashland, NE, **113**
The Suites of 800 Locust
  Des Moines, IA, **29**
Sundown Mountain Ski Area
  Dubuque, IA, **20**
Sunset Zoo
  Manhattan, KS, **44**

Surf Ballroom
  Clear Lake, IA, **16**
Swan Lake
  Bigfork, MT, **96**

T

Table Rock Dam and Lake
  Branson, MO, **79**
Terrace Hill
  Des Moines, IA, **27**
Teton Mountain Bike Tours
  Jackson, WY, **154**
Teton Mountain Lodge
  Teton Village, WY, **158**
Thousand Hills Golf and
    Conference Resort
  Branson, MO, **80**
Thunderhead
    Underground Falls
  Rapid City, SD, **147**
Tony's
  St. Louis, MO, **72**
Topeka Zoo
  Topeka, KS, **38**
Triangle X Float Trips
  Moose, WY, **154**
Triple Creek Ranch
  Darby, MT, **107**
Triple Creek Restaurant
  Darby, MT, **107**

Trostel's Greenbriar
    Restaurant and Bar
  Johnston, IA, **29**
Truman Farm Home
  Grandview, MO, **56**
The Tulsa Zoo
  Tulsa, OK, **133**
Tupelo Grille
  Whitefish, MT, **103**
Tuttle Creek State Park
  Manhattan, KS, **44**

U

Ulysses S. Grant National
    Historic Site
  St. Louis, MO, **66**
Union Cemetery
  Kansas City, MO, **86**
Union Station
  Kansas City, MO, **87**
University of Nebraska State
    Museum
  Lincoln, NE, **113**
Upper and Lower Falls of
    Yellowstone
  Yellowstone National Park,
    WY, **162**
US Cellular Center
  Cedar Rapids, IA, **16**
Utica Square
  Tulsa, OK, **136**

V

Vesterheim Norwegian-
    American Museum
  Decorah, IA, **17**
V. Mertz
  Omaha, NE, **118**
V's Italiano
  Independence, MO, **58**

W

Wall Drug Store
  Wall, SD, **149**
Ward Earthlodge Village
    Historic Site
  Bismarck, ND, **121**
Warren Duck Club
  Tulsa, OK, **136**
Watkins Woolen Mill State
    Park and State His-
    toric Site
  Lawson, MO, **54**
Wells Fargo Bank of Iowa—
    Poweshiek County
  Grinnell, IA, **27**
The Westin Crown Center,
    Kansas City
  Kansas City, MO, **90**
The Westin St. Louis
  St. Louis, MO, **69**
Westport
  Kansas City, MO, **87**

Wheatfield's Bakery Café
  Lawrence, KS, **39**
Whitefish Mountain Resort
  Whitefish, MT, **99**
Whitney Gallery of Western
    Art
  Cody, WY, **162**
Wichita Art Museum
  Wichita, KS, **48**
Wichita Center for the Arts
  Wichita, KS, **49**
Wichita-Sedgwick County
    Historical Museum
  Wichita, KS, **49**
Will Rogers Birthplace and
    Dog Iron Ranch
  Oologah, OK, **131**
Will Rogers Memorial
  Claremore, OK, **131**
Woodbury County
    Courthouse
  Sioux City, IA, **33**
Woolaroc
  Bartlesville, OK, **131**
Worlds of Fun
  Kansas City, MO, **87**
The Wort Hotel
  Jackson, WY, **156**
Wyoming's Rib and
    Chop House
  Cody, WY, **165**

X

Xanterra Parks & Resorts
  West Yellowstone, MT, **99**

Y

Yellowstone Art Museum
  Billings, MT, **98**
Yellowstone IMAX Theatre
  West Yellowstone, MT, **99**
Yellowstone Lake
  Yellowstone National Park,
    WY, **162**

Z

Zoomontana
  Billings, MT, **98**

MISSOURI

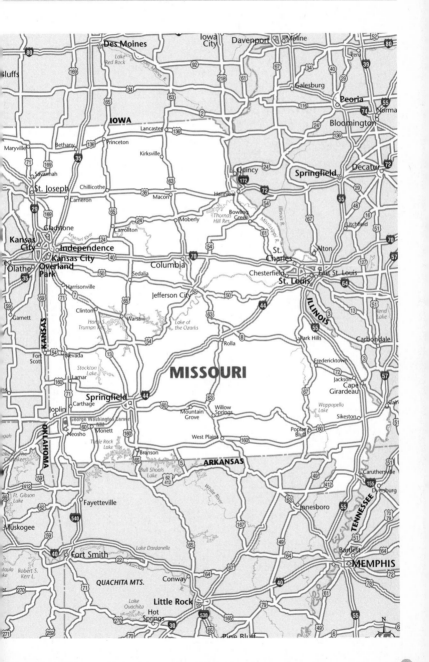

IOWA

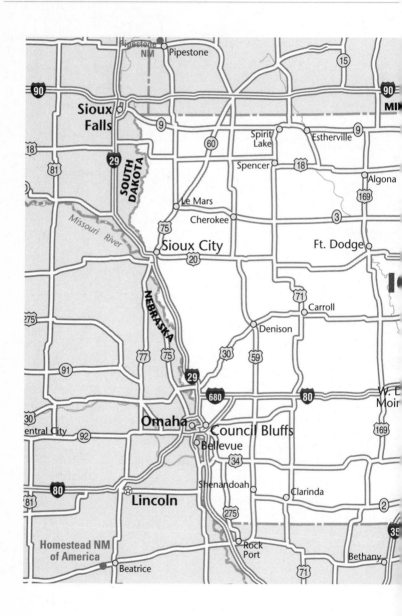

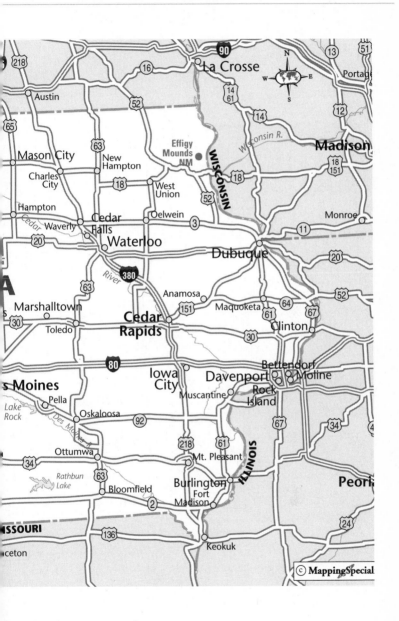

KANSAS

MONTANA

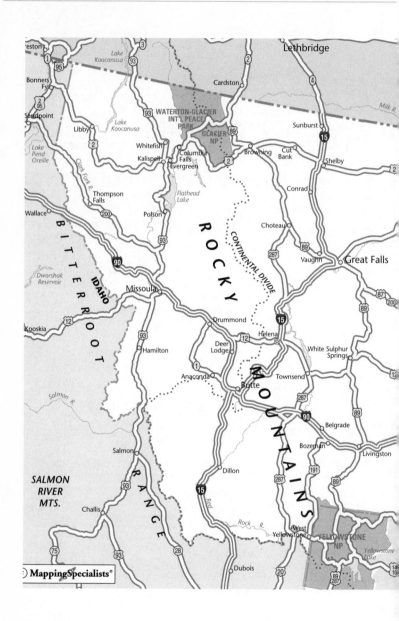

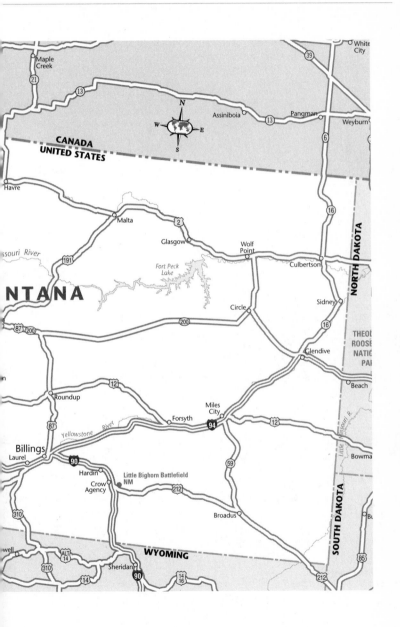

NEBRASKA

NORTH DAKOTA

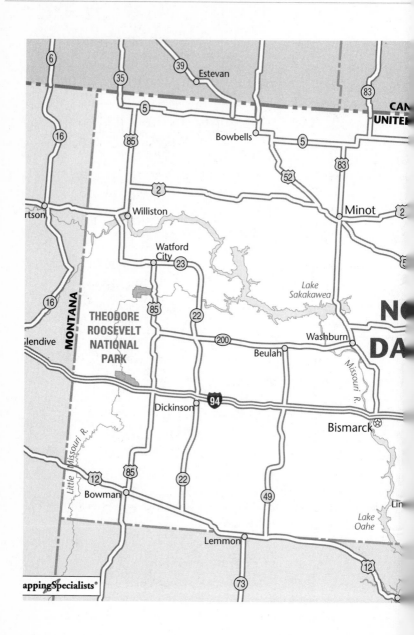

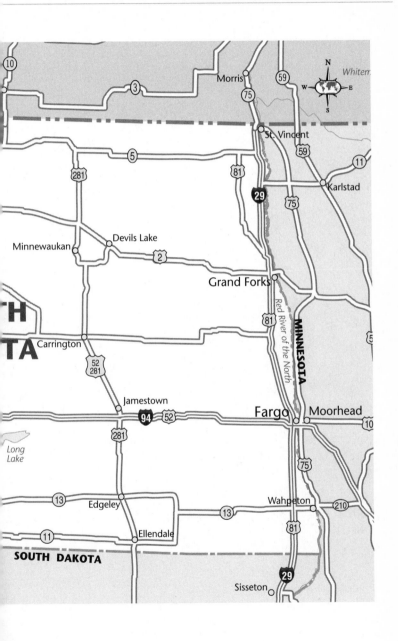

OKLAHOMA

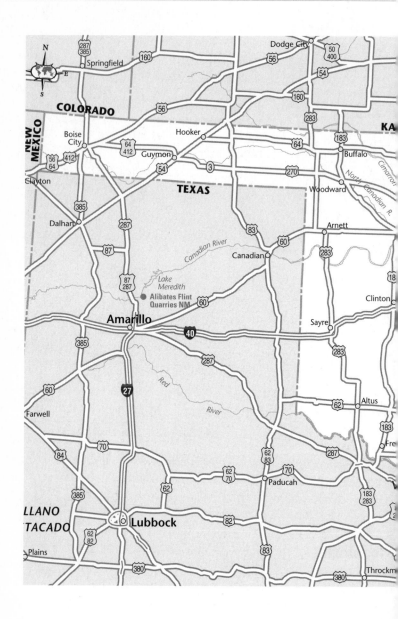

SOUTH DAKOTA

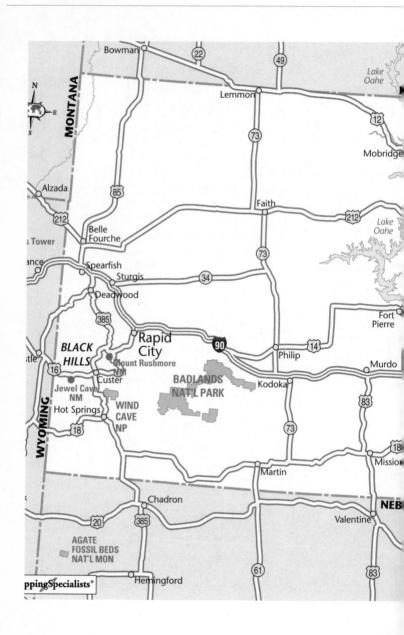

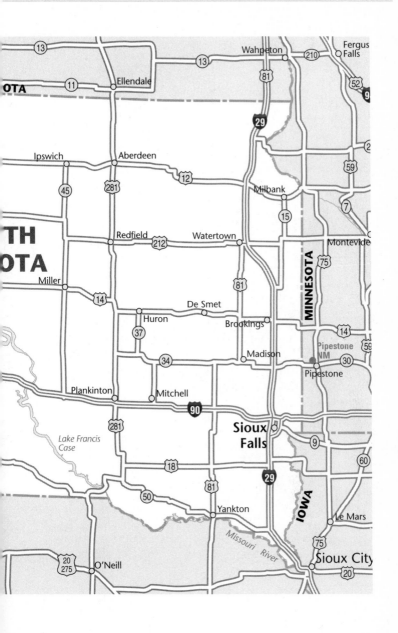

WYOMING

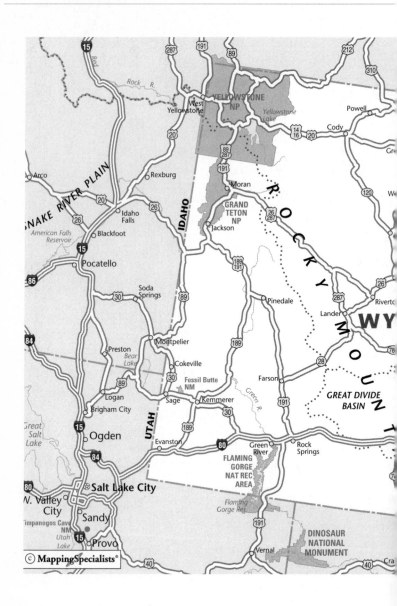

NOTES

NOTES

NOTES

NOTES

NOTES